Advertising and Commodity Culture in Joyce

The Florida James Joyce Series

The Florida James Joyce Series

Edited by Zack Bowen

The Autobiographical Novel of Co-Consciousness: Goncharov, Woolf, and Joyce, by Galya Diment (1994)

Shaw and Joyce: "The Last Word in Stolentelling," by Martha Fodaski Black (1995)

Bloom's Old Sweet Song: Essays on Joyce and Music, by Zack Bowen (1995)

Reauthorizing Joyce, by Vicki Mahaffey (paperback edition, 1995)

Joyce's Iritis and the Irritated Text: The Dis-lexic Ulysses, by Roy Gottfried (1995)

Joyce, Milton, and the Theory of Influence, by Patrick Colm Hogan (1995)

Bely, Joyce, Döblin: Peripatetics in the City Novel, by Peter I. Barta (1996)

Jocoserious Joyce: The Fate of Folly in Ulysses, by Robert H. Bell (paperback edition, 1996)

Narrative Design in Finnegans Wake: *The Wake Lock Picked,* by Harry Burrell (1996)

Joyce and Popular Culture, edited by R. B. Kershner (1996)

Joyce and the Jews: Culture and Texts, by Ira B. Nadel (paperback edition, 1996)

Latin and Roman Culture in Joyce, by R. J. Schork (1997)

Reading Joyce Politically, by Trevor L. Williams (1997)

Gender in Joyce, edited by Jolanta W. Wawrzycka and Marlena G. Corcoran (1997)

Greek and Hellenic Culture in Joyce, by R. J. Schork (1998)

Joyce's Music and Noise: Theme and Variation in His Writings, by Jack W. Weaver (1998)

Joyce, Joyceans, and the Rhetoric of Citation, by Eloise Knowlton (1998)

Advertising and Commodity Culture in Joyce, by Garry Leonard (1998)

Advertising and Commodity Culture in Joyce

Garry Leonard

University Press of Florida
Gainesville · Tallahassee · Tampa · Boca Raton
Pensacola · Orlando · Miami · Jacksonville

03 02 01 00 99 98 6 5 4 3 2 1

Library of Congress Cataloging-in-Publication Data

Leonard, Garry Martin, 1956-
Advertising and commodity culture in Joyce / Garry Leonard.
p. cm.—(The Florida James Joyce series)
Includes bibliographical references and index.
ISBN 0-8130-1632-0 (cloth: alk. paper)
1. Joyce, James, 1882-1941—Knowledge—Advertising. 2. Joyce, James, 1882-1941—Knowledge—Commercial products.
3. Commercial products—Ireland—History—20th century.
4. Advertising—Ireland—History—20th century. 5. Commercial products in literature. 6. Advertising in literature.
I. Title. II. Series.
PR6019.09Z694 1998
823'.912—dc21 98-30330

Garry Leonard is associate professor of English at the University of Toronto. He is the author of *Reading Dubliners Again: A Lacanian Perspective* (Syracuse, 1993).

The University Press of Florida is the scholarly publishing agency for the State University System of Florida, comprising Florida A & M University, Florida Atlantic University, Florida International University, Florida State University, University of Central Florida, University of Florida, University of North Florida, University of South Florida, and University of West Florida.

University Press of Florida
15 Northwest 15th Street
Gainesville, FL 32611
http://nersp.nerdc.ufl.edu/~upf

To KM, Raymond, and Marshall

Contents

Foreword

Garry Leonard's is the first book to deal exclusively with the pervasive economics of commodity culture in Joyce. Leonard reads Joyce through the lens of advertising and merchandising theorist, practitioner, and victim/consumer. The result is not merely a new approach to Joyce studies, but a continuing revelation.

The introduction lays out the extensive scholarly parameters of his investigation, which builds on the Joyce-related criticism of Heininger, Wicke, and Moretti in addition to Kershner and Herr. Leonard is basically a Lacanian whose concern with commodification was shaped by the theories of de Certeau, Baudrillard, Althusser, Irigaray, Deleuze-Guattari, and Jameson. He is so familiar with the theory that he moves through it with grace and ease, omitting anything extraneous to his subject and providing brief but totally understandable explications of sometimes overly problematized concepts, such as Lacan's paramount idea of the individual's sense of a permanent lack, Foucault's theory of sexuality as an effect of discourse and a way to control subjects, and Jameson's dictate to "always historicize."

Leonard's theoretical generalizations are all accompanied by demonstrable evidence from Joyce's text, so the reader is never left with unproven assertions or left wondering where Leonard was coming from. He offers new insights, novel readings, and creative interpretations on every page, and all in a brilliantly funny, irreverent prose that captures the moment or the character like a Joycean epiphany. For example, discussing Blazes Boylan's flashy dressing, Leonard tells us, "Boylan is nearly always described as something flashing past—a hat, skyblue clocks; he is the modern fashion machine incarnate; a jingling juggernaut of jaunty jouissance, not so much a character as a nexus of the latest semerotic signifiers; an erection with an attitude." There is no doubt that Joyce scholars will read and discuss this book long after I and maybe even Leonard are gone.

Zack Bowen
Series Editor

Preface

In Joyce's fiction, advertising and commodity culture, with all its attendant fantasies, both pleasant and unpleasant, is an invisible form of production that makes one's identity intelligible to one's "self" and others. Popular culture operates as a compensatory system offering solace, encouragement, or illusion to people who feel they lack something. As Lacan has argued, the feeling of "lacking something" is the basis of subjectivity and the drive behind desire. In a sense, by presenting, dramatizing, and constructing the cultural artifacts generated by advertising, popular culture, and mass-production, Joyce shows us we do not have to blindly assume that what is represented in a modernist work of "high art" is a complete presentation of the lived experience of modernity as it played itself out in the lives of the historical subjects of his age (or any age).

All "official" metanarratives—such as history, or canonized examples of "high art," or pro-imperial ideology—are both trenchantly embodied and effectively challenged by popular culture and its tendency to record what I call "the history of now"—precisely what "official" history ignores or devalues. Think of the following cultural artifacts in Joyce's fiction: Maria's purse in "Clay," Duffy's ad for "Bile Beans" pasted onto a page in his journal, the gift never purchased in "Araby," the fascination with the object in Stephen's aesthetic theory, or—everywhere present in *Ulysses*—the Plumtree's Potted Meat jingle and the snatch of song from "The Seaside Girls." All of these offer compensation for an historically specific sense of lack experienced by individuals in the modernist era.

As such, it has implications for the construction of gender and subjectivity, the policing of desire, and the politicizing of aesthetics, as well as for relationships between individuals and nations. Advertising would seem to contain both the conscious, hegemonic discourse of its time, as well as subversive encodings that threaten to destabilize historically specific ideology and show how its obfuscation of power relations rewrites itself in the anxieties and desires of the individual subject.

There are many people to thank, as I look back over the history of writing this book, beginning, perhaps, with Robert Spoo, Kimberly Devlin, Ellen Carol Jones, R. B. Kershner, and Bonnie Kime Scott, who formed the "dream team" panel on Joyce and advertising at the International Joyce Symposium in Monte Carlo in 1990. Out of that panel came Spoo's offer to allow me to guest edit a special issue of the *James Joyce Quarterly* on the topic Joyce and advertising. In this effort, I was joined by Jennifer Wicke as coeditor, whose earlier work on Joyce and advertising still stands as a point of departure for anyone working in this area. Murray Beja, Cheryl Herr, Sheldon Brivic, Karen Lawrence, Vince Cheng, Suzette Henke, Berni Benstock, and Zack Bowen are established Joyce scholars who gave much time and effort to encouraging and guiding me at various points in this project. Earlier versions of some of the material in this book appeared in *Novel, Joyce Studies Annual,* and the *James Joyce Quarterly,* as well as in the edited essay collections *Joyce and Popular Culture* (edited by R. B. Kershner) and *Joyce and the Subject of History* (edited by Wollaeger, Luftig, and Spoo).

As always, my deepest gratitude to my family for keeping track of my nonscholarly persona—and insisting I do so as well—however lost I got in Joycean preoccupations. Their patience permitted the completion of this project, a patience only rarely lost, such as in this observation by my eight-year-old son, Raymond, upon discovering I needed to complete a paragraph before joining him in a bike ride: "What are you doing? James Joyce, *again*? James Butthead is more like it." Marshall's contributions (five years old) were more direct as he sat in my lap, hands poised above the keyboard, demanding: "Tell me what to do. Which button should I push?" I wasn't always sure myself, but I leave it to my readers to determine the extent to which I managed to push the right buttons.

Introduction

A Capital Couple—Joyce and Advertising

> A commodity appears, at first sight, a very trivial thing, and easily understood. Its analysis shows that it is, in reality, a very queer thing, abounding in metaphysical subtleties and theological niceties.
>
> Karl Marx[1]

> If I go, I said, I will bring you something.
>
> What innumerable follies laid waste my waking and sleeping thoughts after that evening! I wished to annihilate the tedious intervening days.
>
> James Joyce, "Araby"[2]

I

From the very beginning, according to his brother Stanislaus, James Joyce found his identity underwritten by advertising: "[Joyce] in boyhood and youth was of such a cheerful and amiable disposition that in the family circle he was given the nickname (borrowed from an advertisement for some patent food) of 'Sunny Jim'."[3] This seems innocent enough. Richard Ellmann mentions it in passing, very much as an anecdote. Stanislaus himself can't recall what "patent food" was involved and clearly doesn't feel uneasy about the lapse in memory. But Joyce is fascinated with what I call "the history of now"—the unrecorded yet quintessential fact of everyday lived experience. The only mass-produced chronicle of such trivia is popular culture in general, and advertisements in particular.[4]

The beauty of the everyday as the not yet historicized is enshrined in the most famous Joycean ephemera of all—the epiphany: "By an epiphany he meant a sudden spiritual manifestation, whether in the vulgarity of speech or of gesture or in a memorable phase of the mind itself. . . . these epiphanies . . . are the most delicate and evanescent of moments."[5] As is made clear first in "An Encounter," again in *Portrait,* and yet again in "Nestor," the "official" account of events is good only as something apparently irrelevant for alienated students to recite by memory in order to garner the useless approval of their indifferent teacher. The much-discussed epiphany, as outlined in *Stephen Hero,* shows the subject confronting an object in a period of duration carefully defined as one too brief ever to be "historical" in a traditional sense: "This is the moment which I call the epiphany. . . . when *the parts are adjusted to the special point.* . . . its soul, *its whatness, leaps to us.* . . . *The soul of the commonest object,* the structure of which is so adjusted *seems to us radiant.* The object achieves its epiphany" (213, emphasis added). My emphasis is intended to point out what is often overlooked; the subject is completely passive in this moment. The object, at a "special point," announces itself, and this luminous *structure* makes "the soul of the commonest object" become "radiant." Stephen's theory of the object is also the basis of advertising: to make the "commonest object" appear to "leap to us" and seem "radiant."

Indeed, the first objective of the perfect advertisement is to draw the consumer's attention to the particular product as something distinct from its environment. A savvy advertiser could do worse than establish for any given product or object what Stephen Dedalus calls (after Aquinas) *integritas:* "The first phase of apprehension is a bounding line drawn about the object to be apprehended."[6] Such a "bounding line" is understood by the marketer as establishing a "look" for the product, usually through packaging, which quickly distinguishes it from competing products. A second difficulty in the modern commodity marketplace is that new products are anonymous and have no "recognition value," unless, of course, the ad campaign and the packaging of the object generate *consonantia:* "Having first felt that it is *one* thing you feel now that it is a *thing* . . ." (*P,* 212, italics in the original). The most basic way to make the viewer/consumer "feel now that it is a *thing*" is the "Brand Name," which makes it possible for a consumer to develop a loyalty toward a particular brand of soap, even against the backdrop of other brands of virtually identical soap.

A third difficulty the advertiser must confront arises from the fact that different name-brand products of the same type (soap and potted meat, for example) are not substantially different from one another in terms of their relative use value. The "bestseller" on the market, therefore, will be the product that prompts the consumer, through an easily recognized trademark (for example, "Pear's" soap, "Plumtree's" potted meat), to "discover" the sacred use value of a particular product, thus converting it into a "commodity" where the "exchange value" becomes considerably higher than what it costs to manufacture the object; the object, in other words, through the context of advertising and packaging, must demonstrate and promote *claritas:* "the artistic discovery and representation of the divine purpose in anything or a force of generalisation which would make the esthetic image a universal one, *make it outshine its proper conditions* . . ." (*P*, 213, emphasis added).

Having come this far, the advertiser faces the final and most difficult challenge; having distinguished the product from other similar products, having created an aura that far exceeds its use value, the advertiser must determine how best to sustain brand name loyalty so that the consumer sees the product as possessing a radiant quality ("soulfulness") impossible to find or even imagine elsewhere. The product must achieve *quidditas* in the eyes of the consumer: "You see that it is that thing which it is and no other thing. The radiance of which he speaks is the scholastic *quidditas*, the *whatness* of a thing" (*P*, 213, italics in the original). Stephen's object announces its "whatness"; it becomes, like Coca-Cola, "that thing which it is and no other thing," the real thing.

The object with a soul in Stephen's aesthetic theory is—despite his refusal to see it in these terms—a commodity. In a manner more clear to Lynch than to him, Stephen is outlining two of the challenges of twentieth-century aesthetic theory: how to factor in "low art" and "popular culture," and whether now to include the "kinetic" and the "pornographic" as a "legitimate" element of aesthetic response, or continue to exclude it (as Stephen unconvincingly attempts) as merely a reflex. The relationship between the modern consumer and modern advertising through mass media has changed the relationship of subject to object and, in the process, altered the nature of aesthetic response. Or, rather, it has revealed aesthetic theory, the way it was previously configured, as a particular construction, and not "natural" at all. The phenomenon of "arousal" is not permitted as a reaction to art because this response, more than any other, threatens to draw attention to what is culturally and historically specific about the work. That which is repressed from aesthetic theory, in the interest of defining "timeless" beauty, returns as the epiphany, which redefines the object in terms of immediate response.

If one looks at Stephen's earlier discussion with the dean, one can see Stephen's anxiety stated clearly: "—One difficulty, said Stephen, in esthetic discussion is to know whether words are being used according to the literary tradition or according to the tradition of the marketplace" (*P*, 188). What Stephen appears to be saying, and certainly what he intends to say, is that such a separation can be achieved if one is vigilant. But as I have tried to demonstrate, all the terms in Stephen's aesthetic theory are eminently suited for the marketplace—and even the advertising trade magazine.

What Stephen presents as the essential basis of any aesthetic discussion—separating "works of art" from "commodities"—is precisely what can no longer be done. The more Aquinian Stephen gets in his description of the "spiritual" dimension, that which makes the object "artistic," the more he sounds like Karl Marx, who, far more deliberately than Stephen, discussed the phenomenon of modern commodities as objects with souls capable of inducing a sort of soporific spiritual transcendence: "To find an analogy, one must enter the nebulous world of religion. In that world, the products of the human mind become independent shapes endowed with lives of their own, and able to enter into relations with men and women. The products of the human had to do the same thing in the world of commodities" (Marx, 81). With uncharacteristic generosity, Stephen excessively credits Aquinas as the source of his terminology in order to persuade himself that his words are carefully selected only from the "literary tradition."

What I wish to point out, however, is how the aesthetic theory of modern consumerism is outlined in nascent form by Stephen's concept of the epiphany, and one way to demonstrate this further is to compare it with Bloom's predictably overt commercial desire to imbue commodities with a miraculous "soul" and "radiance" through the secular scripture of advertising:

> What were habitually his final meditations?
>
> Of some one sole unique advertisement to cause passers to stop in wonder, a poster novelty [First we recognise that the object is one integral thing], with all extraneous accretions excluded [then we recognise that it is an organised composite structure], reduced to its simplest and most efficient terms ["the parts are adjusted to the special point"] not exceeding the span of casual vision ["Its soul . . . leaps to us"] and congruous with the velocity of modern life ["The soul of the commonest object, the structure of which is so adjusted, seems to us radiant"].[7]

The fact that Stephen submits his carefully chosen words to the mercy of Lynch's noticeably short attention span ("the span of casual vision," indeed!) proves what Stephen would rather not see: The great artist who sets out to "forge in the smithy of [his] soul the uncreated conscience of [his] race" will have to address ahistorical minds—tuned only to the moment—such as Lynch's (*P*, 253). And it is Lynch—the young man who cheerfully signs his name on statues—who is the future, not Stephen with his pseudo-literary metanarratives, the putrescent nature of which Lynch correctly identifies as giving off "the true scholastic stink" (*P*, 214). Stephen's rather stuffy aversion to anything that excites "kinetic emotions" shuts him off from any awareness of the intense energy of all modes of popular culture.

For Lynch, it is once again only the moment too brief in duration to be recorded that seems closest to authentic consciousness. "—I speak of normal natures," Stephen says, in an effort to eliminate Lynch's contributions to the dialogue (*P,* 205). He may speak of them as much as he wants, but the category has collapsed in the twentieth century. If Freud identified everybody as neurotic, advertisers discovered everybody wants what they are afraid to want, and "normal nature" is an increasingly pathetic strategy of denial.

In *Portrait,* Joyce breaks with the chronological and teleological narration of what he saw as traditional novels of youth by stating his intent to capture "the curve of an emotion," rather than to characterize this or that feeling (*P,* 258). In a similar sense, the "not-yet historicized" evokes the "curve" of an event, the arc of truth, without lasting long enough to reify that event into an "accepted" narration of "what happened." What is "in style," for example, does not seem important, and yet we cannot stop looking. The stylized object, or the commodity, can evoke contempt or envy or a temporary feeling of well-being, depending on whether we refuse to align ourselves with it, wish to align ourselves, or find ourselves already aligned. Fashion and its corollary, style, embody the aesthetic theory of the everyday, that which rivets our attention in the moment yet never strikes us as momentous—except, of course, in Joyce:

> Proud: rich: silk stockings. . . .
> Watch! Watch! Silk flash rich stockings white. Watch! (*U,* 60–61)

Certainly this is just a man trying to look at a woman's nicely stockinged leg—but why the breathless urgency, or the keen, even bitter, disappointment when a tram rolls by and blocks his view at the crucial moment?

Fashion, as Walter Benjamin put it, is a tiger leaping out to devour the past. It is not arbitrary, yet it cannot be anticipated. Style is to history what pantomime is to speech—a gesturing that is evocative rather than a statement that is (presumably) definitive. History, Jameson tells us, is what hurts. Style is not the truth, but rather gestures prompted by the truth, gestures that style embodies, thus evoking a *sense* of something being true. Style, because of its everyday, temporary quintessence, converts the inarticulate pain of history into attitude, performance, and pose. Certainly the "fact" of history is distorted in this process, as much as it is in historical narrative, but the value of style and "the history of now" as it appears in advertising lies in the fact that it is a different sort of distortion of history, one that challenges and subverts "accepted" historical accounts. To put this another way, because it is a different sort of distortion (a curve, rather than a fixed point), it delegitimizes historical discourse as the metanarrative that "recounts" the past, "explains" the present, and "forecasts" the future. In Lacanian terms, the ephemeral and the trivial, because they are ignored by hegemonic discourse, offer a glimpse of the Real—that unrepresented reality excluded by language in order to make the word appear to be the exact equivalent of the world. This equation is never exact; something is always left out. That which is repressed seeks to return, often in the guise of what is unimportant—an advertisement, a bar of lemon soap, a potato, a throwaway, a glimpse of stocking, the straw hat of Blazes, a song about seaside girls.

For Bloom, the missed flash of rich, white stockings is a disappointment that recurs to him throughout the rest of the day, more often, and (apparently) more deeply, than his knowledge that his wife has an appointment to meet Blazes Boylan, her would-be lover. The meeting with Blazes will be "history"—it will "happen" at 4 P.M. Indeed, Bloom's watch stops at about this time in dubious homage to the supposed precision of historical events. But this moment when the possible (will she or won't she?) becomes the actual (she does) is not where Bloom's emotions get played out. If history is what happened, style records what it felt like when it was happening. It is in his passion to immerse himself in a moment configured by "style" that Bloom's pain, hope, and despair all "flash" in front of him. More than that, the incident recalls other times when the same sort of thing happened: "Always happening like that. The very moment" (461). Here is the history of the everyday, the history of now, "the very moment," as Bloom says. And the tramcar blocks his view, making it an event that calls to mind the history of nonevents. "Always happening like that." Like what? In both cases the event is remembered because something anticipated failed to happen.

What if the tramcar had not intervened? Bloom is in a momentary phase of free-floating insatiability; he is attracted not only to a woman's leg, but to a complex of signs that make him think "proud" and "rich." In his moment of anticipation, he does not think "leg"; he thinks "silk" and "stockings." It is not just a woman's body, but the way in which that body is stylized by fashion that arouses him. In this moment of ambivalent yearning, for which a particular configuration of style has served as a catalyst, Bloom not only momentarily focuses his pain and frustration, he also displays his class consciousness. We can see how it promotes his association of wealthy women with finer underthings, leading to an anticipation of greater excitation. In this blocked flash, Bloom is experiencing class distinction (rich), a reluctant yet pleasurable sense of inferiority (she is proud; he is beneath her notice), and a detailed awareness that this flash has been "brought to him" by purchases ("rich!") made in a department store ("stockings!") and then pulled up ("silk!") a woman's leg in the privacy of the home. This was not all done especially for him, in the style of the woman in *Sweets of Sin* ("costliest frillies! all for him! for Raoul!"), but the display is nonetheless available to him if he is alert ("Watch!").

The rapidly changing vicissitudes of style (and the advertising campaigns that support these styles) show there is nothing essential about what is erotic, pleasurable, memorable, or historical in modern culture. Desire is an effect brought about by a convergence of signifiers that makes us feel like the signified—a semiotics of desire, which in this book I have called "semerotics." "Watch! Watch!" Bloom frantically commands himself, while M'Coy drones on in front of him. Satisfaction or satiation is out of the question in this situation, tramcar or no tramcar. Indeed, it is the tramcar that makes this moment extraordinary, not because it blocks Bloom's view of an ordinary woman's leg, but because, by doing so, it alerts him to his own constant and unremitting need to anticipate his own salvation in the various performances of style as they are enacted within the ever-changing framework of fashion.

He must be alert because, like all modern consumers, he is a surreptitious audience. What he wants, and what banishing the tramcar would not provide, is to have her perform for him. How simple, after all, if he could call across the street, "I'm sorry, I missed it, could you do it again?" Or shout, in the parlance of the film director, "Cut! The damn tramcar got in the way. Let's try it again. Take 2!" In advertising, the tramcar never gets in the way, or it does so with the clear message that purchasing the product would halt its approach; even when the glimpse is provided, it is coupled with the requirement to purchase, if one wishes to "own" this moment of "self"-sufficient configuration. In a sense, shopping is a series of epiphanic moments of apparent "self"-fulfillment that turn from anticipatory to frustrating if no purchase is made (as in "Araby") or to a more prolonged suspension if something is bought (all the things Stephen buys with his essay prize before the money runs out).

Unlike the bit of "style" performed in public by the unknowing actress for the unknowable audience, popular culture and advertising, two forces we might understand as the spectacles that empower us to interpret life as spectacle, always protect the moment and deliver it—but only for the moment. The streets are blocked off, so to speak; nothing intervenes; the flash occurs. The future apotheosis of this moment for Bloom is Marilyn Monroe in *The Seven Year Itch*, feigning surprise as the heat vent blows up her dress—a scene that was in fact the result of several takes. Nowadays, if you still manage to miss it, you can rewind the tape and watch it again and again, until you realize nothing has been disclosed, nothing revealed, except your own attraction to moments when something seems about to be revealed. What is in style and in fashion is that which produces these moments with the greatest frequency, and it is the very success of a style that determines its status as ephemeral. The fashionable and the stylish are said to exhibit panache, flair, cachet. They have flash; they are flashy. It is the flash that Bloom feels entitled to and anticipates, and that is denied him: "Silk flash rich stockings white. Watch!"

This is not, as Magritte might have put it, a woman's leg. Where does the word "flash" fit in? One clearly distinct feature of twentieth-century fashion is that, despite the fact it is mass produced, it is marketed as the key to individuality. Wilde's dandy of the late nineteenth century now has to buy off the rack, but he or she must flash individuality nonetheless, which brings us to one of the best-known flashers in literature: Blazes Boylan. Boylan is nearly always described as something flashing past—a hat, skyblue clocks. He is the modern fashion machine incarnate: a jingling juggernaut of jaunty *jouissance,* not so much a character as a nexus of the latest semerotic signifiers—an erection with an attitude.

It is why Molly wants him and yet, at the same time, does not think much of him; he is trivial, irrelevant, disposable, and therefore fascinating and compelling—but only for a little while. Molly Bloom thinks of Blazes in the same terms she might use to describe a well-dressed mannequin in the window of Clery's: "Lovely stuff in that blue suit he had on and stylish tie and socks with the skyblue silk thing on them" (*U,* 617). Her appreciation of Blazes is expressed in terms that are simultaneously erotic and economic, and this language arises, in part, from the frustration she feels at not having the money to advertise her "self" properly. The "it" refers to money, of course, but the shopping, spending, consuming, and displaying all imply something beyond simply exchanging money for necessary goods. What Molly here calls "fine style" will become our own notion of "lifestyle," where one buys in the hope of shoring up a self-image. It is the difference between what the boy feels while moving through the street market in "Araby," and his later nearly unbearable excitement (and equally vivid despair) when he can find nothing to buy at the bazaar. In a sense, what I am trying to do is to read Joyce in a different way by showing how he writes the history of consumption for the first time, and does so in parallel with the oft-written history of the Industrial Revolution.

The idea of men desiring women they otherwise regard as insignificant is a familiar cliché, but the reverse is something to which we still have a blind spot. Among the numerous explanations of how Bloom manages to cope with Molly's afternoon tryst with Blazes the clotheshorse, I have not seen the most obvious explanation: Blazes is a male "bimbo," someone traditionally thought of as only female, who manipulates stylistic signifiers to produce a powerful effect. That is to say, he is a living, breathing advertisement, not so much desirable in his own right, but more in that he causes people to desire (as such he answers to Lacan's description of an object of desire). Bloom knows this ("worst man in Dublin"), and while this knowledge does not make living through the day easy, it might be what makes surviving it possible.

The self-advertisement of one's existence, which I am suggesting now goes under the rubric of "lifestyle," is everywhere apparent in *Ulysses*. Stephen, for example, delivers his kinchlike intellectual pronouncements with the disingenuous air of someone field-testing a new slogan. Likewise, he credits Pyrrhus's immortality to his having coined a phrase that the world remembered. Thus, in Stephen's equation, Pyrrhus's felicitous phrase becomes a clever jingle. The experience of modernity is ahistorical because it is always the history of now. "Style" ambushes the past—a tiger leaping out to devour it—and by doing so sets in motion the hallucinatory experiences (which are, by definition, unrecordable) that occur whenever the sense of the historical is encapsulated in an event of the moment. "The moment in every day," as that anti-historian William Blake put it, "that Satan's Watch Fiends cannot find."

Karl Marx gestures in this direction with his analysis of the commodity as a fetish, but he emphasizes the means of production as the means to power. What Joyce recognizes (as Oscar Wilde did before him) is that controlling the means of consumption (through advertising or the packaging of the "self") is now a rival means of power. Increasingly, those who own machines are dependent upon those who successfully market what the machines produce. To understand Joyce's history of the early days of commodity culture, we must see a synergistic relationship among the machines that produce; the goods that are produced; the advertisements that generate a *particularly* modern, historically *specific* desire to consume; and the consumers who reveal the hopes and anxieties of their time by responding to some appeals and ignoring others. Often in Joyce's fiction, what is beneath notice becomes notable. In such a world, where "value" is no longer part of an agreed upon tradition, constructing and experiencing one's own subjectivity involves a complex theatrics of self-presentation, or "lifestyle."

And what about the adman behind the adman? What about Joyce? It is a truism of modernism—a truism often traced to Stephen's view of the artist as an indifferent God—that the modernist writers cared little about their audience and even less about whether their work was well received. Joyce, by his own account, set into circulation phrases that came back to him in reviews. Like any good marketer, Joyce carefully monitors the rate of his phrase production in order to avoid the problem of a saturated market: "They cannot manage more than about one such phrase every six months," he writes, "not for lack of intelligence but because they are in a hurry" (Letters III, 83). One is reminded of Bloom's own caution to himself, expressed while imagining a perfect advertisement, that the design and intent of the advertisement must be "congruous with the velocity of modern life" (*U*, 592). Only then might it be able to perform the task he imagines for it elsewhere, a task similar to what modernist writers assigned to their own productions: "to arrest involuntary attention, to interest, to convince, to decide" (*U*, 559).

The postmodern end point of such literary advertising might be embodied in the remarks of David Norris, published in the flyer advertising the 1992 Joyce Symposium in Dublin. Norris states, quite astutely I believe, that "even in the harsh realities of world industry," the "name of Joyce"—packaged and commodified by the Joyce industry—creates for Dublin "instant recognisability" and "brand identification." He goes on to thank the major sponsor of the symposium, "Bailey's Irish Cream, an Irish Product, like the works of James Joyce, of international recognition and excellence."

The self-consciously Augustinian aesthetic theory presented by the Stephen of *Portrait* might also be reasonably found in any of the hundreds of manuals for advertising and selling that abounded at the turn of the century. Indeed, the one found in Joyce's library in Trieste is titled, quite significantly, *The* Art *of Selling Goods* (my emphasis).[8] As in Donald Trump's *The* Art *of the Deal,* commercial success is equated with an aesthetic appreciation of how to imbue objects with "soul" and make them "radiant" so the consumer strolling by will "stop in wonder." Indeed, the point is to make one's self an object that makes other people stop in wonder. Through "fashion" and "style" one projects "personality," a performance that exudes the very aura that Benjamin felt mass production was robbing from works of art. The production of "personality" founders on the same paradox as contemporary fashion: it is both mass produced and the assumed essence of "individuality." The history of personality is a chronicle of disorder (which is the way the narrator of "An Encounter" characterizes *The Apache Chief,* the "rubbish" Father Butler confiscates in class), which is to say it is of little interest to the classically ordered Irish historian, and yet of vital interest to the Joyce scholar (*D*, 20).

In the new, improved testament of commodity culture, it is through fashion, style, and performance that one's soul is allowed to shine in the form of an arresting "personality" that makes others stop in wonder, saying to themselves, "Watch! Watch!" Chronicles of disorder are the history of now, and Joyce is our historian of the soon to be forgotten and the not yet historicized. "Know thyself," Socrates advised, with famous succinctness. But here is the conclusion of *The Art of Selling Goods*—one of several new gospels written as part of the new, improved testament: "The real salesman is one who knows . . . himself as well as he does his goods. . . . Let the salesman know as much about the world and about others as he does about himself and his goods. Here is the trinity of success—know your goods, yourself and the world" (166). To which we—devotees of fashion, style, and the performance of personality—can only answer, "Amen." My first chapter, then, argues that, in the absence of universal belief, the images, songs, and messages of popular culture constitute a religion in Joyce's fiction, and the oracular advertisements that instruct us on how best to worship, in the continual hope of achieving inner peace and spiritual fulfillment, are its sacred scripture.

II

Nowadays, of course, we take our popular culture quite seriously. For people of my generation it is the Beatles, for others it is Elvis Presley or Frank Sinatra; the supposedly disposable popular culture of one's youth becomes, in one's maturity, a permanent source of treasured nostalgia. But Joyce anticipates the extent to which popular culture, because it is the only shared symbolic system in twentieth-century culture, inevitably infuses itself with the way we construct our gender, our identity, and our reality. The music hall song "Those Lovely Seaside Girls," for example, was written in 1899, right around the time, Stanislaus tells us, that the teenage "Sunny Jim" was most infatuated (along with his histrionic father) with this form of theater (a form by the way, that we might see as crudely but unmistakably "modernist"). And this "throwaway" song then permeates a novel set six years later, and written yet another fifteen or so years beyond that. Clearly, even when Joyce was actively involved with using this material, it was already quite dated and perhaps not easy to locate. Ephemera, however, is given permanence in Joyce's fiction, a permanence that reality does not reflect. Indeed, Joyce's epic treatment of the trivial is, I believe, one of the central reasons his work continues to grow in importance as we struggle to understand our own time.

In short, we cannot afford to be as casual as Stanislaus was about turn-of-the-century advertising and popular culture because, most certainly, his older brother thought about it often and intensely. The "patent food" that featured Sunny Jim as part of its ad campaign, for example, was a breakfast cereal called FORCE. Sunny Jim was the hero of numerous jingles in which he always cheered someone up, or played the hero, by fixing them a dish of FORCE. One of the jingles went as follows:

Jim Dumps a little girl possessed
Whom loss of appetite distressed.
"I des' tant eat," the child would scream.
Jim fixed a dish of force and cream,
She tasted it—then joy for him,
She begged for more from Sunny Jim.

Why "joy for him"? And are we to view the phrasing "she begged for more," with its barely implicit sexual tension, as a matter of indifference to the young man who bears the nickname "Sunny Jim"? After all, Joyce's alter ego (originally conceived of—with a facetiousness equal to that of "Sunny Jim"—as "Stephen Hero") is a young man who has a fantasy about a woman he wants to want him: "Conscious of his desire she was waking from odorous sleep, the temptress of his villanelle. Her eyes, dark and with a look of languor, were opening to his eyes. Her nakedness yielded to him . . ." (*P*, 223). One way to gloss this adolescent sexual fantasy would be: "Oh, joy for him. / She begged for more from Sunny Jim." Such a gloss does not at all trivialize the fantasy, but rather shows how it mimics the seductive world of advertising, a world where what you want others to do becomes exactly what they wish to do for you—provided you purchase the product.

Advertising—and consumer discourse in general—constitutes a dynamic force every bit as influential on Joyce as, say, the works of Thomas Aquinas, Dante, Shakespeare, or Bruno. Joyce does not cite individual advertisements merely in pursuit of realism or verisimilitude. On the contrary, he presents the overall dynamic of advertising in order to demonstrate the extent to which social relations, nationalist aspirations, power structures, class distinctions, gender constructions, and subjectivity itself all intersect with, and even depend upon, the simulated universe of advertisements.

The key components of this "universe" include actual advertisements, the commodities they imbue with oracular value, and the subjects who negotiate with the various interpellations produced by this intercourse. Indeed, in chapter 1, "Advertising and Religion: The New (Improved!) Testament," I make the case specifically that advertising is the great unauthored metadiscourse of our time—that is to say, the universal religion of the twentieth century—because it transcends three cornerstones of postmodernism: Nietzsche's death of God and rejection of teleological history, Foucault's poststructural "death of the author," and Lyotard's characterization of the postmodern age as one suspicious of metanarratives. It does so because it is apparently unauthored, does not posit a god (a transcendental signified) as the source of its truth value, does not claim the coherency of a metadiscourse or "universal theory" along the lines of Marxism or psychoanalytic theory, and does not depend on any notion of history as cumulative, or even as accessible. Indeed, advertising can be only the history of now. And, despite the apparent modesty of advertising as a source of truth or enlightenment, it is the hyperreal sun we see rising in the sky in "Circe," announcing the dawn of commodity culture as a new pantheism based on coupling the fantasy of completion promised by exchange value with the permanent lack masked by the fiction of subjectivity, and shifting the emphasis from praying to paying as a means toward salvation: "We're a capital couple are Bloom and I. / He brightens the earth. I polish the sky" (*U*, 360).

As this quote suggests, advertising is not a one-way street, inscribing itself on the passive consumer; it is a partnership. Althusser first outlined the idea of "interpellation" as a term for designating the way in which ideology "calls out" to individuals, and appears to offer them a sort of prepackaged subjectivity.[9] In more recent years, Althusser's theory of "interpellation" has been seen as crucial, but limited. Its primary limitation is a failure to see how a subject might react against, or possibly subvert, the interpellative "call." Where Althusser might insist upon seeing ideology dominate the subject, subsequent theorists, notably de Certeau, characterize the relationship between a subject and a given ideology as a negotiation. In de Certeau's view, the subject is an active agent: "The tactics of consumption, the ingenious ways in which the weak make use of the strong lend a political dimension to everyday practices."[10] This idea of the subject and the ad as a two-way street seems much more in line with Joyce's tendency to both celebrate popular culture and suggest its potentially destabilizing influence.

Well before de Certeau and Baudrillard, Joyce understood that advertisements and commodities offer to the subject a wonderfully seductive type of pleasure that might be construed as positive or even welcome. Althusser's notion of interpellation, with its over-investment in the one-way power of dominant ideology, left the consumer in such a passive and defenseless position that negotiation between the "self" of the subject and the "Other" of the advertisement or commodity seemed impossible. Joyce does not see the consumer as being passively interpellated by whatever message producers wish to encode into advertising. The ad that attempts to configure the consumer is, in turn, reconfigured by it. The successful ad cannot engage specifically with a range of fantasies there is no way to predict, but it must, nonetheless, offer a way for the individual to focus his or her desire. Bloom, therefore, has the idea, as an advertisement for stationery, to put women in a glass showcart, ask them to write on paper, and have horses draw the cart through the streets of Dublin.

What is ingenious about Bloom's idea is that no one man will have the same idea about what the women are writing, and yet all will be inclined to think of buying stationery because the spectacle of the women writing will cause them to imagine messages they most desire to receive. Women viewing the showcart will be invited to make a more direct connection to the scene by imagining to whom they wish to write a letter, and what they might like to write. The refigurations caused by an advertisement may not always be pleasant, but, as is suggested by Duffy's "active relation" to a Bile Beans advertisement, they often betray a glimpse of the economic and social constructions underpinning what passes as an individual's "natural" identity, or a society's "common" knowledge. As we can see in "Araby," when the boy feels himself transformed into something wonderful and powerful by the prospect of buying something—only to be inexplicably crushed and humiliated when the bazaar closes down—even though the refiguring may be temporary and problematic, it still functions, however briefly, as an escape. This may explain why, to quote a present-day aphorism, when the going gets tough, the tough go shopping.

One of the most potent gaps left open and maintained by the symbolic economy of advertising is, of course, fantasy. In one's fantasies, one can make passionate love to an emotionally distant spouse (Gabriel in "The Dead"), discover the treasure of Monte Cristo in a pile of candy wrappers (Stephen in *Portrait*), get married to a stranger (Gerty in "Nausicaa"), read the review of an important collection of poems you will never write (Little Chandler in "A Little Cloud"), or become the mayor of Dublin (Bloom in "Circe"). Fantasy produces reality, but this does not so much mean everything is artificial as it means that nothing comprehensible is "natural."[11]

Another part of my argument is that popular culture operates as a compensatory system offering solace, encouragement, or illusion to people who feel they lack something; therefore, such artifacts as Maria's purse, Duffy's pasted ad, and the gift never purchased in "Araby" necessarily offer compensation, or fail to provide it, for an historically specific sense of lack experienced by individuals in the modernist era. In a sense, by examining the cultural artifacts produced by "low art," Joyce shows us we do not have to assume blindly everything re-presented in a modernist work of "high art" is a complete presentation of the lived experience of modernity as it played itself out in the lives of the historical subjects of this age. All "official" metanarratives, such as history or canonized examples of "high art," are effectively challenged by popular culture, and by its tendency to record only "the history of now"—precisely what "official" history ignores or devalues. All "official" representations, in collusion with hegemonic requirements, inevitably distort as "natural" and "inevitable" precisely what most needs to be understood as constructed and culturally specific. The problem is not so much that historical narrative does this, but rather that it denies all knowledge of having done so.

What is needed to analyze the cultural artifacts of "low art" is a theoretical approach that allows one to explore the dynamic relationship between the historical individual and the cultural artifact. The approach I have chosen to work with is known generally as "cultural theory," whereas the results of such an approach are gathered under the general rubric of "cultural studies." Briefly put, cultural theory offers ways to look at the particular way a culture has organized itself, with the understanding that it need not have done so in this one particular way. In terms of my argument in this book, the cultural theory of Lacan, Foucault, Baudrillard, de Certeau, Irigaray, Deleuze, Guattari, and Jameson (to name the most important) allows me to say that "high art" is not simply the incarnation of truth, or a "natural" representation of the desire for universal good, but rather a complex response to a matrix of psychological, sociological, economic, and aesthetic pressures (to name the most apparent).[12] Whereas the Victorian poet and critic Matthew Arnold attempted to universalize the concept of Culture, with a capital *C*, as "the best that has been thought and known in the world," cultural studies offers, instead, scholarly work that problematizes how one arrives at designations such as "the best," or how one organizes and reconstitutes perceptions into what is then understood as the "known." Thus, from the perspective of cultural studies, "low art," or popular culture, becomes an important source of the cultural reality that an artist reconfigures into "the best" of what is "known."

Throughout my argument, I use Lacan's central thesis that identity is based upon a permanent sense of lack.[13] We compensate for this lack by understanding ourselves through symbols. Through the creative perception and rearrangement of these symbols, we construct a "myth of the self." Such a myth compensates for the primal sense of lack but can never eliminate it. Lacan maintains that the object of desire for the human subject is never *what* we desire, but what *causes* us to desire. The object may compensate for insatiable lack, or distract us from experiencing it, but can never absolve it. Lacan's sense of the human being as needing to compensate for lack through the constant consumption of symbols makes his theory a powerful way to factor in the influence of the birth of advertising, popular culture, and commodity culture on the fiction of James Joyce. To put this another way, when Ulysses is reincarnated in Joyce's novel, he becomes Leopold Bloom, an ad canvasser in 1904 Dublin, whose "final meditations," just before drifting off to sleep at the end of a long day, are "of some one sole unique advertisement to cause passers to stop in wonder . . . reduced to its simplest and most efficient terms." Joyce's fiction also permits—even insists upon—a "final meditation" on the "low art" forms of commodity culture, in search of essential clues about the historically specific, lived experience of individuals in the early part of the twentieth century.

Foucault's theory of sexuality as an effect of discourse, and as a way to control subjects, is employed by me to argue that the apparently "natural" phenomenon of what we call "pleasure" also has a history.[14] Here, as elsewhere in the book, my approach heeds Jameson's credo "always historicize." Relative to the early twentieth century, the historicization of "pleasure" requires an understanding of the social and psychological matrix generated by new technology (especially photography and cinema), new products to consume, new marketing strategies to promote this consumption, and new ways to construct what I call "pleasure scenarios," in which "satisfaction is guaranteed"—or at least a simulacrum of satisfaction. In chapter 3, "Power, Pornography, and the Problem of Pleasure: The Semerotics of Desire and Commodity Culture," my example of this, boldly stated, is that the technology that permitted the mass production of erotic postcards *for* male consumers also led to the mass production of erotic fantasies *within* consumers. Advertising acts as a sort of software that permits us to organize and print out "pleasure scenarios" featuring our "selves" as the focal point of a symbol-generated experience of "pleasure."

Specifically, I look at Gabriel's erotic reverie in "The Dead" as a particular packaging of desire—culturally, historically, and even technologically specific—designed to yield, as countless ads also promise, an apparently unproblematic "abode of bliss." Furthermore, just as the commodity erases all trace of the human labor that produces it, as well as any way to analyze the configuration of power brought about by an individually specific relationship of economics and identity in a given subject, Gabriel's reverie also promotes pleasure *while* obscuring relationships of power, and amplifies it *by* obscuring relationships of power—even though it is these very relationships of power that provide the infrastructure for the sensation of "pleasure" in any given scenario. Such moments of pleasure need to be further deconstructed and historicized as the specific strategy of a middle-class bourgeois husband, within a colonial culture, who is uneasy about feeling attracted to the idea of physically imposing himself on his partner as a direct way to meet sexual needs, many of which arise from the ambivalence caused by being a colonial subject of Ireland.

In more general terms, I demonstrate how mass media in general, and advertisements in particular, frequently offer Joyce's characters (the narrator of "Araby," for instance) a way to frame reality, to configure desire, and to fantasize about what is needed to complete the self. Instead of being a sacred language available only to the approved supplicant (i.e., one who has been baptized), advertising is a secular language available to all consumers, although "communion" (i.e., purchasing the product) is possible only to those with cash or approved credit. In both cases, however, the discourse offers transcendence in exchange for compliance. "Pay for me" and "pray for me" amount to the same thing. In our own time, the relationship between heaven and a shopping mall is increasingly obvious. Like cathedrals, malls are vaulted spaces full of resonant iconography and sacred objects (the heavily advertised commodity), calling out to the faithful (those with credit cards) to enter the various shrines and p(r)ay. But once again Joyce anticipates this similarity when the narrator of "Araby" likens the closing of the bazaar to the conclusion of a Catholic mass: "I recognised a silence like that which pervades a church after a service" (*D*, 34).[15]

III

There is still more to consider relative to Stanislaus's offhand remark about Joyce's childhood nickname of "Sunny Jim." Joyce's family—his father, one suspects—superimposed an entire advertising campaign on their son by nicknaming him "Sunny Jim." We can speculate that such a process wields a powerful influence on Joyce's formation of self because he presents the power of such a process in the opening few lines of *Portrait*. When Stephen's father reads a story to him about "a nicens little boy named baby tuckoo," the effect on his sense of self is so immediate and direct as to become his identity: "He *was* baby tuckoo" (*P*, 7, emphasis added). Indeed, the process does not stop there; he further identifies a street in the story as identical to the one near where he lives: "The moocow came down the road where Betty Byrne lived: she sold lemon platt" (*P*, 7). Note how the "reality" of Betty Byrne living in Dublin and selling lemon platt becomes seamlessly joined to the presumably fictional road and moocow mentioned in the story. In a sense, the young Stephen Dedalus had not made any connection among such things as roads, traveling, and stopping off for a treat until the story helped him organize these apparently random events into both a pleasant memory and an anticipation of future consumption (and the revisiting of a scenario of pleasure).

A child in another century hearing this story might have used it as an organizing principle for a very different perceived reality. My point is that the child uses this early narrative to organize his behavior as a consumer, and this, at one and the same time, both grants him an identity and provides a primitive "pleasure scenario." There does not appear to be anything sexual about Stephen's reverie, but consider the way, as an adolescent, he organizes an erotic reverie of himself traveling down a road in "Nighttown," waiting to be called over by some woman selling a treat: "He would follow a devious course up and down the streets. . . . The whores would be just coming out of their houses. . . . He would pass by them calmly waiting for a sudden movement of his own will or a sudden call to his sinloving soul from their soft perfumed flesh" (*P,* 102). It is significant that he is not describing something that is happening, but rather something he is anticipating will happen. This links him not only to the narrator of "Araby," but also to his infantile self imagining the road past Betty Byrne's as identical to the one mentioned in the story his father told him. Although guilt and desire heighten the tone of this adolescent sexual daydream, one can nevertheless see it as similar to a consumer's imagining a walk down the aisle of a store, or the corridor of a mall, waiting for the "sudden movement" of an impulse to buy, or the "sudden call" to him of an ad designed to seduce.

Nicknaming Joyce "Sunny Jim" is not merely descriptive, but also inscriptive; he is to be the child who cheers everyone up, quite miraculously, by performing in such a way as to distract other family members from their depression. As John Joyce was no doubt a primary cause of family depression, small wonder he connected his son's identity to an ad campaign that promised, miraculously, to introduce bliss into the home without requiring anyone to change or even examine his own behavior or attitudes. Now this sounds like a jingle more familiar to us, doesn't it? "What is (the Joyce) home without ('Sunny Jim') Plumtree's Potted meat? / Incomplete. With it an abode of bliss."

The opening pages of *Portrait* also give a glimpse of an Edenic family setting where a young boy, with the alacrity of a vaudeville hoofer, keeps his family entertained and distracted: "[His mother] played on the piano the sailor's hornpipe for him to dance." He learns suddenly, like Adam, that he is naked ("He hid under the table"). His defense is not quite a prayer and not quite a poem, but rather an advertisement of his fear, written with the hypnotic, apparently impromptu persistence that mimics the form, if not the content, of a Sunny Jim jingle: "*Pull out his eyes, / Apologise, / Apologise, / Pull out his eyes*" (*P*, 8). The content, of course, is completely—perhaps deliberately—antithetical to the spirit of an ad jingle, since it both demands self-degradation and threatens bodily harm. Poor Sunny Jim; there is no "joy for him." He has become, in this sudden reversal, the very girl he once knew how to cheer up—but who will mix up some FORCE and cream for him?

As for the young boy depicted in "The Sisters," who certainly does not appear to be anything like Sunny Jim, we should note that this whole story bears the strain of some momentous change relative to the boy's role in the family's psycho-drama. Although once Old Cotter's companion, he is now sullen in his presence. His uncle notes his moody withdrawal by calling him "that Rosicrucian there" (*D*, 11). This boy has clearly begun to separate from the family narrative, to draw less and less attention to himself, even refusing to eat crackers because they might be too noisy. The point is that this is new behavior, and the family seems at a bit of a loss about how to compensate for the boy's precipitous withdrawal from his designated position. For his part, the boy is glad to be out from under something stifling and oppressive, only vaguely understood by him as connected to Father Flynn, but clearly connected to his own family as well.

Nevertheless, while he may have abandoned a role the family assigned to him, this former Sunny Jim goes right back to advertisements in search of a new, self-generated (or so he thinks) reality: "I walked . . . *along the sunny side of the street,* reading *all* the theatrical advertisements in the shop-windows as I went. I found it strange that neither I nor the day seemed in a mourning mood . . ." (*D*, 12, emphasis added). This subtle use of the word "all" reveals a sophisticated notion about advertisements on the part of Joyce. Unlike our use of more traditional sources of information, when we look for advertisements, we do so because we do not know what we want. In the boy's case, he does so for the additional reason that he does not know who he is. Having abandoned the identity assigned to him by the family, he cannot go back to them for reassignment, but the colorful ads with their adventuresome spirit "call" to him in a manner we might express this way: "Feeling like a gnomon? Incomplete? Both pleasant and vicious at the same time? Try this and feel like a parallelogram again!" Although mentioned only briefly here, the extent to which a young boy shapes and is shaped by popular culture is a subject taken up in more detail in the following story, "An Encounter."

In Althusser's terms, the narrator wants to be "hailed" by something, and then experience his (apparently) new-found identity in relationship to this "interpellation." But as my analysis of Stanislaus's Sunny Jim anecdote suggests, it is more complicated than this. In the twentieth century, as Joyce's fiction richly illustrates, mass culture, mass media, and popular culture are the crucial discourses that allow us to formulate and reformulate who we are, how we desire, and what we experience. Neither the narrator of "The Sisters" nor Stephen Dedalus is a blank slate; quite the contrary. At various times, and with varying degrees of success, each of them tries to extricate himself from a particular family, nation, or religious history (the "nets" Stephen vows to fly past) so he can articulate "his story." The text of advertisements, the process of shopping and desiring, the fact of popular culture cheaply available all permit an experience of "self" that operates as a crucial antidote to the poisoning and debilitating effects of unchallenged hegemonic discourse, which, if unchecked by the individual subject, inevitably produces "moral paralysis" in Joyce's fiction.

Examined in a certain light (i.e., from the perspective of poststructural theory), "low art" cultural artifacts such as advertisements reflect a type of immediacy at least somewhat equivalent to what the historical individual of the time might have experienced. Anxieties about gender, for example, might be occluded in a hegemonic narrative, while everywhere exemplified in the advertisements of the day. In the case of a 1904 advertisement, for example, whether actual or in literature, the historical viewer of the ad wonders, in a complex but relatively unexamined way, whether or not to buy the product. The "popular" in commodity culture is that which people are willing to spend money to experience, whether the content of the experience consists of gazing at an advertisement, going shopping, being "entertained," or consuming a particular product with its attendant advertising and packaging. For this reason, I would argue, Joyce presents "low art" cultural artifacts and "chronicles of disorder" as symbolically imbued with the anxieties, hopes, desires, and fantasies of an age in a way that is different from, but no less important than, the texts produced by practitioners of "high art" and "official" history.

My exploration of the importance of advertising in Joyce's fiction shows several new reasons for scholars of modernism to continue the ongoing project of dismantling the traditional modernist distinction between "high art" and "low art." In addition to demonstrating how Joyce's fiction shows a collapse between "high" and "low" culture, I also offer an explanation of why this artificial separation was so carefully maintained in the first place: the barrier between "popular" art and "timeless" art appeared to authenticate the fiction of an independent and aesthetically pure sense of "self" that could distinguish (supposedly) the central from the incidental, the ephemeral from the enduring. And it did so precisely at a time when the "self" as a fiction, and "gender" as a performance, grew increasingly apparent.[16] Accordingly, in chapter 2, "Kitschy, Kitschy Coup: 'Life' and 'History' in a World of Mass-Produced Objects," I look at the way "history" is configured in a commodity culture. Here we find Joyce fascinated with the not yet historicized (and not likely to be) artifacts such as advertisements, magazines, and items of kitsch.

From a colonial perspective, it is the forgotten events and lost objects "beneath" history that retain, for Joyce, a more accurate imprint of what it felt like to be a subject of imperialism. Stephen's indifferent history teaching in "Nestor," for example—accompanied by his interior, fervid questioning of what happens to the "possibilities" ousted by history's "actualities"—suggests why Joyce was so fascinated with advertising and popular culture: it is never an "official" discourse; it is never authored from a monologic perspective (or even by a single, identifiable author); its purpose is to promote impulses rather than contain them; its success will be determined by how much profit it generates rather than by how well it obscures relationships of power. Thus, an advertising campaign, in order to compensate historical subjects and prompt them to buy, will subvert reigning ideology if to do so creates consumer demand for something. Shopping can be an act of unconscious rebellion. Finally, the necessity that it be "popular" assures its peculiar salience to the *lived* experience of being a subject at this particular place and time, regardless of how successfully hegemonic discourse domesticates the authorized and legitimated metanarratives of an era.

Looking at Joyce from the perspective of commodity culture also demands that we look at the history of commodity culture *as* a history, and not merely as something that happened along the way (which is the way commodity culture tends to represent itself). Indeed, Joyce comes out of a "tradition" of commodity culture that has been neither understood as important nor recorded as history.[17] We need a history of commodity culture in order to historicize it as a specifically modern phenomenon. We know about the history of the Industrial Revolution, which is also the history of machines and their effect on labor and society, but we know infinitely less about the history of the things these machines produced, and their effect on modern configurations of subjectivity as demonstrated through historically and culturally specific constructions of identity, gender, desire, and pleasure. Commodity culture is modern, in part, because it relies on technological advances in visual presentation, such as photography, and improved methods of printing, such as lithography. These advances permitted, in turn, cheap production of the plethora of images and advertising that provided the infrastructure of what we now call "mass media." In a parallel development, the ability of machines to mass produce objects connected with a powerful—that is to say, profitable—counterpart in the new-found ability of advertisers to mass produce images and discourse designed to make these innumerable objects appear valuable and necessary.

Added to this, urban populations were swelling, making possible the sales of goods to large numbers of people at a rate never imagined before. The dependably high volume of sales made producing commodities even cheaper, freeing up capital for more and more involved advertising strategies, and thus laying the groundwork for a shared discourse among the rich and poor alike, understood now as "popular culture."[18] In yet another separate but convergent phenomenon, electricity became readily available, thereby permitting the pedestrian areas of the city to be well lit and thus spawning what now goes under the generic term of "night life." Inside the stores, the fact of electricity permitted shop owners to display goods by splendidly bathing them in light, in prearranged settings, safe from the distracting bustle of the street. Cheap printing also brought about modern packaging and modern advertising; thus, one selected from several brands of soap or meat or ointment, all of them roughly the same, but each made distinctive by a successful or unsuccessful advertising campaign. Plate-glass windows, in conjunction with electric light, permitted magical tableaux designed to instill in the viewer complex feelings of hope, envy, discontent, and desire for fulfillment. Although these tableaux, as layered as a dream rebus, were readily available to the eye of everyone, nonetheless an inch of glass ensured that active participation in the fantasy was reserved for those who could afford it.

England's Great Exhibition of 1851 was, as a cultural historian tells us, "devised by a think tank to become a sort of semiotic laboratory for the labor theory of value."[19] But having been planned as a valorization of labor and machines, the Great Exhibition, housed in an enormous building called the "Crystal Palace," became instead "a monument to consumption, the first of its kind, a place where the combined mythologies of consumerism appeared in concentrated form" (Richards, *Commodity Culture,* 7). The original point was to highlight the power and efficiency of the machines that had made all the new products of modern living possible. But the crowds who came to the Crystal Palace found the machines static and uninteresting; they chose to marvel, instead, over the bewildering variety of mass-produced items that the machines were able to produce. For these primitive shoppers, "the era of the spectacle" (as well as the era of the gadget, the gizmo, and the commodity) had begun. By contrast, in a street-market atmosphere, which was the earlier form of commercial exchange, items of food and hand-made products are set up under the indiscriminate light of the sun. The price is not fixed, and the items are readily available for handling. The unromantic bartering and jostling of the street market are not at all reassuring to the narrator of "Araby," who describes his strategy for surviving it in religious and military terms, saying he must "[bear his] chalice safely through a throng of foes" (*D*, 31).

In the Great Exhibition, however, items, for the first time, were displayed; that is to say, they were illuminated by artificial light, deliberately placed just out of reach of the observer, and offered to the public as something precious that would soon be cheaply and readily available in innumerable quantities. Rather than seeking edification through the process of looking, as one might do in a museum, the observer is persuaded that looking must now be experienced as a prelude to possessing. If one once admired objects in order to appreciate them in the light of an agreed-upon aesthetic theory, and a commonly valorized notion of style, the point now became to view objects as much more "active" forms of property capable of bestowing on the owner a "self"-generated "lifestyle." The social construction of one's identity, gender, and value through consumption makes "reality" a much more readily malleable phenomenon because communal values need not be addressed (indeed, should not) when, to paraphrase Ezra Pound, one "makes it new." And yet, the ads that encourage one to express "individuality" by transcending communal values make this pitch to the entire community.

When an object, through advertising, is characterized as unique and personally fulfilling and is at the same time readily available to everyone, shopping takes on the seductive escapist quality that has brought us to our current consumer credo: "Shop till you drop." But while the Crystal Palace is one easily defended place to begin a history of modern consumption (a history that needs to be understood as distinct from the much more studied phenomenon of the history of production), I do not wish to position it as the only one. To do so is to reproduce the teleological, monocausal sense of value and tradition that commodity culture effectively brought to an end. A movement from a set notion of style to the individual production of "lifestyle" generates a new form of symbol generation independent from history in a way never possible before. While commodity culture defies hegemonic historical narrative, it is not at all ahistorical. Commodity culture brings about a nonteleological history based on multiple points of origin, rather than a single, agreed-upon narrative that operates in conjunction with a monological presentation of cause and effect.

From this perspective, the Paris exhibit of 1900 must also be seen as one of the explosive starting points of modern commodity culture. A journalist of the time described with dismay the "India Bazaar" at the Paris exhibit, where the "treasures" of India were on display: "A whole phantom-race dies there and suffers in famine. India is not only a warehouse, it is a cemetery."[20] And, this might prompt us to ask, what is Ireland? What does it mean when a young boy in a colonized country rushes breathlessly to the commodified spectacle of another colonized country with the vague idea of consummating his love—"The syllables of the word Araby were called to me through the silence in which my soul luxuriated and cast an Eastern enchantment over me" (*D,* 32). At the very least, a historical perspective on commodity culture complicates our reading of the boy's final disillusionment—a disillusionment that is accompanied by both the sound of people speaking in the accent of Britain and the clink of dropping coins; it is the very jingle—in both senses of the word—of cultural imperialism.

Indeed, Joyce's allusions to the holy grail in the story (often noted by commentators) represent Joyce's "modern" translation of the grail search into a shopping expedition! Nowadays, if we are to judge by Joyce's revision, Sir Lancelot might say to King Arthur, "I'm going to the mall, can I get you anything?" And the King would then reply: "Bring back the Holy Grail and—O yes—some Oreos." Once we understand just how radical the rise of commodity culture was in Joyce's time, we can see that Joyce's reduction of the holy grail quest to a shopping expedition is a prelude to his making the great Odysseus an ad canvasser. This is not a thin joke, but a profound revelation. The holy grail of our culture is the promise of completion held forth by every advertised commodity. What Joyce saw in his time has continued into our own; consumers are perpetual pilgrims, traveling down "the sunny side of the street," looking for the (w)holy advertisement that will bring divine whol(i)ness into their lives. If Bloom gets his wish, it will be he who designs this perfect ad; every night, as we learn from *Ulysses,* the fantasy of creating the perfect advertising poster is his last thought as he is falling asleep.

But the humiliation the boy feels at the Araby bazaar, which far exceeds his disappointment about Mangan's sister, is also the humiliation the colonial subject feels standing before the ideology of cultural imperialism, an ideology that designates him a "creature" with no inherent worth, someone who is told to regard his least attempt at self-empowerment as grotesquely futile vanity. Joyce critiques British imperialism by examining the seductive quality of its cultural exports, rather than by depicting the unsubtle, too easily despised exportation of its army. And yet, again in a manner that Michel de Certeau characterizes as the "tactic" by which the oppressed avoid the "strategies" of their oppressors, Joyce also shows the enlivening quality of popular culture, independent of its political basis (de Certeau, *Practice of Everyday Life,* xix). Bloom's relationship with the Nymph of the Bath or Maria's relationship with her purse stamped "*A Present from Belfast*" suggests a subject not entirely, and not necessarily, subjected to the demoralizing mandate of British cultural imperialism.[21]

This quality raises another fascinating question: What did it mean that Yeats insisted that the true story of Ireland could issue forth only from the mouth of a peasant—that is, an uncommodified person? What did it mean that Yeats also strove to set up an "Irish" theater, while Joyce frequented the commercial theater and declared that the music hall (with its constant celebration and critique of commodity culture), not poetry, was a criticism of life? Can one find in these distinctions an implicit explanation of why the "Celtic Revival" went one way and Joyce went the other? Certainly Stephen's metaphor of modern Ireland as "a pawn shop" is directly at odds with Yeats's characterization of it as an untapped warehouse of mythological treasures. As Joyce makes clear in his story "A Mother," the supposedly commercially pure Celtic revival was in fact big business: "When the Irish Revival began to be appreciable Mrs Kearney determined to take advantage of her daughter's name and brought an Irish teacher to the house. Kathleen and her sister sent Irish picture postcards to their friends and these friends sent back other Irish picture postcards" (*D,* 137).

IV

A sociologist studying consumer culture has recently remarked: "The story of the great transformation of the West has been consistently told from the point of view of the industrial revolution. What has been consistently neglected is the consumer revolution that was a necessary companion of industrial developments."[22] Both modernism and advertising show the various interconnections among the "consumer revolution," the reconfiguration of desire, and the social construction of reality. When James Duffy pastes an advertisement for Bile Beans onto the first page of his cryptic journal, we can safely assume this does not reflect the intention of the marketers of the product. Instead, this product's hyperbolic claim for purging all sorts of melancholia is used by Duffy to remind himself that his little sentences "inscribed from time to time" will no more redeem him than the occasional ingestion of a spurious patent medicine.

Modernism in particular, as sociologist Rob Shields notes, has resisted seeing the connection among commodities, patterns of consumption, and cultural production: "In general, the modernist separation of economy and culture has left little room for serious engagement with consumption practices" (37). Margorie Perloff argues more specifically that Eliot's theorizing about modernism made the literary text a privileged space, immune to, and therefore removed from, economic, social, and ideological influence:

> For T. S. Eliot, form and content were inseparable and hence a poem or novel or play was never primarily what we now call a social text, whose political unconscious might reveal much about the ideology and culture of the early twentieth century but first and foremost a unique work of art. As such, any literary text inevitably raised the issue of value, the unavoidable question being not "What are the ideological underpinnings of X?" or even "What does X mean?" but "Is X a good poem?"[23]

The interesting result, to extrapolate from Perloff's remarks, is that literary texts might well be discussed in terms of a naive sort of use value—"Is X a good, better, best poem?"—but never in terms of a more problematic exchange value: "What are the ideological underpinnings of X that might contribute either to its canonization or marginalization (i.e., its success or failure as a product)?"

If commodity culture has a tradition, Joyce also has a predecessor in the honoring of that tradition: Oscar Wilde.[24] James Joyce and Oscar Wilde are two fellow colonial exiles who developed a modern "personality" (what Wilde called a "mask," and Joyce called "the enigma of a manner") in order to combat an imperialist ideology designed to make them feel inherently inferior and creatively bankrupt, except as comical espousers of witty sayings. In a paradox that Wilde would have appreciated, any tendency in the last decade to dismiss his work as witty but insubstantial is widely viewed by contemporary scholars as the mark of a superficial mind. What was often dismissed as "shallow" in Wilde's work by his contemporaries—his high regard for the ephemeral "trivia" of fashion, style, and manner, for example—is, I argue, precisely what made him fascinating to Joyce. For Joyce, Wilde is an Irishman who out-Britished the British, and his disastrous fall from grace was punishment for that, as much as it was the logical result of institutionalized homophobia.

For the colonial subject, appearances *are* far more meaningful than the ponderous Victorian platitudes that passed for philosophy. Whereas people like Haines and Mr. Deasy extol notions of "character" that privilege the maintenance of pro-imperial ideology, Wilde celebrates the self-generating aura of importance made possible by the cultivation of a "personality." Personality is a packaging of the self. In the same way that a lowly commodity, or a tawdry bazaar like Araby, can be made to appear "magical," a colonial subject, through fashion, wit, and impersonation can fly by the nets of prejudice, snobbery, and racism. For example, Deasy's idea of wisdom is contained in the treacherous Iago's advice "Put but money in thy purse"; Iago, of course, is most insistent in this advice with the various people he plans to rob. His is the advice of the imperialist to the colonist: Work hard, fill your purses, because I represent a system that will systematically empty them into my coffers.

Joyce elaborates upon Wilde's brilliant reading of the twilight of the Victorian age of "substance" as the dawning of an age of "spectacle." Mass media is the new infrastructure of this age in which superficial appearances have become—in an exceedingly complex way—everything. As Lady Bracknell says of Algernon, "[he] is an extremely, I may almost say an ostentatiously, eligible young man. He has nothing, but he looks everything."[25] Formerly, in order to qualify as "someone," one needed to own property and come from a suitably impressive family bloodline. But with the rise of the mercantile class, a class able to make vast fortunes by advertising and marketing such packaged items as spurious health pills, one could also achieve upward social mobility by "posturing"; that is, by repackaging the "self" as a "personality." As Lord Henry points out in *Dorian Gray,* "With an evening coat and a white tie . . . anybody can gain a reputation for being civilized."[26] Indeed, having a "reputation," a liability once upon a time, became, in Wilde's time, a useful and even essential component for the construction of a "personality."

Naturally, the art of posturing, because it was so effective at infiltrating social boundaries, was attacked as being insincere by the very people whose boundaries were being infiltrated. Wilde demonstrated that sincerity is the luxury of the inclusive; it is the self-affirming principle of people of wealth and property who control access to their own society, and who use it as a shibboleth to exclude others. Sincerity, one might say, is in the eye of the key holder. Buck Mulligan's relentless insincerity, like Stephen's "kinchlike" cynicism, are variations of Wildean dissembling. Personality, in this case, is a composite of "tactics" permitting one to enter the enemy camp of British imperialist society and subvert the "strategies" designed to make colonial subjects feel inherently inferior. What Wilde taught, both in his socially mobile life and in his writing, is that sincerity is important in one sense only: once you have learned to fake it, you've got it made.

Victorian wisdom, as Wilde presents and lampoons it in his satirical epigrams, promotes self-serving behavior and crass objectives under the guise of presenting lessons that have been learned after centuries of trial and error. "Young people, nowadays, imagine that money is everything," Lord Henry's uncle pontificates in *Dorian Gray.* "Yes," Lord Henry replies, "and when they grow older they know it" (82). In short, Wilde was a droll prophet of the coming commodity culture apocalypse, shouting out, in the noisy wilderness of a burgeoning new marketplace ruled by image, fantasy, and desire (the dominant reality of his time and ours), his misgivings as well as his delight. His conscious relationship to his theater and public audience should be viewed as one of his workshops for exploring subjectivity with decentering analytical techniques that are now lumped under the general rubric "poststructural." It is Dorian Gray who, sounding amazingly like Jacques Lacan, "used to wonder at the shallow psychology of those who conceive the ego in man as a thing simple, permanent, reliable, and of one essence. To him, man was a being with myriad lives and myriad sensations . . ." (102). The "individual" not only performs for an audience, he or she experiences a sense of "self" by acting as his or her own audience. "We watch ourselves," states Lord Henry in *Dorian Gray,* "and the mere wonder of the spectacle enthrals us" (127). In the age of spectacle, we are no more or less than what we imagine other people see when they look at us. This awareness of spectacle causes Gerty MacDowell to lean back and Bloom to ejaculate when she does so.

Another important link between the two writers is their understanding of aesthetic theory as politically motivated, something I discuss in detail with reference to Stephen's aesthetic theory in the concluding chapter. Wilde's aesthetic theory, often summarized as "art for art's sake," concerns itself more with altering perception than discussing reception. The kinetic and the pornographic, usually excluded by the aesthete because they are unpredictable and unintellectual, are both factored in by Joyce and Wilde for these same reasons. For Wilde, the artist becomes a criminal in the sense of calling attention to implicit laws by breaking them, and Joyce sees the artist as a con man who forges checks to better illustrate where cultural bankruptcy lies. Every effect is produced by the performative—and none more so than the normative: "Being natural is simply a pose," Lord Henry states, while defending himself against accusations of posing, "and the most irritating pose I know" (23). The fact that everything is a pose does not mean that everything is artificial; rather, it means that nothing is "natural," and therefore everything is neither more nor less artificial than everything else.

This insight is what Baudrillard has called the "simulacrum" phenomenon in the "age of spectacle." When a package states that it contains "real fruit juice," in what precise sense is the juice more "real" than "artificial" flavor? When we watch thirty minutes of "world news," is it really about the world and is it really news? Reality, in an age of mass media, seems to be a convention that is formed in opposition to whatever polarized point of view we choose to view as "artificial." Nowadays (to use a favorite word of Wilde's), whoever acquires the most information about something is in a position to declare their point of view "genuine." As Lyotard has suggested, information is now "nature" for postmodern man. When Dorian Gray says "it is personalities, not principles, that move the age," the point to be made is not that principles are "genuine" and personalities are "artificial," but rather that "principled" people pose as much as "personalities." The whole difference between the two poses is that the former mode of being is out of fashion, hence ineffective and laughable, and the latter is more "in style," hence powerful and influential.

Postmodern theorists, with their denaturalization of "innate" principles such as "reality," "truth," and "goodness," have set the stage for a more profound appreciation of what Wilde and Joyce intuited about an age of spectacle—an age in which everything is both on display and for sale. "Nowadays," Lord Henry observes, "people know the price of everything and the value of nothing" (*Dorian,* 104). The struggle to define "value" in some manner unrelated to marketability is at the center of both late-Victorian aestheticism and late-Victorian angst; we have moved from the image of a consumer studiously buying only what he or she came for, to the image presented in Toyota commercials: consumers in mid-air, frozen in leaps of joy from which we never see them descend. The endlessly varied expression of "personality" has replaced the less spectacular maintenance of preestablished "principles." Dorian Gray is reluctant to forward an expensive bill to his guardians, "who were extremely old-fashioned and did not realize that we live in an age when unnecessary things are our only necessities" (92). The trivial and the ephemeral simply are more important than anything posing as permanent, because "personality" and the sensation of "the moment" constitute "reality" (as the Toyota ad has it, in a contemporary version of history as a shout in the street: "Oh, what a feeling!").

Stephen's ineffectual history lesson can be compared to an outmoded form of the market, where events were recorded because of their "significance" and objects were bought for their "use value." Now, at least to himself, Stephen questions where actualities unrecorded by history go. He questions history's claim to be a metanarrative that records all that is worth noting. Pyrrhus, as I've already suggested, is remembered for a slogan; meanwhile, the battlefield is littered with anonymous dead who will not make it into the history books. Stephen seems to read this as a lesson that only the skillful ad campaigner can be sure to "make history." It is not what happens, but how what happens is packaged that makes it "history." In today's media, we know this as "spin control."

In this light, the greatest ad campaigner of all time is Jesus Christ, the man who brought you the communion wafer: "Hey, everybody! It looks like a piece of bread, but wait . . . !" He is an adman sent by the home office to set up a chain of local franchises (churches) and to disseminate numerous slogans, which will then be woven into the fabric of people's everyday life like a sort of sacred Sunny Jim jingle: "To Caesar what is Caesar's, to God what is God's. A long look from dark eyes, a riddling sentence to be woven and woven on the church's looms" (*U*, 22). Christ's parables, which entice and puzzle, are perfect advertising copy because they keep the listener/consumer mesmerized in a position of fantasizing all the myriad ways the message might yet complete their lives and transform them. "Man does not live by bread alone," Christ reminds us, and modern advertising would be ineffectual, irrelevant, and incomprehensible if he were wrong.

Through the new testament of advertising, giving unto Caesar (shopping and paying) feels the same as giving unto God (attending Mass and praying), and that is why it is the new religion of the twentieth century. Just as the distinction between "high" and "low" culture has collapsed in art, the "sacred" and the "secular" world are likewise meaningless polarities in commodity culture. To shop is to worship; to pay is to pray. As Bloom makes clear when he pops into a Catholic Mass, one secret of the communion wafer's success is the careful ritual that precedes its consumption: "Good idea the Latin. Stupefies them first" (*U*, 66). It is an adman's dream product, easily and cheaply made, and yet able to attract, in the context of a Mass, worshipful masses who come forward to p(r)ay.

V

Joyce's first short story was printed in an agricultural journal just above an advertisement for mineral water ("Sparkling Montserrat. The Drink for the Gout & Rheumatic") and another advertisement for dairy equipment ("Refrigerating Machines; Cream Separators; Mild Pumps"). It was only after Joyce saw the story printed that he introduced Eliza's famous verbal slip of "rheumatic wheels" instead of "pneumatic wheels." Thus the eminently forgettable soda advertisement ("The Drink for the Gout & Rheumatic") generates the momentary slip of the tongue.[27] The "language of the marketplace," which Stephen Dedalus is so anxious to keep separate from the "language of the artist," has already been collapsed into the nonhistoricized moment. Stephen is fighting a battle in *Portrait* that was lost before it even occurred to anyone to fight it; the distinction between supposedly "timeless" art and the conveniently ephemeral marketplace is—as we like to say nowadays—history.

Stephen himself seems to be coming around to this point of view in the closing page of *Portrait,* where he refers to his own behavior as opening the "valve" of "the spiritual-heroic refrigerating apparatus, invented and patented in all countries by Dante Alighieri" (*P,* 252). This choice of metaphor takes us back again to the advertisement published next to Joyce's first published work, which announces the availability of "Refrigerating Machines." This might be said to be the anxiety not of influence, but of invention. Stephen is taking further Oscar Wilde's idea that life imitates art; now, however, the artist is an inventor who markets his creation to people, in all countries, working on the machinery that will produce their "personality." Dante was a genius, but he also wrote good copy.

In chapter 4, "The Virgin Mary and the Urge in Gerty: Praying, Buying, and the Packaging of Desire," I look at the religious fetish and the commodity fetish in "Nausicaa" from both a post-Freudian (Lacan, Irigaray, Kristeva, Zizek) and post-Marxist perspective (Baudrillard, de Certeau, Foucault, Jameson) to show how both function as objects of desire that purport to "complete" the subject, but really only serve as catalysts for a subject's fantasy of completion. As in the "Nausicaa" chapter itself, I reverse perspective in this chapter to demonstrate how Joyce explores what it feels like to *be* an object of desire, and how he represents the effect of such a position on the experience of desire (what does the object of desire want?). I argue that sexual desire generated in the commodity culture of the twentieth century is culturally specific, historically determined, and dependent upon a commercially generated, sacred iconography made culturally intelligible by a current advertising campaign.

The particular gender construction urged by advertisements plays a crucial role in the formation of fantasies by which the male and female reach each other.[28] If, as Lacan claims, the sexual act is a complex masquerade whereby the woman pretends to be what she is not, so the man can become what he pretends, then advertisements provide the latest dance steps in this waltz of orgasmic misrecognition; far from being unpleasurable, such misrecognition is necessary in the production of a scenario of pleasure. Likewise, the aura of commodities depends upon our mistaking them as being representative of what we need to complete our "selves."

Before modern mass production, "style" was a way to indicate where one stood in relation to a preexisting social hierarchy, but, with the advent of mass-produced images, clothes, and advertisements in the twentieth century, "style" became more personal, more a way to declare one's independence from the existing order. Whereas earlier one would assume a given style in order to "fix" oneself at a certain point in the social hierarchy, by the turn of the century, in a move pioneered by Wilde, attention to style indicated the exact opposite ambition: one's determination to move freely in and around, up and down a social hierarchy that had become unfixed. Such a use of style, as Wilde's career indicates, was of particular benefit for someone from a colonized country where "the natives" were white; the ability of the Irish to mimic the imperialists, therefore, was unimpeded by the presence of easily stigmatized physical characteristics such as skin pigmentation. If Mulligan enjoyed traveling to England and merging him"self" with "oxy chaps" at Oxford, Stephen, with his "Latin quarter hat," appears to have enjoyed being a bohemian artist of no readily apparent origin while in Paris (*U,* 6, 14). And, put in this wider context, Gerty's ruminations about her underwear seem more savvy about how to market herself in a competitive market, than they seem the silly preoccupations of a vain girl.

My penultimate chapter turns to the "Penelope" chapter of *Ulysses* and examines in detail what Jennifer Wicke has called "Molly's work of consumption" (Wicke, *JJQ,* 174). When Molly complains that "sure you cant get on in this world without style all going in food and rent when I get it Ill lash it around I tell you in fine style" we can see in her juxtaposition of ideas, as well as in her awkward repetition of the word *style,* that she is trying to articulate an urge to be a modern consumer with a "lifestyle" (and not merely a woman anxious to dress in the latest "style") (*U,* 618). Her phrase "you cant get on in this world," for example, indicates that in "this world"—that is to say, Molly's contemporary world—an individual whose money is "all going in food and rent" lacks what we now call the "discretionary income" needed to support a lifestyle that solicits the gaze of others. A lifestyle, even though privately manufactured by a consumer, nevertheless must be made visible to others, or it cannot be said to exist at all.

In my final chapter, "When a Fly Gets in Your I: The City, Modernism, and Aesthetic Theory in *A Portrait of the Artist as a Young Man,*" I broaden my focus considerably and suggest issues ultimately beyond the scope of this book, but nonetheless connected to it. I discuss *Portrait* in detail in order to show how Joyce's form of modernism is not a representation of modernity but a symptom of it. More specifically, Joyce's fiction makes a strong connection between the experience of modernity and the rise of the modern city, and I argue that what is specifically "modern" about the city in the twentieth century is the sense of publicly signifying systems of desire, circulated in an unprecedented manner through improvements in mass media, and amplified as never before through sophisticated rhetorical strategies (most notably, advertising).

In this regard, setting up the aesthetic and the pornographic serves the important task of polarizing and categorizing sensory response in such a way that any dialogue about desire becomes an exercise in taxonomy, obsessed with "self"-defensively sorting out the "perverse" from the "normal." This is a very Catholic oscillation that Stephen has already lived out in his own body, literally shuttling between the "pornographic" realm of Nighttown and the "beautiful" aura of the Virgin Mary: "her names were murmured softly by lips whereon there still lingered foul and shameful words, the savour itself of a lewd kiss" (*P*, 105). But this oscillating process is also, from a historical perspective, an attempt to maintain some distance from, and thus achieve some resistance to, the newly seductive visual extravaganza of the modern city.

Earlier writers (Gissing, for example) managed to weave the phenomenon of advertising spectacle into their novels with a sort of naive indignation, but Joyce deliberately presents only a peripheral view of actual advertising spectacle in his fiction in order to highlight the entire phenomenon of commodity culture—including ubiquitous advertising, the constant introduction of "new" products, increasingly sophisticated strategies of display—all combining to provide the post-Cartesian subject with a new system for ordering consciousness. For example, by setting Bloom's consumption of Gerty (and her consumption of his consumption) on a deserted Irish seashore, but nonetheless in strict accordance with the semiotics (one might say the semerotics) of the sexualized leisure space in British resorts such as Brighton, Joyce makes the point that advertising can structure gender, desire, and what we take to be "reality"—Sandymount strand "becomes" Brighton beach, and Bloom's orgasm, in this sense, is produced by a plethora of absent advertisements, popular songs, and fashion images.

In other words, advertising can colonize space as well as consciousness, but this same process also can open up unexpected space, both in one's fantasies and in intersubjective relationships, for a possible semerotic reconfiguration of the social construction of identity, gender, and nationality. Eveline's conception of the exotic place of "Buenos Ayres" (fresh air) where she will "be somebody," is analogous to the "spaces" opened up by mass culture. As a result of traversing these oddly exciting, wide-open spaces, interspersed throughout dear, dirty Dublin, Eveline is able to imagine, in a fragmented way, traveling much further to a far-off land where "people would treat her with respect then" (*D*, 37). In places such as these, not unlike the space of the Araby bazaar, everyday experience is commodified into "entertainment," and escape seems plausible in the form of a satisfaction that is anticipated as complete, even as it is impossible to actually bring about in any concrete way.

Stated most simply, my project throughout this book is to demonstrate how Joyce's fiction consistently asserts that what is disposable, insignificant, ephemeral, dead, or forgotten may nevertheless—may especially—influence and shape our sense of reality and self more profoundly than those objects, texts, and images that have been designated as worthy representatives of eternal truth. Advertising—the protean incarnation of what Stephen Dedalus rather archly considers the language of the marketplace—influences the way Joyce's characters think, consume, desire, and despair. In one instance, Father Arnall explains the unique properties of hellfire, unintentionally employing the language of the marketplace: "the sulphurous brimstone which burns in hell is a substance *which is specially designed* to burn for ever and for ever with unspeakable fury" (*P*, 121, emphasis added). In another instance, Bloom admires how effectively the Catholic Church utilizes complex slogans to market the communion wafer. In a third instance, Stephen conceives an image of his prayers mounting up as a giant cash register in the sky. Everyone in Dublin dreams, at one time or another, of buying cheap and selling dear.

By presenting consumption as equivalent to an act of faith, Joyce underwrote the experience of modernity in the twentieth century. His fiction is always concerned with "now," sandwiched as it is between the unrepresentable past and the inscrutable future. If his fiction has long been characterized as "classic," my study may contribute to our appreciation of it as forward-looking, as, well, the novelistic equivalent of what Burger King has recently called its latest breakfast muffin: an "instant classic."

1

Advertising and Religion

The New (Improved!) Testament

What past consecutive causes, before rising preapprehended, of accumulated fatigue did Bloom, before rising, silently recapitulate?
... the advertisement of Alexander Keyes (Urim and Thummim). . . .

(*U*, 599)

Urim and Thummim: A means of revelation used by the High Priest. . . . Revelation was thought to have been given by light flashing or by the protruding of certain letters from the breastpiece stones. It is striking that even in the face of repeated defeats, after obeying each time the instructions received by using the Urim and Thummim, the revelation received was not questioned.[1]

Joyce teaches us that insignificance is curiously powerful, precisely because it dwells beneath the notice of history. Perhaps it is the general status of advertisements as "ephemeral," "trivial," and "vulgar" that has caused many critics to regard their presence in Joyce's fiction as indicating nothing more than his passion for factual and "realistic" details. Increasingly, however, as my introduction outlines, scholars are paying closer attention to these "disposable" features in Joyce's fictional reality. After all, the famous "throwaway" handed to Bloom announces the most important event, from a Judeo-Christian perspective, since the world began: "Bloo . . . . Me? No. Blood of the Lamb. . . . Elijah is coming" (*U*, 124). While Alexander J. Dowie's throwaway intends to announce the coming of Elijah, preparatory to the second coming of Christ, in Judaic tradition it is also Elijah who will reappear to usher in the Messiah and the final redemption of mankind. In *Ulysses,* the ephemeral and disposable—a "throwaway"—figure forth the apocalypse and provide a promise of closure to the painfully open-ended experience of being human. Modern advertising's promise of completion, redemption, and the attainment of paradise is the equivalent of holy scripture for Joyce, the new (improved!) testament, promising completion and bliss if purchased, and warning of permanent gnomonic despair if spurned.

Like the modern advertisement intended to arrest the gaze of the urban pedestrian, the biblical Urim and Thummim also presented itself as a mesmerizing display; precious stones set in a breastplate gave forth light or shifted into the formation of different letters when a prophet wore the breastplate into the presence of God. One property of the message, which made it especially potent, is that it was supposed always to give a perfect and complete answer. In the treacherous world of biblical prophecy, only for this message was complete satisfaction guaranteed. In this sense, it was seen as unique and distinct from either oracles or dreams—both of which might be false to begin with, or might be true and still be misinterpreted. The message of the Urim and the Thummim was highly valued because it could not be false, and—even more astounding—could not be misinterpreted. It was the purest form of communication, with no loss of meaning as a result of transmission; to see it as a signifier was to discover that one was what it signified.

Nevertheless, as the quote I cite above makes clear ("It is striking that even in the face of repeated defeats, . . . the revelation received was not questioned"), circumstances would often contradict the message. Contradiction, disappointment, and disillusionment, oddly enough, never caused people to doubt it the next time it appeared. Can we not equate this to modern advertising? A startling message appears, arresting enough to make us stop in wonder; the revelation seems complete—indeed, it seems to complete us. We do its bidding; that is to say, we buy the product and use it; we are disappointed that the result is less than apocalyptic. But another message appears . . . what does it say? No matter, we do its bidding, "obeying each time the instructions received."

In the case of the prophet David, his particular method for eliciting a revelation was to ask direct questions and obtain affirmative answers. *The Encyclopedia Judaica* reports, "In point of fact no examples of negative answers are anywhere recorded."[2] This may give a clue about why the message was sought and obeyed, again and again, and the revelation never questioned, "even in the face of repeated defeats." In essence, David asks a question to which he hopes to receive the answer "yes." The message formed and illuminated by the Urim and the Thummim is persistently believed, despite "defeats," because it only answers those questions already formed in the mind of the questioner, and it never says no. The message is nothing more than a presumably objective reflection of what the questioner needs to believe. The attraction of this form of "revelation" is that a dimension outside the self seems to confirm what the self needs to believe if it is to experience itself as complete. All it really reveals, of course, is the exact opposite, that subjective consciousness is built around a forgotten but irrepressible sense of loss and incompleteness. Our need to search for substitute objects to mitigate this loss is insatiable and unending.

As Lacan would have it, language, symbols, and objects are all replacements for a permanent "lack-in-being" that can be temporarily assuaged, but never eradicated. The object of our desire, he asserts, can never be what we want, but only that which causes us to want. Built into the sense of satisfaction and completeness that the object or message gives us is an inevitable disappointment causing us to want again; this paradox of human desire makes a commodity culture both possible and profitable. Like the advertisement making a manufactured commodity appear as an object of desire, the message from the Urim and Thummim creates repeat customers by offering a powerful mix of absolute reassurance specifically tailored to a preexisting anxiety. The fact that this reassurance is then followed by a disappointment only stimulates the need for further reassurance.

People surreptitiously seek personal affirmation and reassurance even as they claim to be simply in search of "the truth." Though they choose to view this reassurance as an objective and indifferent prophecy, the fact that it does not come true does not relieve them of the compulsion to go through the process again. Knowledge of this human phenomenon—that the self needs to be authenticated and authorized by something perceived as beyond the self—makes the successful marketing of a new product—or a new belief—possible. When Bloom muses about the perfect poster before falling asleep (and we are told he does so "habitually"), he imagines it as "unique" in a way that makes the perceiver "stop in wonder" and somehow (mis)recognize the "uniqueness"—available to all—as intended solely for him (*U*, 592); in other words, whatever your hope, your ambition, your fear, the advertisement replies: "Yes! You will! Yes! Yes!"

I am arguing that Joyce consciously links the power of advertising with the power of revelation in the Judeo-Christian tradition, but, even beyond that, he sees the impulse that draws us to advertising as the same impulse that draws us to any form of mysticism. When Bloom stares at the label of a Bass Ale in the "Oxen of the Sun" episode, the point is made—first by the narrative style, and then more succinctly by Buck Mulligan—that Bloom is having an other-worldly experience such as a prophet or high priest might have before passing on the "revelation" to the wider community:

> It floats, it flows about her starborn flesh and loose it streams, emerald, sapphire, mauve and heliotrope, sustained on currents of the cold interstellar wind, winding, coiling, simply swirling, writhing in the

> skies a mysterious writing till, after a myriad metamorphoses of symbol, it blazes, Alpha, a ruby and triangled sign upon the forehead of Taurus. (*U*, 338)

> He was laying his hand upon a winejar: Malachi saw it and withheld his act, pointing to the stranger and to the scarlet label. Warily, Malachi whispered, preserve a druid silence. His soul is far away. (*U*, 340)

The triangle on the Bass Ale bottle, with its symbolical allusion to Alpha from the book of Revelation, indicates that the message, whatever its specific content, has something to do with origins and destinations, birth and death: "I am Alpha and Omega, the beginning and the ending, saith the Lord" (Rev. 1:8). Any object, label, slogan, or symbol that indicates to us it knows the beginning and the end—including our beginning and end—would appear to us as reassuring, as able to fill in what is lacking, if we could only learn how to associate ourselves with it or how to pay it homage.

In the case of Plumtree's Potted Meat, authored by Joyce, we have a brilliantly representative ad in which the product knows what we need and, by extension, both knows and pities what we lack. But the product, like God, can only do so much; the product helps those who help themselves—that is, who help themselves to the product. From this position of absolute knowledge, the product is able to offer a guaranteed remedy and absolute reassurance. A sense of lack and incompleteness is deliberately evoked in order to set the stage for an onset of unexpected, thus "blissful," completion. The emphasis, with both Bass Ale and Plumtree's Potted Meat, is on nondenominational clairvoyance; the consumer mesmerized before the product is presented as a degraded version of the supplicant in ecstasy before a religious vision. "Bliss" is a word denoting "supreme happiness," but it is also a theological term meaning "the joy of heaven." Indeed, the narrator's description of the slowly forming revelation from the Bass label is not unlike the purported mystical "swirling" of the Urim and Thummim; there, too, stones glow, shift, and finally protrude from the breastplate until "after a myriad metamorphoses of symbol," an unequivocal message appears.

Commodity culture also uses repetitive messages to stimulate repetitive behavior, as does religious ritual. From this perspective, as I discuss in detail later, Bloom sees the communion wafer as the most successfully advertised "product" in the world. Adherence to the Catholic faith becomes a profound example of what marketing strategists call "brand loyalty." Joyce presents the overall dynamic of advertising, as well as the broader social phenomenon of what we might call "commodity culture," in order to demonstrate the extent to which social relations, nationalist aspirations, power structures, economic disparities, gender constructions, and even consciousness itself all depend upon, and interact with, the simulated universe of consumerism, cultural imperialism, and commodity culture.[3] As Franco Moretti has suggested, "reality" is always a cultural construct in *Ulysses:* "There is nothing but ideology in this novel: it is a universe of false consciousness" (206). I would like to take this observation one step further by suggesting that, in Joyce's fiction at least, "consciousness" is always "false" because the "universe" within which we experience "consciousness" is always a cultural and linguistic construct. But this falsity, what Baudrillard would call a "simulacrum," is no more or less than the inevitable mediation that follows when the world is replaced by the word.

Joyce recognized that advertising had come to influence the structure of the human subject's "universe" with a dominance and pervasiveness previously reserved for religion. As Jennifer Wicke states, "*Ulysses* conceives advertisement as the substitute for holy communion. . . . the multiple reception of advertisements is a simulacrum of religious ceremony" (*Advertising Fictions,* 147). The connection between advertising and religion is not original with Joyce, however. The idea of advertising as a sort of New Testament is already implicit in this excerpt from an American advertising manual of 1870: "No monarch's slaves ever scattered at his bidding so fleetly or faithfully, or in such bewildering numbers, as the literary messengers that bear your individual word to the people of this great nation" (qtd. in Wicke, *Advertising Fictions,* 79). "The people" of a "great nation" are united by advertisements and the dynamic of paying rather than by religious creeds and the dynamic of praying. Indeed, I wish to argue that Joyce demonstrates how, in the twentieth century's phase of late capitalism, it is the construct of the consumer, rather than that of the supplicant, that supplies the new blueprint for the myth of the self within the universe of commodity culture. Bliss, formerly a religious revelation that leads to a glimpse of heaven and an all-knowing God who completes us and guarantees our worth, is now something we experience by consuming the "all-knowing" product.

The ideology embedded in all advertisements practices, to use Jameson's felicitous phrase from *The Political Unconscious,* "strategies of containment."[4] Advertisements offer simulations of reality that help the subject suppress any potentially subversive contradictions in the narrative of his or her own history. Advertisements, and the commodities that they elevate into the realm of sacred relics, permit the subject to maintain a relatively utopian view of a self-determined "reality." They help the subject perceive his or her "self" as the originating force of what is in fact a socially constructed "reality." This simulated universe is a product of the complex interaction between the insatiable structure of human desire and the exigencies of economic necessity. By relying on the paradoxically insatiable structure of human desire to assure a market for a potentially infinite number of new commodities, and by constantly celebrating the consumer's freedom of choice, advertisements help sustain the modern mythic structure of individual autonomy as well as the illusion of free will.

This myth of the unmediated "self," in its turn, helps preserve the illusion that a capitalist economy provides everyone with a just economic environment where all people are free to compete on equal terms with one another for financial and material gain: "If *Ulysses* expresses the cultural dialectics of liberal capitalism in agony, then it will necessarily linger upon the dissolution of the figure of the petty bourgeois—the free producer, economically independent and intellectually proud of his own autonomy—so relevant within the Anglo-Saxon ideological system in the eighteenth and nineteenth centuries" (Moretti, 198). Moretti goes even further and explains the suicide of Bloom's father as the sad result of an individual "not wanting to abandon the heroic ethic of the free market" (199).

In a commodity culture, the highly valued myth of individual free will is reified (one might say "deified") into the sacred notion that we are free to express who we are because we are free to buy what we want. What this equation leaves out, of course, is that the consumer has been persuaded to believe in what he or she wants, and has been further conditioned (as a side effect of this ideological seduction) into no longer wanting what he or she already has. In a more concrete description of this process, going shopping bestows a temporary state of grace on the consumer; it is a state of grace—as powerful as it is temporary—not unlike that which the faithful experience during the ritual of participating in a church service. As an ad canvasser, Bloom frankly admires the ability of the Catholic Church to attract "repeat customers." He interprets the structure and content of the Catholic mass as an effective advertising campaign—one that is, from his point of view, ingeniously designed to attract consumers eternally.

In *Ulysses,* advertising seems to be the central feature of a new religion (consumerism) that makes a congregation of unified believers out of even the most culturally disparate group. As Jennifer Wicke puts it: "Where channels of public speech have broken down—the church pulpit, the town meeting—advertisements' illusory surface of collective discourse finds a place" (*Advertising Fictions,* 16–17). Nowhere is this more evident than in "Wandering Rocks," where the posters featuring Eugene Stratton and Marie Kendall smile benignly at all people passing, regardless of their race, creed, or gender. "The advertised ones seem to grab the noblesse oblige for themselves" Wicke says of these two posters; "they smile their ecumenical smiles at all and refuse to bestow especial grace on the powerful ones, who, themselves, become part of the pageant passing before the ever more contained power of advertisements" (*Advertising Fictions,* 150). One needs to note, however, that Wicke seems in danger of reifying these two advertisements into objects that exert force independent of the participating presence of a consumer. I would argue that there is no political or mythic dimension for advertisements that is not connected to the equally political and mythic structure of the "autonomous" subject; advertisements cannot be anything more than what they persuade us to think we are doing, and who they allow us to think we are.

In Joyce's fiction, the "self"-generated Cartesian subject is replaced by a new matrix of over-determined signifiers, and we might call this latter day Prometheus "the consumer." Descartes's philosophy, long ago reduced to a single line that has the pithiness of a slogan or a bumper sticker, "I think, therefore I am," has been recast into a new slogan, of which an actual bumper sticker I saw recently may serve as a succinct example: "I owe, I owe, so it's off to work I go."[5] In a commodity culture, the modern presumption about subjectivity is that we may not always be able to think what we choose, but we will always be free to verify the individual autonomy of our "self" by choosing what we buy. In the act of shopping, so we come to believe, we are "free to be ourselves." But as Baudrillard has pointed out, "free to be oneself" in fact means free to project one's inarticulate desires onto products that have been pre-articulated by advertisements.[6] In Joyce's time as well as our own, the mode of production, so central to Marx's philosophy, has been replaced by an ahistorical mode of consumption—a mode where pieces of the Berlin Wall can be marketed to the public using the same strategy that years ago made pet rocks an apparent necessity. The question becomes "who controls the mode of consumption?" In the case of Joyce's Ireland, the answer is England.

When Bloom is appalled by his mental image of the arid wasteland of the Middle East, it is the ahistorical reflection that he must begin performing Sandow's exercises again that brings him relief:

> Desolation.
>
> Grey horror seared his flesh. Folding the page into his pocket he turned into Eccles street, hurrying homeward. Cold oils slid along his

> veins, chilling his blood: age crusting him with a salt cloak. Well, I am here now. Yes, I am here now. Morning mouth bad images. Got up wrong side of the bed. Must begin again those Sandow's exercises. On the hands down. (*U*, 50)[7]

In "Circe," Bloom the amateur astronomer is placed within the self-referential hermeneutical constellation of advertisement and product. As Bloom's bar of lemon soap mounts into the sky, announcing as it does so, "We're a capital couple are Bloom and I. / He brightens the earth. I polish the sky" (*U*, 360), his "reality" becomes a closed loop of signification, a simulated universe, that forecloses any knowledge of the unconscious dimension that nonetheless continues to exist as something Real (to use Lacan's term) beyond the "complete" universe of representation that the advertisement presents so vividly and soothingly.[8]

"Consumption is not a passive mode of assimilation," Baudrillard asserts, "[it] is an active mode of relations (not only to objects, but to the collectivity and to the world). . . . material goods are not the objects of consumption: they are merely the objects of need and satisfaction" (*Selected Writings,* 21). This statement is particularly true of Gerty's underwear: "As for undies they were Gerty's chief care and who that knows the fluttering hopes and fears of sweet seventeen (though Gerty would never see seventeen again) can find it in his heart to blame her?" (*U*, 288).[9] Here the narrator is explicit in pointing out that it is what her underwear represents about the possibilities of marriage—and the emotional and financial security she imagines this will bring her—and nothing about its use value (that is, its reality as a simple piece of cloth), that causes her to care for it, and even meditate about it, as though it were a sacred relic. My point is that those objects of consumption most central to our sense of our "selves" have an importance for us that is equal to the importance sacred relics have for parishioners in an organized religion. In both cases, the over-determined signification of the object, what we might call its "Alpha and Omega," imposes meaning on the disconcerting chaos of subjective experience.

Gerty is a product in the sense that how well she packages her "femininity" will most likely determine whether or not a "manly man" purchases her for his home. Indeed, the relationship between advertising and femininity seems to have been understood even by the pioneers of national advertising (many of whom wrote dozens of advertising manuals in the latter half of the nineteenth century). Giving advice to would-be advertisers in 1890, Nathaniel C. Fowler wrote, "A woman who would not read advertisements would not be a woman, consequently all women read advertisements."[10]

Or, in sacred terms, a sinner who refuses to acknowledge God is damned and, thus, no longer a child of God, and no longer worthy of his protection and love. The point Fowler is making (rather unconsciously, one suspects) is that products that are advertised with a promise to confer "femininity" onto a female consumer will, by virtue of this fact, actually serve to define what "a woman" should be. For Gerty, the act of shopping recollected in tranquillity is poetry. While the men in the background recite a litany to the Virgin Mary, the urge in Gerty produces a litany of orgasm. Nathaniel C. Fowler was all too correct in claiming, "A woman who would not read advertisements would not be a woman." Many theorists of popular culture, taking their cue from F. R. Leavis, have argued for the need to resist advertising as an unfortunate force that cuts us off from some linguistic Eden where we once assigned words to their proper objects with the ease of Adam naming all the animals as they filed past him.

One cannot logically, however, accuse advertisements of falseness because they never pretend they are real. We all know toilet paper can't talk, soap can't sing, and Green Giants do not live in a valley. In fact, most advertisements actively call attention to their own deliberately amusing falseness in order to make more real the supposedly inviolable autonomy of the consumer who practices "free will" and "self determination" when he or she "chooses" what to buy. The myth of subjective consciousness as an unmediated "reality" that serves as the pure origin of experience is as much a simulation as the self-reflexive universe of advertising. Advertising provides the images that help construct the simulated phenomenon of social exchange. In this sense, it is the advertisements, and the process of consumption they incite, that are real, and the consumers who imagine themselves in relation to this "reality." Baudrillard argues:

> The truth about consumption is that it is a function of production and not a function of pleasure, and therefore, like material production, is not an individual function but one that is directly and totally collective. . . . Pleasure would define consumption for itself as autonomous and final. But consumption is never thus. Although we experience pleasure for ourselves, when we consume we never do it on our own (the isolated consumer is the carefully maintained illusion of the ideological discourse on consumption). (*Selected Writings,* 46)

This insight explains why the actual number of commodities we possess, as well as their particular use value, is completely incidental to our desire to continue immersing ourselves in the process of buying whatever it is we haven't got. Purchasing some advertised commodity seems like a way to verify the transcendent quality of our subjectivity. We believe this as an article of faith, which is why the strength of our anticipation does not depend on whether or not we actually know what it is we want to buy, or whether what we buy satisfies us for very long.

In fact, the object we buy eventually is merely the convenient end point of a ritual of consumption we will enact again and again, just as the faithful must attend mass again and again in order to feel like part of a collective. The communion wafer, like the heavily advertised commodity, has an entirely symbolic value and would be beneath notice (nothing more than a tiny bit of bread) if it were to be offered to an individual independent of the rites and sacraments of the Catholic Church. Bloom's dual status as a non-Catholic and as an advertising canvasser causes him to explicate the Catholic mass strictly in terms of its brilliant marketing strategy: "The priest went along by them, murmuring, holding the thing in his hands. He stopped at each, took out a communion, shook a drop or two (are they in water?) off it and put it neatly into her mouth. Her hat and head sank. Then the next one. Her hat sank at once. . . . Good idea the Latin. Stupefies them first" (*U*, 66).

Bloom's admiration of the strategic use of Latin to mesmerize the communicants mirrors a basic strategy of advertising copy: associate unfamiliar buzzwords with a product in order to produce a unique association in the mind of the temporarily confused consumer. A modern-day example of this (1929, actually) is Listerine's use of the word "halitosis" essentially to invent the concept of bad breath. Victorian advertisers of patent medicines were always searching for new words to describe general states of discomfort or anxiety; words such as "neuralgia" and "rheumatism," by virtue of their repetitive use in advertising copy, moved from being specialized medical terms to being household words.

The entire structure of the mass, from the point of view of an advertising canvasser, builds anticipation for communion. The sense of drama inherent in the Catholic mass can be seen, in predictably degraded form, in daily commercials advertised during TV soap operas. The Wisk commercial, for example, opens with a scene of daily life—husband and wife at a cocktail party important to the husband's career—followed by a devastating dislocation: "ring around the collar." Indeed, there is no person present at the party to correspond to this thundering voice-over, which can only be said to come from the sky. The scene cuts from the party to private scenes of the woman failing to solve the crisis: "You try rubbing it out. You try scrubbing it out, but still—'ring around the collar'."

The one practical consideration this commercial elides, of course, is that if clean collars are so important to the man's career, he might think to wash his neck once in a while. Instead, the woman is placed in the hopeless and helpless position of being responsible for the effect of someone else's dirt. The solution to her trumped-up problem, when it arrives, is nothing short of a miracle. Wisk, like the communion wafer, assures her that, although she should be doomed, divine mercy has provided a way out she may embrace through the ritual of consumption: Wisk gets the dirt out. Go in peace. In Bloom's crude but shrewd analysis of the Catholic mass, religious ritual makes the communion wafer a symbol of transcendent subjectivity. An effective advertising strategy, as Bloom is at pains to explain to anyone who will listen, creates a similar repetitive environment that eventually gives a commodity the status of a sacred object. The marketplace where one purchases products is a huge church where, no matter how privately and discreetly one buys, one is participating in, as Bloom says of the people receiving communion, "Something going on: some sodality" (*U*, 66).

The modern consumer is the twentieth-century recuperation of the somewhat faded glory of the "autonomous" Cartesian subject. The consumer is the modern Prometheus who needs advertising—and the resulting marketplace of "sacred" commodities—in order to maintain the illusion that personal experience is still the basis for the presentation of that privileged form of "reality" that we call "consciousness." Commodity culture is a powerful religion that attracts everyone to the altar of the marketplace because it has no creed except, perhaps, for the sign I have often seen posted above cash registers: "In God we trust. All others pay cash." But even this crassly worded creed promises "sodality"; it reaffirms the "autonomy" of all those who p[r]ay for whatever object has been made sacred by the religious and commercial ritual of "mass" media. Baudrillard describes this paradox very neatly: "Advertising tells us, at the same time: 'Buy this, for it is like nothing else!' ('The meat of the elite, the cigarette of the happy few!' etc.); but also: 'Buy this because everyone else is using it!' And this is in no way contradictory. We can imagine that each individual feels unique while resembling everyone else: all we need is a schema of collective and mythological projection—a model" (*Selected Writings*, 11).

In a similar vein, Plumtree's Potted Meat sanguinely promises to "complete" *any* "home." The advertisement both credits everyone with having a unique home life, and then paradoxically promises to "complete" everyone inside the home, regardless of how different various people might be. This concept of universal uniqueness can find its echo only in the biblical discourse, issued from the point of view of God, where we are all God's children, and yet unique in his eyes.

Of course it is not "home" that is incomplete, but the human subject, who, as Lacan maintains, is based on lack. The psychological dimension of the Plumtree ad, therefore, with its bold pledge to "complete" whatever is lacking in the consumer's life, is archetypal. Indeed, the structure of its advertising pitch conforms precisely to what Baudrillard describes as "the heart of the project": "At the heart of the project from which emerges the systematic and indefinite process of consumption is a frustrated desire for totality. Object-signs are equivalent to each other in their ideality and can proliferate indefinitely: and they must do so in order continuously to fulfill the absence of reality. It is ultimately because consumption is founded on a lack that it is irrepressible" (*Selected Writings*, 25).

Bloom's idea about how best to advertise Hely's stationery also exploits the tendency of subjects/consumers to be attracted to anything that shows promise of "completing" them: "I suggested to him about a transparent showcart with two smart girls sitting inside writing letters, copybooks, envelopes, blottingpaper. I bet that would have caught on. Smart girls writing something catch the eye at once. Everyone dying to know what she's writing. Get twenty of them round you if you stare at nothing. Have a finger in the pie. Women too. Curiosity. Pillar of salt" (*U*, 127). His ad is designed to catch the attention of men, something we realize when we see his addendum "Women too."[11] Bloom's further references to "curiosity" and "pillar of salt" make it clear that he is a precursor to the modern-day adman in the sense that he seeks to exploit the most basic psychological constructs of the human subject. Lot's wife could not resist looking, even when there was a high price to be paid, and, given the right ad, modern consumers will not be able to resist looking either.

I would like to spend a little time historicizing the theory of advertising as it was understood in Joyce's time (and even well before his time) in order to strengthen further the connection I am drawing between religion and advertising. In the nineteenth century (and even today), writers who addressed themselves to the subject of advertising often turned to religious metaphors to express either their approval or their disapproval of the rise of commodity culture. Railing against a heavily advertised patent medicine called Morison's, Thomas Carlyle wrote in 1843, "Men and women . . . fancy that their religion . . . shall be a kind of Morison's Pill which they have only to swallow once and all will be well. . . . I advise thee to renounce Morison; once for all, quit hope of the Universal Pill."[12] Having chastised the loyal communicant/consumer for what he insists is a blasphemous belief in the efficacy of a product, Carlyle goes on to deplore the fact that manufacturers work harder to create myths around the object than they do to create objects that have a higher use value: "The Hatter in the Strand of London, instead of making better felt-hats than another, mounts a huge lath and plaster Hat, seven feet high, upon wheels; sends a man to drive it through the streets; hoping to be saved thereby. He has not attempted to make better hats, as he was appointed by the Universe to do . . . but his whole industry is turned to persuade us that he has made such! He too knows that the Quack has become God" (qtd. in Turner, 80).

By 1887, Carlyle's outraged description of what he saw as the immoral motives of the advertiser reappears as an amoral, commonplace tip in a manual called *An Advertiser's Guide to Publicity:* "The usefulness and value of most things depend, not so much upon their own nature as upon the number of people who can be persuaded to desire and use them."[13] In 1903, Walter Dill Scott's articles in the *Atlantic Monthly* discussed advertising in terms of how the advertisement must invent the experience of pleasure for the consumer, regardless of the "nature" or use value of the product: "How many [advertisements] describe an undergarment so that the reader can feel the pleasant contact with his body?" (qtd. in Turner, 167).

In an even more confident tone, Burton offered this description of Christ in a 1925 best-seller entitled *The Man Nobody Knows:* "He would be a national advertiser today . . . as he was the great advertiser of his own day." In explaining what was so special about Christ, Burton explains that, as a copywriter, Christ was without equal: "take any one of the parables, no matter which—you will find that it exemplifies all the principles on which advertising text books are written. Always a picture in the first sentence; crisp, graphic language and a message so clear that even the dullest cannot escape it" (qtd. in Turner, 212). Father Purdon, in the short story "Grace," presents a parable to an assembly of businessmen in much the style described here. Cheryl Herr notes that his real-life counterpart, Father Vaughan, was on record as stating that he was "a member of the oldest advertising firm in religion on this planet." Vaughan further advocated that the Catholic Church could not afford to scorn the power of advertising, which employed human psychology as a means of "arresting attention" (Herr, 239).

In this context, Bloom's professed fantasy of creating "one sole unique advertisement to cause passers to stop in wonder" again posits him as the true Elijah who has come to write the new gospel of modern living. He envisions this gospel as "a poster novelty, with all extraneous accretions excluded, reduced to its simplest and most efficient terms not exceeding the span of casual vision and congruous with the velocity of modern life" (*U*, 592). Once again, we can see a paradox in the fact the "unique" ad will also be the one that somehow effectively arrests the attention of everyone. This corresponds to the paradox of the consumer who feels like an individual endowed with free will when he or she gazes at a poster that has this effect on everyone who looks at it. A year after Burton's bold explanation of Christ's true merit, *Printers' Ink Monthly,* an advertising trade journal, made explicit what was already implicit in Joyce's *Ulysses:* "[advertisements are] beginning to occupy the place in inspiration that religion did several hundred years ago" (qtd. in Turner, 201).

In Carlyle's comment about the moral demise of hat makers, he defends the image of God as a benevolently divine being who approvingly watches a "natural" hat maker make a hat with humble reference to some Platonic ideal of what a hat should be. Instead of this "natural" scenario, what advertising has wrought is a simulated universe where "the Quack has become God." Carlyle's denouncement of the blasphemous power of advertising might be seen as a harbinger of Alexander J. Dowie, that prophet out for profit who assures his congregation of p[r]aying consumers, "The Deity ain't no nickel dime bumshow. I put it to you that He's on the square and a corking fine business proposition. . . . He's got a coughmixture with a punch in it for you, my friend, in his back pocket. Just you try it on" (*U,* 349). If we accept Dowie's description of God, we would be forced to acknowledge that Christ learned the advertising trade from his father.

For Dowie, one supposes, the communion wafer is the world's most successful patent pill, consistently advertised for 2000 years, and the exemplary result of a brilliant ad campaign launched by that divine copywriter, Jesus Christ. In our own time, of course, we've moved from religious statues that come to life praising God, to raisins that form a rock and roll group in order to sing about cereal. The dynamics of consumption, like the dynamics of worship, promise the subject, against all evidence to the contrary, that the world is still a fair competition among free producers, all of whom are judged impartially. The fact is, in the increasingly competitive environment of twentieth-century capitalism, Carlyle's "Quack" is more capable of reassuring the subject about a benevolent universe than Carlyle's "God." In addition, the "Quack" stands to make a good deal more money in doing so.

As a final example of how commodity mythification comes to sustain the myth of the subject's autonomous "self," let me return to my discussion of "Araby." As I have already suggested, the narrator succumbs to an overriding sense of purpose that is imposed on his thoughts after he offers to bring back, from the "magical" land of Araby (magical because he knows of it only through advertising), the product that will produce a communion between himself and Mangan's sister. But he arrives too late; the shop is closing. Workmen further break the enchantment by shouting to one another about the mechanics of dismantling the elaborate illusion. The lights have been dimmed, making the products all look tawdry ("shopworn," as Gerty would say). The salesgirl is too tired even to try to convince him that a transaction would be in any way special, and the day's take (which is the "real" purpose of the bazaar and which has been obscured by the "self"-reflective universe of advertising) is being noisily counted. The imaginary world of Araby, a world that was to have authenticated the reality of his love for Mangan's sister, inverts itself to become a marketplace that is real in contrast to the fantastic image of himself as an autonomous consumer/ subject. His image of himself as autonomous is vanquished by the terrifying glimpse of him"self" as a creature of a commodifying process that he has failed to resist.

This process is what Baudrillard calls the "deterrence machine" of commodity culture (*Selected Writings,* 172). In Joyce's fiction, the mythic aura of completeness and totality that advertising attaches to the commodity is synonymous with the myth of the autonomous self that the consumer embraces in order to compensate for the lack that is the basis of subjective consciousness. The world of advertising is a "deterrence machine" to which the subject willingly submits because the supposed falseness of this advertised world strengthens the illusory reality of the mythical self. Joyce's fictional world is not "a universe of false consciousness," it is a simulated universe of "reality," constructed in a manner that invites us to explore the intertwining influences of commerce and desire that render all forms of consciousness a fantasy of the self.

2

Kitschy, Kitschy Coup

"Life" and "History" in a World of Mass-Produced Objects

The tactics of consumption, the ingenious ways in which the weak make use of the strong lend a political dimension to everyday practices.[1]

It was hard to know what to buy and all she could think of was cake.

(*D*, 102)

I

The word *kitsch* makes its first appearance in 1939, according to the *Oxford English Dictionary.* In its early usage, the word was a term of disparagement whereby purveyors of "good taste" in works of art legitimated their position as experts by pointing out examples of "bad taste," which they labeled "kitsch." One reason objects of kitsch seem to be automatically disqualified as objects of art is that they are often machine-made, which means they are duplicated in such vast quantities that nearly anyone can afford to own them. But, precisely because objects of kitsch are so valueless, they afford the consumer a type of interactive experience that works of art in a museum do not. One can, for instance, frame them, generously protect them from the imminent destruction they seemed designed for, and even doodle on them: "The Nymph: . . . You bore me away, framed me in oak and tinsel, set me above your marriage couch. Unseen, one summer eve, you kissed me in four places. And with loving pencil you shaded my eyes, my bosom and my shame" (*U*, 445).

What becomes emotionally resonant about kitsch is not what it represents, but what it comes to represent after someone chooses to interact with it: "She [Maria] took out her purse with the silver clasps and read again the words *A Present from Belfast.* She was very fond of that purse because Joe had brought it to her five years before when he and Alphy had gone to

Belfast on a Whit-Monday trip" (*D*, 100). Maria, who is rather desperately clinging to a version of reality that is at least five years old, highly values this "trivial" object as one of her most important props. It is, like many of the commodity objects with which we surround ourselves, more real than she is because it offers her a vantage point from which she is able to imagine the coherency and importance of her existence. With an increasing lack of subtlety, her family seems to wish she would stay always in the Dublin by Lamplight laundry, practically dead if not literally, instead of, every Halloween, escaping from the grave to which they have consigned her and haunting them all anew. The purse, therefore, is a worthless item with a priceless function: it helps her to feel she is loved in the face of life circumstances that suggest she is—far from being gone but not forgotten—in fact, forgotten but not gone.

Maria, who constantly hears remembered compliments playing through her head with the soothing consistency of elevator music, also values this "trivial" object as an important prop in her masquerade of contentment. What matters to Maria is not what the object is—a purse—but how it is advertised. This curious dislocation reminds me of Magritte's famous painting in which he drew a hyperreal representation of a pipe—kitsch, we might say—and wrote beneath it, in an imitation of advertising copy, "Ce n'est pas une pipe," entitling the painting *The Treachery of Images*. For Maria, this is not a purse. Given the time-honored association of the purse with female sexuality, we can see that Maria, unlike her purse, suffers from the fate of being imprecisely labeled—she's neither a nun, a mother, nor a prostitute, so she is incongruously placed in a laundry for reformed prostitutes and allowed a little spending money. She is seen as beyond the margins of what can be labeled; she is insignificant, yet dislocated and therefore dangerous—a witch, or, as Magritte might put it, "Ce n'est pas une femme."

Mass-produced items afford a different sort of value to the consumer because they are resolutely the same thing to all people. The Pepsi you sip is the same Pepsi that Madonna sips; all her glamour does not procure for her a better can of soda. Indeed, if one offered a million dollars, one could not buy a better can of Pepsi than what is available for seventy-five cents, from any machine, in the basement of any number of laundromats. The heavily advertised commodity achieves a transcendent democracy that is as cool and inviolable as the carefully coy smile of Maria Kendall, who displays her charms equally, and without stinting, to both Paddy Dignam junior and the Lord Lieutenant of Dublin. Kitsch souvenirs are so abundant, and so cheap, that one can commemorate the events of a single day—or even several events in a given day—by purchasing something at periodic intervals. When traveling somewhere out of the ordinary, we enjoy thinking about buying something (usually quite ordinary) to bring back for someone else.

Indeed, most of the items we might buy in such a place are completely ordinary objects like ashtrays, cups, and pencils, but they have been stamped with the name of the exotic place we are visiting. The producers of the Araby bazaar have successfully employed the modern marketing technique of creating an exotic place for the sale of spuriously exotic kitsch right in the unpropitious middle of dear, dirty, dubious Dublin: "The syllables of the word *Araby* were called to me through the silence in which my soul luxuriated and cast an Eastern enchantment over me" (*D,* 32). Predictably, the narrator is obsessed with buying something in this "enchanted" space that will commemorate his vague yearning for Mangan's sister. The notion of going somewhere in order to buy something for Mangan's sister is such a compelling idea for the boy that he does not need to speculate beforehand on what this something might be; nor does he worry about getting Mangan's sister a gift that he is sure she wants, needs, or even comprehends. It is strictly his anticipation of the satisfying process of consumption that dominates all his other thoughts. The "use value" of kitsch, if any, is usually slight and never important. Many objects of kitsch are also unlikely looking gadgets; trying to guess how they could possibly be of any use to anyone becomes part of their essential kitschiness.

Indeed, nowadays, one's response to a mass-produced bauble or gadget offered as a gift might be to say, "Thank you so much—what is it?" While we may have become somewhat jaded in the buying and giving of kitsch, the narrator of "Araby," not unlike Maria in "Clay," allows the contemplation of purchasing a commodity to "annihilate the tedious intervening days." Maria, after all, visits two cake shops and elaborately discriminates between them like the contemporary shopper stunned by the nearly psychotic variety presented by the modern mall. Buying something is everything to Maria; her day—one suspects her life—revolves around anticipated purchases, and when she nearly cries at discovering the loss of her plum cake, we need to reflect, to paraphrase Magritte again, "This is not a piece of cake." The point, in a commodity culture, is never what is purchased, but what the process of purchasing is being made to configure, relative to the configuration of the commodity, by advertising, as an object of desire. The commodity fits Lacan's description of the *objet a* (object of desire); it is not what we want, but what causes us to want.

For most of us today, as for the narrator of "Araby," what the recollection of purchasing a kitsch object calls to mind is the first time we spent our own money on a gift for someone else. Think about what you bought for Mother's Day when you were between the ages of nine and fourteen. Father's Day? Valentine's Day? Perhaps your mind is flooded with long-gone disposable objects of the past (which the recipients, as a testament of their affection for you, swore they would keep forever, despite the object's ineluctable worthlessness). The first time we enter the marketplace as young consumers, our meager funds virtually guarantee that our first purchase of a manufactured item as a gift for someone will probably qualify as kitsch. But because this is one of the first times we have personally immersed ourselves in commodity culture, the purchase will include an emotional investment that will perhaps never be equaled by our later purchases of more expensive items. The narrator of "Araby," as a would-be first-time consumer, is made literally breathless by the titanic promise of pleasure and contentment signified by advertised and displayed commodities.

At the Araby bazaar, everything is a label first and an object second. "A Present from the Araby Bazaar," unlike "A Present from Belfast," is no longer connected to a recognizable object. The narrator's inability to make the connection leaves him unable to continue imagining his own coherency as a subject. He becomes arbitrary—a signifier among signifiers—rather than a signified attracting (purchasing) signifiers. This dislocation of self is recorded by the "Araby" narrator as "seeing himself"—from a previously unsuspected and unimaginable vantage point—as someone falling apart. Something similar might occur to Maria were she to lose her purse. Although she feels it is she who gives the purse meaning, in fact the relationship is reversed, and it is Maria who imagines her coherence in relationship to the purse. One could go a step further and say that since Maria is an aging virgin unattached to such culturally intelligible roles as nun, prostitute, sweetheart, or wife (as the game makes clear), then she is an empty purse, and also a disposable one, tossed into a heap with other used-up purses (aging prostitutes). It would seem that Maria, with her never-filled purse, and the former prostitutes, with their worn-out purses, would be at opposite ends of the spectrum, but in another sense they are exactly the same thing: objects of desire no longer desirable (no longer able to cause desire), or—what amounts to the same thing—commodities no longer in circulation.

For the narrator of "Araby," the combination of vague and frustrated desire awakened by the vision of Mangan's sister, followed by the sensation of imminent and complete fulfillment as a consumer in the modern marketplace, is nearly enough to drive the boy mad. Small wonder that, as Thomas Richards points out, late-Victorian advertisers not only "discovered" but also partly invented, and profited from, the concept of adolescence: "adolescence now provides a biological basis for consumption by coordinating it with physiological changes that issue from the consumer's body" (*Commodity Culture,* 224). In a commodity culture, the process of consumption and gift-giving (a process that, courtesy of mass production, is inexpensive enough for nearly any adolescent with a modest allowance) is such a powerful form of being that what the actual gift might be, or what its use value is, no longer exists as the rationale for the purchase. Indeed, the cheap, ready-made availability of kitsch, with its frequent blatant imitations of more valuable objects, allows nearly anyone to enter the marketplace as an excited shopper, but one who is likely to experience disappointment when confronted with the actual objects that have been made to seem magical by advertising. And yet, although an object of kitsch may appear astonishingly trivial as an actual object, it still has a crucial economic and psychological function because it serves as a child's entry point into the enchanting bazaar of modern commodity culture. As a consumer, if not as a lover, the narrator in "Araby" loses his virginity.

Buying and giving objects of kitsch are forms of expressing ourselves. Consumption in a commodity culture is as much a psychological process as an economic one because the connection between what we purchase and what we actually need has been completely severed. Unlike the street market, where the boy is required to accompany his aunt in order to bring necessary parcels home, the curiously erotic market of the Araby bazaar attracts him with a thoroughness that drives out every other consideration; he "knows" that the object he finds there will complete him, even though he has no idea what that object is. Part of its erotic component derives from the fact that there is no necessity for him to be there; it is slightly taboo in the sense that neither his aunt nor his uncle has any but the murkiest idea about the bazaar, and they wonder whether it is suitable for him to go there. It is also where Mangan's sister would like to be, in explicit opposition to the retreat she must attend. And so he "believes" that something he might buy there will complete him, and the success of his equation for satisfaction depends on the fact that he entertains no conscious preconception of what that object is. By contrast, when he and his aunt set out for the open street market, they do so with a clear idea of which household supplies have been depleted, and therefore need to be replenished. It is a strict equation of supply and demand that, far from encouraging fantasies of fulfillment, pushes the narrator into an attitude of "self"-preservation: "I imagined that I bore my chalice safely through a throng of foes" (*D,* 31).

The case of Maria is instructively similar, even though she is the recipient of a gift. It is unlikely that she specifically asked Joe and Alphy to buy her a purse. Had they not bought it for her, she would not have missed it, and yet she has now used it every day for five years. Recipients of kitsch, such as Maria, may venerate the object as "priceless" when they have strong feelings about the person who gave it to them. Conversely, they may ignore it when they do not. Treating a trivial object as though it were precious will gratify the person who gave it as a sincere token of his or her love, but it will embarrass the person who did not. One might easily be deeply hurt if a person one loves treats a Valentine's Day gift like the disposable item that it very often is; such an emotional and economic paradox underscores the fact that actual market value plays no objective role in these exchanges (except that it produces the items that are readily and cheaply available as, quite literally, tokens of affection). Because the kitsch object's status as "worthless" remains consistent, both the giver and the recipient are better able to objectify and quantify their feelings in this complex exchange process that might be called an economy of emotion. The exchange of a valuable gift confuses this dimension because any gratitude expressed by the recipient might easily be directed more at how much was apparently spent, than at how much they care for the person who spent it.

What can make an object of kitsch emotionally priceless, therefore, is the fact that it is an object designed to be economically worthless; thus, personal emotions can be more effectively highlighted. The kitsch object can be invested with emotion more easily because it has no capacity to reflect any other sort of value. At the same time, it can be treated at face value as an inexpensive and trivial item. There is a good deal of irony in the fact that Joe and Alphy decide to buy a purse for a woman who has so little to put into it. The extent of their involvement with this gift, I would suggest, is that they needed to get her something, and so they grabbed the first thing they saw that had "A Present" printed on it. In this context, they did not really buy Maria a purse at all; they engaged in a brief, inexpensive exchange in the marketplace that helped keep her frightfully needy situation at a safe distance from their own rather precarious peace of mind.

Souvenir kitsch quite often consists of common household objects, readily available back home, that are given a temporary veneer of value by having the exotic place of their purchase stamped upon them. In this way, the souvenir object stands in for all the money, time, and trouble that went into locating ourselves in a given souvenir shop that is impressively far from home. Had the boy arrived at the bazaar earlier, before the lights were shut out, he might have been able to preserve his faith in the transcendent power of kitsch long enough to actually buy something. The Araby bazaar, as a prototype of the modern department store, brings objects into an interior space and floods them with light in order to give them the same sort of transcendent aura that might normally surround any sacred relic that is compellingly displayed, beneath directed lighting, in the hushed confines of a church. Once the lights are out, objects are no more magical than they would be if offered by a street vendor in the undifferentiated light of outdoors.

In his discussion of the production and sale of souvenirs during Queen Victoria's Jubilee (1887), Thomas Richards remarks, "Jubilee kitsch . . . was an article of faith" (*Commodity Culture,* 106). He also makes the point that, for the British, buying kitsch objects for the home was a way of celebrating imperialism: "jingo kitsch came in the wake of Jubilee kitsch and relied on the . . . same strategy of making individual articles bear the weight of immense social significance, here not of the monarchy but of the Empire at large. The roster of articles produced during this period reveals a salmagundi of kitsch charged with the task of legitimating the Empire" (*Commodity Culture,* 133).

Examining the very different political dimension of objects in the Irish homes of Joyce's characters is beyond the scope of this book, but let me just mention that the "colored print of the promises made to Blessed Margaret Mary Alacoque" hanging on the wall of Eveline's home (*D,* 37) is a far cry from the "jingo kitsch" that Richards describes: "The new imperialism adopted the idea that there was direct correlation between commodity production and territorial expansion and so drove home the imperial importance of manufactured objects . . ." (*Commodity Culture,* 133). No wonder the disillusionment of the boy in "Araby" is deepened when he hears the shop girl talking with two men and cannot help noting "their English accents" (*D,* 35).

One of the conditions for the phenomenon of kitsch, according to Richards, is that kitsch objects, in order to "enchant" the consumer, must be displayed within "the saturated space of materiality" (*Commodity Culture,* 103–4). The Araby bazaar was elaborately constructed to be just such a place. To convey people to this elaborately constructed space, a special train was commissioned: "At Westland Row Station a crowd of people pressed to the carriage doors; but the porters moved them back, saying that it was a special train for the bazaar" (*D,* 34). Compare this "magical" place to Stephen's desultory encounter with a flower girl in the streets of Dublin:

> A hand was laid on his arm and a young voice cried:
> —Ah, gentleman, your own girl, sir! The first handsel today, gentleman. Buy that lovely bunch. Will you, gentleman?

> The blue flowers which she lifted towards him and her young blue eyes seemed to him at that instant images of guilelessness; and he halted till the image had vanished and he saw only her ragged dress and damp coarse hair and hoydenish face. (*P*, 183)

The woman's wares are held in her hand in broad daylight, rather than carefully displayed beneath light that has been artificially directed. She has to grab his arm as he passes—a technique for attracting consumers that is far more crude than the boy's experience of riding "a special train" until "[i]n front of me was a large building which displayed the magical name" (*D*, 34). And yet, something similar happens to both the boy and Stephen—an initial moment of enchantment suddenly vanishes because the atmosphere in which the objects are offered for sale is revealed to be nothing more than a vulgar point of exchange that demystifies the merchant, the consumer, and the commodity.

Richards draws attention to the enormous change that occurred in the marketplace when commodities were brought indoors and flooded with artificial light: "Unlike the grand aisles of the Great Exhibition [1851], the streets of mid-Victorian London did not provide an antiseptic ambience for commodities; in the open air a commodity was still preeminently an inert thing handled by human beings, an everyday item available for purchase, and an object of use" (*Commodity Culture,* 45). In *Portrait,* the crudeness of the street scene, combined with the flower girl's all too evident desperation to sell her wares, permeates Stephen's view of her and overwhelms his initial attempt to see her as an ideal of Irish girlhood. In the marketing system that takes place on the street, the people presenting the goods are also, by and large, the same people who need to sell them in order to survive. With the advent of the store, and the hired shop clerk, there was less connection between the products displayed and the seller's financial or emotional status. One result of this shift was that bartering became obsolete (the price was fixed), and a bland sort of uniform courtesy became the norm (quite different from the urgent atmosphere that ensues when the flower girl grabs Stephen's arm).

We know from Joyce's story "Eveline" that girls who sell commodities inside a store, rather than on the street, are constantly reminded by supervisors that they must remain as relentlessly cheerful as all the bright commodities that surround them; "Look lively, Miss Hill, please" is a refrain that echoes in Eveline's head as she contemplates leaving behind her life in Dublin. Significantly, Eveline aggravates her anxiety about what it might be like to leave Dublin by reviewing the various trinkets that constitute her notion of "Home": "Home! She looked around the room, reviewing all its familiar objects which she had dusted once a week for many years . . ." (*D*, 37). The extreme contrast between Eveline's depressed state of mind while at home and the perky persona she is expected to project at work emphasizes the extent to which the modern department store was designed to be an ahistorical place where political, economic, and emotional issues are suspended.

In Stephen's theory of the epiphany, as I have suggested, it is the object that is said to achieve its epiphany, and the presence of the subject is identified as merely the catalyst that allows the object to differentiate itself from all other objects. This is precisely the intended effect on a consumer of a carefully advertised and displayed commodity: to incite the illusion of autonomy in the subject by declaring that a given product is uniquely different from all other products, thereby allowing the subject to express his "individual free-will" by honoring this "fact" when he or she enters the modern marketplace.

One of the most frightening experiences for Stephen Dedalus occurs when he is walking down the street in Cork with his father, and, suddenly: "He could scarcely interpret the letters of the signboards of the shops." Simultaneous with this partial aphasia, he is overcome with a frightening feeling of hyperinsularity in which "Nothing moved him or spoke to him from the real world unless he heard in it an echo of the infuriated cries within him. He could respond to no earthly or human appeal . . ." (*P*, 92). Significantly, the next portion of the novel details the temporary joy Stephen feels as he establishes social relations with the people around him through buying things with the money from his essay prize: "For a swift season of merrymaking the money of his prizes ran through Stephen's fingers. Great parcels of groceries and delicacies and dried fruits arrived from the city. . . . In his coat pockets he carried squares of Vienna chocolate for his guests while his trousers' pockets bulged with masses of silver and copper coins. . . . Then the season of pleasure came to an end" (*P*, 97–98).

Stephen's "season of pleasure" suggests the extent to which merchandise is eroticized by twentieth-century advertising and marketing techniques. In fact, in an interesting transition, the last of his essay money is spent on the most overtly erotic product of all: his first encounter with a prostitute. While *Portrait* presents—in gradual, "inevitable" increments—Stephen's growing awareness of himself as an artist, it seems important to me (and, I think, was important to Joyce) to ask whether or not Stephen's pursuit of an artistic vocation would have even manifested itself at all had his prize money been magically replenished. "How foolish his aim had been!" he rather piously declares about his unabashed orgy of consumerism—but only after he has run out of money (*P*, 98). Commodity culture is a powerful religion that attracts everyone to the altar of the marketplace.

The circulation of kitsch objects in Joyce's fiction—including objects that are purchased, objects that are received, and objects that fail to enchant—allows Joyce to make explicit the volatile link between consumerism and consciousness in the twentieth century. Bloom's several purchases of his breakfast kidney, his cheese sandwich, the novel *Sweets of Sin,* and a bar of lemon soap (as well as his complex contemplation about whether or not to buy Molly some lingerie) are all actions that might be said to form the superstructure of his day, built up from the infrastructure of his desires and anxieties. Indeed, the primary manner in which Bloom summarizes June 16 is to list everything he has bought. Conversely, many of the "crises" that occur to Joyce's characters (as I have tried to show in my discussion of "Araby") directly result from some type of disruption in the process of commodity consumption. In *Dubliners,* for example, there is Farrington's rage that the money he received for pawning his watch is not enough to get him drunk. In an oddly similar vein, Maria's most difficult moment in "Clay" occurs when she cannot find the plumcake that she had purchased with such extraordinary care: "Downes's plumcake had not enough almond icing on top of it so she went over to a shop in Henry Street. Here she was a long time in suiting herself . . ." (*D*, 102).

Michel de Certeau suggests that "from advertising to all sorts of mercantile epiphanies, our society is characterized by a cancerous growth of vision, measuring everything by its ability to show or be shown . . ." (*Practice of Everyday Life,* xxiv). The overriding "reality" that completes Little Chandler's despair turns out to be a purchase he made on credit that is visible all around him: "Could he not escape from his little house? Was it too late for him to try to live bravely like Gallaher? Could he go to London? There was the furniture still to be paid for" (*D*, 83).

In the case presented in "Two Gallants," Corley brags that the maid he is "dating" always brings him "souvenirs" to commemorate the furtive sex they sometimes have in a meadow in Donnybrook: "It was fine, man. Cigarettes every night she'd bring me and paying the tram out and back. And one night she brought me two bloody fine cigars—O, the real cheese, you know, that the old fellow used to smoke . . ." (*D*, 51). The central tension of the story is whether Corley can get her to move up to bringing him money instead of middle-class commodities. Ironically, he has gained her trust by lying to her about his former place of employment: "I told her I was out of a job. . . . I told her I was in Pim's" (*D*, 51). Pim's was a "wholesale-retail empire in south-central Dublin. . . . The Pims were Quakers and were widely regarded in Dublin as models of sober commercial reliability."[2] Selling over-the-counter commodities, once disregarded as a type of desperate street existence, has now become a type of employment that suggests reliability.

I have defined *kitsch* as cheaply produced objects that are so widely available, and so inexpensive, that any individual in a commodity culture can commemorate the ephemeral sensations of everyday life by purchasing them. This is hardly an exhaustive definition of this term, nor is it intended to be one. I have set forth this limited definition in order to suggest that the phenomenon of consumerism is by no means simple. Michel de Certeau, for one, devotes much of his work to the need for a more thorough explication of this practically invisible, but nonetheless central, everyday practice: "The purpose of this work is to make explicit the systems of operational combination which also compose a 'culture,' and to bring to light the models of action characteristic of users whose status as the dominated element in society (a status that does not mean that they are either passive or docile) is concealed by the euphemistic term 'consumers'" (*Practice of Everyday Life*, xi). I have tried to trace out some of the ramifications of the machine-made commodity in Joyce's fiction by noting how it pervades actual and contemplated gift buying, as well as more improvised rituals of exchange (the slavey bringing cigars to Corley, for instance). Joyce not only presents and examines twentieth-century commodity culture in his fiction, he also explores the pattern and process of consumption by which people interact with objects of the marketplace in a manner that betrays their fears, aspirations, and desires relative to other people.

One further point I would like to make, by way of historicizing the phenomenon of kitsch, is that, at the turn of the century, when inexpensive commodities flooded the market, there seemed to be very little anxiety about inadvertently revealing "bad taste" by giving someone a gift that the giver considered valuable, but that the recipient regarded as kitsch. There seemed to be a prelapsarian innocence concerning the commodity; any manufactured object was a good object and therefore equally worthy of display. Clearly this is no longer the case. All the postwedding wrap-up discussions that I have been a part of always get around to discussing the gifts that are regarded as kitsch. Expensive wedding gifts become invisible in such discussions, and my sense is that people often pay a good deal of money for presents (that is to say, more than they think the recipient is worth) in order to ensure that their presents—and thus they themselves—are not subjects of ridicule. In fact, the practice of self-consciously giving out items of kitsch as presents has become an oddly sophisticated thing to do in our time (or so I believe), but only when the gift giver clearly indicates that he or she understands the comically "worthless" quality of what they are imposing on another person. The implication is not "I like you enough to buy this for you," but "I like you enough to share a joke with you."

The horror we all privately fear is that we will give a gift to someone in a manner that telegraphs our high regard for it, only to have them judge it as kitsch, and then gleefully show it to others in this light when we are not around to defend ourselves (and the only effective defense is to insist that we knew it was kitsch all along, so the joke is on them). In the gift-giving world depicted by Joyce, however, there seems to be a simple belief that commodity objects are always fascinating, and that no shame can descend on anyone for buying them. Here, for example, is Gerty MacDowell's rumination about what sort of gift she might buy her confessor, Father Conroy. She feels particularly indebted to him because he was kind enough to inform her that menstruation was just another part of God's inscrutable plan, and therefore not actually a sin: "He was so kind and holy and often and often she thought and thought could she work a ruched teacosy with embroidered floral design for him as a present or a clock but they had a clock she noticed on the mantelpiece white and gold with a canarybird that came out of a little house to tell the time the day she went there about the flowers for the forty hours' adoration because it was hard to know what sort of a present to give or perhaps an album of illuminated views of Dublin or some place" (*U*, 294).

Several points that I have already tried to make about kitsch are illustrated in this paragraph. First, the process of contemplating the purchase, and not just the object itself, is a part of what we might designate as kitsch. Second, objects of kitsch are, by definition, highly interchangeable, and so one looks forward to the experience of being surrounded by objects in the marketplace, rather than planning out the necessity for buying a specific item. Even Gerty's rather specific gift idea of "an album of illuminated views of Dublin" is immediately undercut by her completely random thought "or some place."

The final point suggested to me about kitsch in this quotation is that people already have a great deal of kitsch objects in their homes, and thus it is "hard to know what sort of present to give." The only possible failure for shoppers, a failure that is increasingly possible in a world of mass-produced objects, is that they will give someone an object that is identical to one they already own ("but they had a clock," Gerty says). Nowadays, of course, since all items of kitsch are even more prevalent, and even more overtly useless, it hardly matters when we have a few extra. Indeed, if recipients see you don't know they already have what you just gave them, the highly disposable nature of your gift allows them to greet your present with delight, while making a mental note to throw out its duplicate before you discover it. What I find fascinating about Gerty's rumination is that she is already aware of the difficulty of buying presents for people who have everything. One reason people have everything is that mass-produced objects are designed and marketed in a way that makes it possible for everyone to own them. When we go shopping for someone else in a commodity culture, therefore, we can easily get the feeling that anything we might buy is likely to be something that everyone already has.

Anywhere that buying, selling, or giving is featured in Joyce's fiction, we can also see the complex tactics and strategies that people employ to constitute the experience of their everyday life. *Tactics* and *strategies* are two terms for which de Certeau offers a detailed definition in his attempt to highlight the political dimension that is present in each "trivial" act of consumption:

> A tactic insinuates itself into the other's place, fragmentarily, without taking it over in its entirety, without being able to keep it at a distance. It has at its disposal no base where it can capitalize on its advantages, prepare its expansions, and secure independence with respect to circumstances. . . . Strategies, in contrast, conceal beneath objective calculations their connection with the power that sustains them from within the stronghold of its own "proper" place or institution. (*Practice of Everyday Life,* xx)

In a very real sense, all Irish consumers must employ tactics against the strategies levied against them by "the stronghold" of British imperialism. As Richards demonstrates, commodities manufactured in Britain are marketed elsewhere by employing an ideology that makes British imperialism the "proper place." The offering of the British commodity for sale to the Irish becomes an invitation for the members of a marginalized Irish culture to briefly participate in the dominant power apparatus that routinely oppresses them. As Diane and Geoffrey Hindley suggest, the British ad agencies, late in the nineteenth century, mounted what was virtually a second colonizing attack on Ireland: "[A British advertising man] writing in his own press directory in the 1890's, was recommending Ireland as a relatively virgin field for exploitation by his advertiser clients. One of the market's major advantages was, apparently, the decent instincts of the Irish themselves. 'The Irish gentry still retain their simpleness of heart and a consequent belief in the goodness of mankind; hence they answer advertisements very easily'."[3]

More specifically, we can see Dilly Dedalus employing a "tactic" of consumption that attempts to "secure independence" with respect to her dire circumstances:

> —What have you there? Stephen asked.
> —I bought it from the other cart for a penny, Dilly said, laughing nervously. Is it any good? . . .
> He took the coverless book from her hand. Chardenal's French primer.
> —What did you buy that for? he asked. To learn French?
> She nodded, reddening and closing tight her lips.
> Show no surprise. Quite natural.
> —Here, Stephen said. It's all right. Mind Maggy doesn't pawn it on you. I suppose all my books are gone.
> —Some, Dilly said. We had to.
> She is drowning. Agenbite. Save her. Agenbite. All against us. She will drown me with her, eyes and hair. (*U,* 200)

Dilly's instant embarrassment at having been discovered in the act of exercising this tactic leaves no doubt that her purchase will prove futile in the long run. In a rather uncharacteristic act of compassion, Stephen tries to convince her that he views this profoundly pathetic tactic of consumption as a successful strategy: "Show no surprise. Quite natural." And yet his next comment—"Mind Maggy doesn't pawn it on you"—inadvertently highlights the fact that her tactic only "insinuates itself into the other's place, fragmentarily, without . . . being able to keep it at a distance." In Stephen's metaphor for Dilly's tactic of consumption, the French primer happened to float by, and, although she has convulsively grabbed on to it, she is still drowning. Since Stephen, just like Dilly, has no permanent footing in "a place that can be circumscribed as proper," any attempt to rescue her would drown him too.

I would suggest that those who believe in kitsch, in the sense that they give and receive such objects without irony, tend to practice a tactical consumption that is designed to keep the demeaning force of a dominant economy at bay. On the other hand, groups who identify kitsch for the express purpose of ridiculing it might be seen as exercising a "strategy" that is designed to further secure their central position as the "proper" arbiters of "taste" (i.e., power and wealth) within a given culture: "A strategy assumes a place that can be circumscribed as proper . . . and thus serves as the basis for generating relations with an exterior distinct from it" (de Certeau, *Prac-*

tice of Everyday Life, xix). That is why, to put this most simply, what "we" like is art, and what "they" like is kitsch, but I will reserve my discussion of commodity culture and aesthetics until later.

My apparently trivial topic about supposedly trivial items (kitsch) is intended to identify the distinctly modern phenomenon of consumerism and commodity culture in Joyce's work. Kitsch is not simply a designated object. It is a way of thinking and acting that is sometimes defensive and sometimes aggressive, sometimes tactical and sometimes strategic. It may be a strategy for consolidating power, or a tactic for outwitting the totalitarian principles of "good taste." Strategies and tactics of consumption set in motion "the calculus of force relationships" (de Certeau, *Practice of Everyday Life,* xix). As a phenomenon, objects of kitsch, as well as the way these objects circulate (in the form of commodities, gifts, and souvenirs), constitute a complex historical configuration made possible by the advent of advertising, "material spaces" (modern department stores), and commodity culture in general.

In Joyce's time, as in our own, we are, to an increasing extent, what we buy and how we buy; or, as Barbara Kruger puts it, in her photograph of a woman's hand holding up a credit card, "I shop, therefore I am."[4] These words, I might add, are stamped on the card, making the card itself, and the license to buy it represents, the equivalent of Maria's transcendent purse. What we like to think of as our individual moral structure is likewise reflected and refined in our shifting strategies of consumption (shoplifting, clipping coupons, using credit cards, watching for sales). When all else is confusing, a trip to the mall—the cathedral of our time—can always be counted on to feel like a return to the familiar because, here in the twentieth century, the past and the future appear to have been collapsed into the mercantile epiphany generated by the displayed object.

II. The history of now: Commodity culture and everyday life in Joyce

Ephemeral objects, we are told, both appear and disappear beneath the notice of history because the duration of their existence is too brief ever to be notable. And so the ephemeral would seem to be the unimportant. The fact that the ephemeral is quickly forgotten, so we reason, is appropriate to its presumed status as the eminently forgettable. The ephemeral, we reassure ourselves, can never be timeless or timely because it leaves no trace in time beyond the momentary. "If very short, lasting only a single day," reports a medical textbook of 1880, "it is an ephemeral fever."[5] Not to worry. But what of something very long, lasting only a single day? What of Joyce's

Ulysses? Or, for that matter, what of the characters in *Dubliners*, most of whom are presented to us, within a twenty-four-hour framework or less, like so many literary mayflies (Latin term *ephemeroptera*)? Time's winged chariot has more the character of an incoming missile in Joyce's short-story collection.

Indeed, because of the short duration of time within which Joyce presents his characters, their every thought, act, and gesture—while clearly ahistorical and ephemeral—nonetheless seem imbued with what I might call nonhistoricized significance: "[A]nd in the end," gravely pronounces the Joyce narrator, thus closing off the final recorded moment of Joe and Maria's long day, "he [Joe] had to ask his wife to tell him where the corkscrew was" (*D*, 106). Here, we encounter the description of a moment manifestly devoid of historical significance presented in a tone ("and in the end") implying the appropriate close of a historical narrative. And yet, at the same time, it is clearly not an insignificant moment, recalling, as it does, both the missing verse of Maria's recital, and the "castration" of the hapless Joe. Paradoxically, such apparently trivial, ephemeral, and arbitrary moments are often presented in *Dubliners* as fundamentally more authentic than "historical events" precisely because they are "insignificant" (i.e., impossible to distort into a historical narrative). Joyce's fiction consistently presents what is beneath notice as that which is most notable.

In "An Encounter," moments we might recognize as historical do not even produce a complete sentence, whereas everyday moments threaten to eclipse the rote recitation of hurtful history: "This page or this page? This page? Now, Dillon, up! *Hardly had the day*. . . . Have you studied it? What have you there in your pocket?" (*D*, 20). What Dillon has, clearly of more interest to him than "official" history, is a cheaply printed text—*The Apache Chief*—detailing events that Father Butler denounces as ahistorical and as that most ephemeral thing of all—garbage: "What is this rubbish? . . . Is this what you read instead of studying your Roman History?" (*D*, 20). The servile connotations of Father Butler's name ought to sensitize us further to Joyce's complex irony; a man who is in the service of England historicizes British imperial ideology by valorizing as "history" an earlier and excessively heroic account of imperial conquest. His dismissal of *The Apache Chief* as "rubbish" is equally a dismissal of any possible authority the victims of imperialism might have to tell their own story.

The narrator, on the other hand, once free of the environment of school, finds himself drawn, with an inarticulate and visceral urge, to the once ephemeral story of the colonial hero, now pronounced to be irredeemable "rubbish" by the loyal lackey Father Butler: "[W]hen the restraining influence of the school was at a distance I began to hunger again for wild sensations, for the escape which those chronicles of disorder alone seemed to offer me" (*D*, 20–21). A chronicle is a chronological record of events, a specific sort of history, so a "chronicle of disorder" is, on the face of it, an oxymoron; that is to say, a chronicle that is disordered ceases to be a chronicle. But, as I suggested in my introduction, a "chronicle of disorder" is the nonchronological experience of impossible-to-historicize moments, which nonetheless allows for a sense of continuity in one's identity over time. Or, put another way, a chronicle of disorder (popular culture) signifies, in a manner unfairly dismissed as "rubbish," a nonnarrational history of the everyday as distinct from the narrative history that Haines blames, with famous self-serving vagueness, for causing any problems Ireland or Stephen might care to name.

The "escape" afforded by chronicles of disorder is not an escape from history but rather an escape from the historicized to the not yet historicized, where the colonial subject may have access to possibilities ousted by the sham actualities imposed by historical narrative. "From its own niche," Senn suggests, "*Ulysses* may have helped to change our views of what history also is; we have now learned to read an age not solely in terms of its great masterpieces and dominant philosophies, but particularly in its newspapers, its advertisements, or its fashions."[6] But I would not want to lose sight of what the narrator of "An Encounter" tells us. Such sources as newspapers, advertisements, and fashions are not an overlooked source of history; they are "chronicles of disorder," or records of a different kind of history. We should not use them to "correct" the record of dominant historical narrative, but to become aware of a different record—the history of everyday experience operating beneath, beyond, and in between the exhaustive yet still limited monocausality of historical narrative.

In "Eveline," it is the dust Eveline has contended with for as long as she can remember that orders and pervades her world—and even makes its insignificant yet indomitable presence felt in the lining of her nose: "[I]n her nostrils was the odour of dusty cretonne" (*D*, 36). Joyce's oddly clinical word choice ("nostrils") shows an obsession with precisely those details of reality that cannot possibly be historicized, but which, still, undeniably, exist. Joyce presents details about the characters in *Dubliners* almost the way an anthropologist presents details of a two-thousand-year-old human. In the case of the anthropologist, what this person had for breakfast—certainly an ephemeral event at the time—now holds clues for determining his historical circumstance. If he ate corn, how was the corn prepared, with tools that bespeak the iron age or the age of bronze?

In "Araby," to offer another example, an object the narrator never specifies nonetheless becomes something he "knows" he cannot afford. In the famously depressing conclusion of the story, the narrator is interpellated as a colonial subject who experiences the failure of trying to shrug off the weight of the historical by placing himself in a protective constellation of the ephemeral: "I lingered before her stall, though I knew my stay was useless, to make my interest in her wares seem the more real" (*D*, 35). In Althusser's theory of interpellation, the subject is always "called" or "hailed" by something that offers spurious subjectivity in the form of ideology. But in "Araby," the narrator is hailed by nothing ("Remembering with difficulty why I came I went over to one of the stalls" [*D*, 35]), and it is within this peculiarly Joycean "political theater," as Mark Wollaeger puts it, that "efforts to interpellate the individual as a subject—the coronation ceremony, the Mass, recruiting posters—are staged in the liminal space where an individual's experience of the world confronts institutional attempts to shape that experience."[7] Writing the history of the everyday through cultural consumption is an attempt to offset the debilitating inscription of blameful history.

III. Historicizing reality: Psychosis?

Poststructuralist theorizing on the nature of historical narrative, and on the process of historicizing reality, from theorists such as Lacan, Lyotard, Foucault, Benjamin, de Certeau, and Jameson, while disagreeing on a great deal, nonetheless contains one common denominator already present everywhere in Joyce's fiction: a privileging of "now" as a fulcrum point of power and knowledge. Jameson, for example, offers a lamentation: "Note that as temporal continuities break down, the experience of the present becomes powerfully, overwhelmingly vivid and 'material'."[8] This is not at all a positive state of affairs for Jameson. Like Baudrillard, he likens the sensation to that of the schizophrenic: "[S]chizophrenic experience is an experience of isolated, disconnected, discontinuous material signifiers which fail to link up into a coherent sequence. The schizophrenic . . . does not know personal identity in our sense, since our feeling of identity depends on our sense of the persistence of the 'I' and the 'me' over time" ("Postmodernism," 119).

There is, however, something suspiciously chummy about Jameson's stark distinction of "us" and "them." He beckons the reader over to the side of sanity—to his side—when he states, "the schizophrenic . . . does not know personal identity *in our sense*" (my emphasis). What could this communal notion of "our sense" be—how could it be articulated—when one has only to turn on MTV, as Jameson himself notes, to experience the schizophrenic, ahistorical, ever-present, ever-changing "now"? Jameson stigmatizes contemporary experience by making it analogous with psychosis because he sees it as irredeemably ahistorical, and he warns us grimly of "the disappearance of a sense of history, the way in which our entire contemporary social system has little by little begun to lose its capacity to retain its own past, [and] has begun to live in a perpetual present . . ." ("Postmodernism," 125). What is disappearing is not "a sense of history" but rather a sense of history as a discourse that speaks "the truth" from a position of unassailable authority and authenticity.

The disappearance of this certitude is disconcerting and decentering, but not purely negative and not necessarily psychotic. As Kaplan notes, in her discussion of the MTV phenomenon, "Jameson's Marxist critique retains the notion of history as a discourse that speaks from a perspective of 'truth' and this . . . is problematic."[9] Nowhere is it more problematic than in a colonized country, such as Ireland, where, as Stephen Dedalus notes when confronted with student apathy during history class, "For them too history was a tale like any other too often heard, their land a pawnshop" (*U,* 21). Indeed, a pawnshop is where commodities go to die—stripped of all illusion, no longer packaged, no longer artfully arranged on the shelf, bereft of all the aura produced by advertising. The experience of learning history for the colonial subject is the experience of the subject in a pawnshop who can only pay again for what he or she once owned, and the repurchase must take place in an atmosphere of dimly lit chaos. The stock of the pawnshop consists of disenchanted commodities signifying disillusioned lives. To purchase something there is the antithesis of "shopping" because everything in the store has already been bought by someone.

By contrast, the "Imperial" experience of shopping in a department store involves an interaction with the new and the untouched (significantly, this is *not* Gerty MacDowell's experience at Clery's department store, since all she can afford is an item from a nondescript bargain bin that is "slightly shopsoiled"). The department store categorizes and illuminates the apparently actual, while eliding the fact that the arrangement represents only one of many possibilities. The goods are put on display after hours, so that they appear to the shoppers to have always been there, independent of human labor, just as historical narrative displays the "facts" to the charmed reader as if they were not the product of mediation and arrangement; it is the humanly possible posing as the divine actual. By contrast, the pawnshop is the room of ousted possibilities, the nightmarish by-product of the department store's aggressive—dare I say psychotic?—presentation of a mythical "truth."

Rather than events emerging from a determinate origin in an identifiable pattern of sequence and causality, history is a theatrical production that manufactures the past while purporting to discover it. History, as de Certeau characterizes it, is always the production of a profitable form of the present by obscuring the possibility of multiple versions of the past: "Within a socially stratified reality, historiography defined as 'past' (that is, as an ensemble of alterities and of 'resistances' to be comprehended or rejected) whatever did not belong to the power of producing a present."[10] Jameson's apparently reasonable and communal "sense of history" depends on a "natural" past offering itself equally to all who care to explore, like an undiscovered continent with no inconvenient aboriginal life already there. But de Certeau points out what can be "legitimately" conceived of as the past has already been predetermined by historiography—that is, by "acceptable" styles of "recording" history—thus setting the stage for multiple possibilities to become an actuality that can only masquerade as inevitable.

For Lacan, the organization of a predetermined past into an apparently inevitable history is a way for the individual subject to misrecognize the endlessly disorienting, eternally present, schizophrenic "now" of the imaginary order, and turn it into the false, totalizing certitude of the symbolic order, which is the hallmark of acceptable historical discourse: "Events are engendered in a primary historization. In other words, history is already producing itself on the stage where it will be played out once it has been written down, both within the subject and outside him."[11] Stephen Dedalus speculates that "time" has branded and fettered events "in the room of the infinite possibilities they have ousted" (*U*, 21). But time is no more to blame for this than history. Time is the result of this process, not its progenitor, and, as we have seen, Jameson notes, perhaps too comfortably, "our feeling of identity depends on our sense of the persistence of the 'I' and the 'me' over time" ("Postmodernism," 119). But the comedian Stephen Wright reports to his audience, "I tried to make instant coffee in my microwave oven and I almost went back in time," suggesting that the postmodern "I" and "me" are a "feeling of identity" now dependent on the "schizophrenic" history of the everyday.

Cheryl Herr points out that even hefty volumes of contemporary Irish history rarely mention Joyce, and this makes perfect sense to me since Joyce is presenting the history of the everyday, the significance of ephemera, the memorable quality of the forgotten experience, the peculiar and particular permanence of anything that has disappeared before being historicized.[12] The nonhistoricized haunts us, and the historicized acts as an oft-repeated incantation to keep it at bay. The paradoxical strength of the ghostly is that, because it lacks substance, it is far more durable than anything substantial. The actual department store (historical narrative) invites us to fantasize a purely substantial, ghost-free future, while the pawnshop (personal narrative) startles us into mourning the haunting past anew; the possible past is the ghost of the actual present, just as the forgotten everyday is the ghost of historical narrative.[13]

Unlike Jameson, Joyce favors apparently ephemeral moments of ever-present now because any "awakening" from history will necessarily be experienced as a schizophrenic, identity-fracturing moment. Far from being ahistorical, such moments expose the phenomenon of history to be a fictional construct; such exposure then permits the subject to resist its interpellative "hailing" component. In the case of Ireland, an imperial view of history that permits what Jameson calls "our sense of the persistence of the 'I' and the 'me' over time" must be interrogated—as Stephen silently does with Deasy in "Nestor"—to see what sort of "I" and "me" is being preserved, and by what right it is presented as the communal time matrix within which each subject must make sense of him- or herself. Baudrillard describes the "moment" of the schizophrenic subject (the epiphany?) as "bereft of every scene, open to everything in spite of himself. . . . [the subject exists in] the absolute proximity, the total instaneity of things, the feeling of no defense, no retreat. It is the end of interiority and intimacy, the overexposure and transparence of the world which traverse him without obstacle. He can no longer produce the limits of his own being, can no longer produce himself as mirror. He is now only a pure screen, a switching center for all the networks of influence."[14] To exist continually in this state would be insanity perhaps, but to glimpse it momentarily is to slip backstage and see the machinery that sets in place the scenes before which we choose to act in the performance of *Our Sense of History.*

Indeed, Baudrillard's description of this moment is remarkably applicable to Gabriel's swoon in "The Dead," a swoon where he loses all ability to sustain his "I" over time, and becomes instead a passive screen of absolute proximity: "His own identity was fading out into a grey impalpable world: the solid world itself which these dead had one time reared and lived in was dissolving and dwindling. . . . His soul swooned slowly as he heard the snow falling faintly through the universe . . . upon all the living and the dead" (*D*, 223–24). The "transparence of the world which traverse[s] him without obstacle," writes Baudrillard, an apt description of Gabriel, who, against "our sense" of the world, miraculously "hears" snow falling everywhere in the universe, on all those living, and on those who have ever lived; it is a moment of wondrous and unbearable instaneity. Whereas Jameson and Baudrillard seek to eliminate the possibility of this state of being, Joyce features it as a not-to-be-dismissed awakening, albeit a brief one, from "our" nightmarish addiction to certitude and to a myth of sequential cause and effect.

3

Power, Pornography, and the Problem of Pleasure

The Semerotics of Desire and Commodity Culture

> It [the "erotic postcard"] was essentially a low-cost industrial product, with a high novelty content. . . . These factors assured an enormous popularity for the postcard as soon as it appeared. . . . In 1910, 125 million cards were printed in France alone.[1]

> The sordid details of his orgies stank under his very nostrils: the sootcoated packet of pictures which he had hidden in the flue of the fireplace and in the presence of whose shameless or bashful wantonness he lay for hours sinning in thought and deed. . . .
>
> (*P*, 115)

> [P]ornography reveals current regimes of sexual relationships as "a coincidence of sexual phantasy, genre and culture in an erotic organization of visibility."[2]

I

The technology permitting the mass production of erotic postcards also led the way to the mass production of erotic fantasies. When Stephen Dedalus comes upon the word *Foetus* carved into a desk at his father's university in Cork, he is "shocked . . . to find in the outer world a trace of what he had deemed till then a brutish and individual malady of his own mind" (*P*, 90). But the "traces" are everywhere—erotic postcards, posters (think of the excessively coy Marie Kendall), and advertisements. In the twentieth century, it is nearly impossible to have "a brutish and *individual* malady of [one's] own mind" (emphasis added). Every conceivable stimulus to pleasure is produced and marketed by what I am calling the semerotic pleasure machine of commodity culture. So much of what might have formerly been stigmatized as perversion has since been constructed by commodity culture into acceptable and accessible productions of purportedly innate pleasure.

Such pleasure scenarios are similar to pornographic scenarios in general, and the sequential narratives of erotic postcards in particular, in that they offer to the consumer an "erotic organization of visibility," promising the production of pleasure without the potentially debilitating by-product of guilt or shame. Indeed, there is nothing "individual" about Stephen's "malady"; instead, for the purposes of making possible the production of pleasure, he has simply severed the connection between this forbidden and sinful (and therefore titillating) "den of monstrous images," and the mass-produced "sootcoated packet of pictures which he had hidden in the flue of the fireplace" (*P*, 115).

One historian of the erotic postcard quotes Havelock Ellis in order to insist that the postcard was detailing pictorially what Ellis was trying to describe clinically: "[A]s Freud, and other sexologists of the period like Krafft-Ebing, Moll, and Ellis, were building their theories of sexual symbolism the lowly picture postcard was merrily and consciously proposing its pictorial usage."[3] According to Ellis, any depiction of "erotic symbolism" became attractive to the viewer because it contained, by virtue of the way it was constructed, "a certain amount of power of concentrating the attention on a point outside the natural path of instinct and the ability to form new mental constructions around that point" (qtd. in Hammond, 8). Of course, the proliferation and popularity of erotic postcards make it clear that the "natural path of instinct" is an unrealistically narrow footpath cut through the thickets of human sexuality, one that is easily widened once "new mental constructions around that point" are mass produced in the ongoing search for new markets. Indeed, Ellis's choice of metaphor suggests a curious resemblance to the modern practice of taking over an unremarkable tract of disorganized land, with a few meandering paths through it, in order to erect a shopping mall where the consumer will be directed down miles of aisles lined with products, all marketed differently, and yet each subscribing to the one dynamic featured in all forms of twentieth-century advertising, marketing, and pornography: "We will resolve for you (by obscuring it) the problematic relation between pleasure and power."

Consistently in Joyce's fiction, women who speak their minds, thus advertising their own desire for pleasure, both confuse and frighten the men who inadvertently stumble into conversations with them. There is "that Lily," for example, who sends Gabriel scurrying out of the room when she offers her frank appraisal of the contemporary male character: "The men that is now is only all palaver and what they can get out of you" (*D*, 178). There is Molly Ivors, who so unnerves Gabriel with her pointed questions and well-timed observations he cannot conceive of her as a woman at all: "Of course the girl or woman, or whatever she was, was an enthusiast . . ." (*D*, 190). Gretta, especially, is expected to "speak," silently, with her body, what he needs to "hear" with his soul. Her "language" is to be meaningful gestures performed against a backdrop of silence:

> He would call her softly:
>
> —Gretta!
>
> Perhaps she would not hear at once: she would be undressing. Then something in his voice would strike her. She would turn and look at him. . . . (*D*, 214, Joyce's ellipsis)

This apparently simple erotic daydream is anything but simple. A theatrical work of considerable subtlety, Gabriel's briefly imagined scene of mounting excitement involves a script, costuming, stage direction, and a silent tableau of literally unspeakable pleasure indicated by Joyce's—and Gabriel's—ellipsis. Furthermore, the scene has a rigidly imagined sequence; one thing simply must follow another. If not, all traces of the desired effect of the reverie will be utterly dissipated. The scene cannot begin, for instance, if Gretta already happens to be looking at him; nor could it continue were she to ask indifferently, perhaps while continuing to look down at a troublesome button on her dress, "what is it?" The reverie is charged with pleasure because it is wired with a sequential circuitry of details. One break in the circuitry, at any point, and the mental machinery will lose its ability to produce pleasure.

Gabriel further requires that Gretta's looking up must not be cued by the too ordinary stimulus of merely hearing her name pronounced. Instead—and rather oddly, at that—he dictates that hearing her name is to have no immediate effect on her ("perhaps she would not hear at once"). The use of "perhaps" introduces a crucial note of uncertainty in a sequence of events that otherwise seems to be imagined as inevitable. As Robert Stoller notes, "[E]xcitement is an oscillation . . . the oscillation is between success and failure. . . . the person experiencing the excitement is also its author and has, in advance, scripted a pseudo risk guaranteed to work out well and therefore lead to pleasure."[4] In one's own reverie, "pseudo risk" is inserted in order to better enjoy seeing it overcome. Implicit in Gabriel's imagining "perhaps she would not hear at once" is the more recognizably erotic scenario of Victorian pornography: "Perhaps she would not submit to my caresses at first." With an almost tiresome predictability, hesitant women in the erotic scenarios of Victorian pornography protest against sexual advances in order to highlight, and even showcase, their sudden and dramatic acquiescence; it is this hesitancy, followed by complete submission, that, in turn, foregrounds the irresistible ministrations of their masculine admirer (and, through fantasy, the masculine reader).[5]

When Gabriel tries to actualize his reverie, however, it is in fact the "pseudo risk" of the fantasy that becomes actual and breaks the circuitry of his pleasure production. Technically speaking, Gretta does come when her name is called, but her look is one of exhaustion and preoccupation rather than impulsive, impassioned abandon. But in his reverie, because she does not hear at first, Gabriel imagines himself free to enjoy watching as the tone of his voice, not what he has said, "strikes her." The "something" in his voice that he imagines she will "hear" remains nebulous precisely so that he may more convincingly envision it (and, by extension, himself) as powerful and dominant. From a visual perspective, Gabriel anticipates watching his voice penetrate Gretta; such a tableau will stimulate the requisite visual foreplay he hopes will further stimulate his desire to penetrate her literally.

Gabriel's visual (one might say cinematic) reverie was being mass produced at an astonishing rate with the advent of the erotic postcard. I argue in this chapter that with the invention of photography, and the production of easily affordable sexual images it made possible, we have an example of the extent to which pleasure may be seen as a construct with a constantly fluctuating history—technological, social, and psychological—rather than an innate and ahistorical by-product of subjective experience. The erotic postcards so popular in Joyce's and Gabriel's time were typically sold in sets that depicted, through a sequence of photographic scenes, a mounting production of pleasure. In one such set, figures 1 and 2 show a mass-produced version of Gabriel's erotic reverie. In figure 1, a man has silently entered the woman's bathroom. He gazes upon her, observing with pleasure her body, while she conducts herself in a manner that indicates she is oblivious to his presence. Then, after he announces himself, she turns, looks, and suddenly gives him an expression of welcome as she accepts his flowers. The man's hand, clutched to his heart, is the visual equivalent of Gabriel's ellipsis of ineffable satisfaction when he imagines Gretta turning to look at him with a look of passionate understanding.

Gabriel's curious insistence that Gretta will come to him after his tone "strikes her" is a continuation of his submerged wish for dominance that has been provoked and strengthened throughout the evening by the humiliation he has suffered at the hands of Lily and Molly Ivors: "Gabriel took his seat boldly at the head of the table and . . . plunged his fork firmly into the goose. He felt quite at ease now . . ." (*D*, 197). As he follows her up the stairs of the Gresham, we read, "only the stress of his nails against the palms of his hands held the wild impulse of his body in check" (*D*, 215). The strange, subtle tension of Gabriel's erotic reverie is the result of an oscillation he sets up between, on the one hand, a desire to dominate and subjugate her to his desire ("something in his voice would strike her"), and, on the other, a need to see this subjugation as her desire too ("She would turn and look at him").

In the paradox of his reverie, he experiences the excitement of dominating his partner at the same time that she relieves him of feeling guilty about this exercise of power by telegraphing to him her hitherto secret desire to be dominated. The reverie clarifies and amplifies Gabriel's anticipation of pleasure by obscuring and muting the exercise of power that implicitly makes it possible.[6]

In addition to introducing "pseudo risk" within a framework of inevitability, a successful erotic reverie allows the exercise of power within an environment that is guilt-free because those who are subjugated announce this very subjugation as (surprise!) the central feature of their own scenario of pleasure. Issues of power are implicit in Gabriel's reverie, and the precise construction of the reverie can be understood as the configuration necessary to allow him to remain ignorant of this same fact. Indeed, as I argue in some detail, any given erotic fantasy is effective only to the extent that it maximizes pleasure while minimizing the relationship between excitement and power that is always an organizing factor in the production of pleasure. Likewise, in the brief reverie depicted in the erotic postcard set, the coercive and voyeuristic configuration of power implicit in a man's sneaking into a woman's bathroom to gaze upon her naked body is transformed from dominance to delight when the woman "discovers" that his impulsive desire has "awakened" in her an absolutely compatible desire.

Similarly, in a different set of cards, we can see another "production of pleasure" in which a woman undresses, unaware she is being watched (much less photographed!). After she has progressively removed her clothes in initial pictures, her gaze discovers the photographer, but once again she bestows a knowing look. Her look suggests that she knows what the voyeur wants, even if he doesn't, and there is no hint of reproach or offense at having been spied upon. What we see both in these postcards and in Gabriel's reverie is the incorporation of a former "perversion"—voyeurism and fetishism—into a new "erotic organization of visibility" that is presented as a natural cause of innate human pleasure. In both cases, however, pleasure is a result of a careful production that is profoundly influenced by the recently developed technology of photography.

Actualizing the reverie begins auspiciously for Gabriel because he is able to bide his time until the proper initial scene presents itself. He carefully picks the moment that approximates, to an exceptional degree, his earlier reverie:

> She had taken off her hat and cloak and was . . . unhooking her waist. Gabriel paused for a few moments, watching her, and then said:
>
> —Gretta! (*D*, 216)

She does turn, she does come toward him, but "Her face looked so serious and weary that the words would not pass Gabriel's lips" (*D*, 216). The point where the actual scenario stumbles is the point where the previous reverie soared into an ineffable expression of satisfaction. When Gabriel says that "the words would not pass [his] lips," what is he talking about? There were no "words" in the previous reverie beyond the annunciatory word "Gretta," and even that, as I have suggested, was less a word than an opportunity for Gabriel to imagine witnessing the tonality of his voice operating upon the unsuspecting Gretta like a powerful aphrodisiac. In reality, as soon as the single word fails to achieve the effect imagined in fantasy, Gabriel no longer has any defense sufficient to protect himself from his own urge to dominate: "If she would only turn to him or come to him of her own accord! To take her as she was would be brutal. No, he must see some ardour in her eyes first. He longed to be master of her strange mood" (*D*, 217). In his reverie, Gabriel's utterance of a single word guarantees that Gretta's "ardour" will be an extension of his own desire, and that the tone of his voice will be sufficient to make her the compliant handmaiden of his erotic scenario.

His initial reverie, in other words, successfully completes, although with decidedly erotic overtones, the mission of his biblical counterpart, the archangel Gabriel. The archangel Gabriel is presumably dispassionate when he informs Mary she is to be impregnated by God, but his problem, the same one we see in Gabriel Conroy's erotic reverie, is how to subjugate her to the desire of a male figure without betraying any element of coercion. The solution, also identical to Gabriel Conroy's imagined solution, is to have her freely confess that to be the object of this desire is her desire as well. What if Mary had declined? It is certainly possible, as the story is told, for her to have done so. But the possibility of her declining seems a "pseudo risk" intended to make her acquiescence certain, and therefore pleasurable, rather than inevitable, and therefore unexciting. Of course, Joyce's Gabriel imposes an erotic dimension on Gretta's acquiescence that is conspicuously absent in the biblical story of the Annunciation.

The story of the Annunciation, in its narration of the events leading up to a girl's being impregnated by a God, is also a retelling of the story of Leda and the swan, but in the Christian version of the story, all evidence of eroticism, power, or pleasure has been either suppressed or made obscure. In the story of Leda and the swan, there is no role equivalent to the delicate diplomatic mission of the archangel Gabriel. In the sexual relations depicted in Greek mythology, the relationship between pleasure and power is much more easily discerned; indeed, it seems clear the act is pleasurable to the god precisely because he takes Leda by force. In Yeats's version of Leda and the swan, for example, no archangel appears to explain to her what will happen; "a sudden blow" is all the annunciation Leda receives.[7] The Christian version, in contrast, avoids even the implication of divine rape; instead, the Virgin Mary immediately expresses a desire to comply to the unusual request—though not a passionate desire, certainly—and she does so the moment she hears the word of God. Were Mary to refuse this verbal call, were she not to "come to him of her own accord," the archangel Gabriel would be in the same spot as his human counterpart: "To take her as she was would be brutal." Both Gabriels expect to excite compliance with simple pronouncements: "Hail Mary, full of grace," in the Catholic rosary prayer and "Gretta!" in the other version. Recall here, also, that Gabriel Conroy begins to desire his wife physically only after he sees her poised at the top of the stairs and notes that "there was *grace* . . . in her attitude, as if she were a symbol of something" (*D*, 210, emphasis mine).

Both the biblical and the Joycean Gabriels require the woman's unconditional compliance if all urges toward domination and mastery are to be suppressed effectively. The construction of pleasure in the Annunciation is strictly confined to piety and obedience, whereas the modern-day Gabriel wishes to see Gretta "coming to him of her own accord," in a manner suggesting to him that she, too, is in active search of her own pleasure. Mary, understandably enough, wants to be sure she and the angel Gabriel are talking about what she thinks they're talking about; and so, while she stops short of refusing, she does inquire, with superb delicacy, as to the intended mechanics of this impregnation: "How shall this be, seeing I know not a man?" (Luke 1:34). Mary acknowledges some awareness of the existence of sexual intercourse but strictly within the context of a duty a woman submits to, with a legally designated partner (a man she "knows"), rather than an impulse indulged in with a stranger (a man she desires). Her concern, quite properly, is whether God's intentions are honorable and whether this impregnation will take place within the accepted context of marriage.

The archangel Gabriel then delivers a description of divine sex that is a masterpiece of strategic vagueness: "The Holy Ghost shall come upon thee, and the power of the Highest shall overshadow thee" (Luke 1:35). A more cynical Mary might fairly have inquired, "Come on, what's it going to be like, really?" The archangel Gabriel's statement is so charged with denial of the very domination and eroticism with which it is imbued that it describes the manner of conception with metaphors that promise overpowering ecstasy, yet it makes no mention of how this pleasure is to be produced, or for whom it is to be produced. If God has occasion to use a pick-up line, we might have expected it would be this well crafted. In any event, we can imagine it is just such a statement of overpowering ecstasy that Gabriel

Conroy wishes to convey to Gretta through the ineffable "something" in his voice that will "strike her." Mary's famous reply to the archangel's sketchy description, were it to be Gretta's actual reply, would have completed Gabriel Conroy's earlier erotic reverie in wondrous fashion: "Let it be done to me *according to thy word*" (Luke 1:38, my emphasis).

Each of the three scenarios I have analyzed—Gabriel's erotic reverie, his failed attempt to actualize it, and the archangel Gabriel's successful Annunciation—all present the potential rewards and considerable difficulties for the construction of pleasure by the "masculine" subject, especially if the pleasure of the "feminine" subject is to be taken into account. Gabriel's problem is that he both wants to "master" Gretta, and he wants her to understand this and recognize it as an enactment of her own desire, too. In the scene of the Annunciation, there is no suggestion that Mary acquiesces to God's "word" in order to construct her own scenario of pleasure; still, her immediate and unconditional consent is featured as the immensely satisfying climax of the scene. In Joyce's updating of this scene, the implicit eroticism is thoroughly restored (this is the same writer who made Molly Bloom considerably less chaste than her classical predecessor). More than this, the twentieth-century Gabriel produces a scenario of "masculine" pleasure that requires Gretta to be, for want of a better word, turned on: "[H]e must see some ardour in her eyes first." The connotations of *ardour*—warm feelings, heat, fervent desire—bring the issue of the woman's pleasure into the forefront in a way that Luke's recounting of Mary's cool compliance does not.

Just as the commodity erases all trace of the human labor that produces it, as well as any suggestion of the relationship among power, economics, and identity in such production, Gabriel's reverie also functions as a commodity in that it promotes pleasure while obscuring relationships of power—even though it is these very relationships of power that produce the pleasure. According to Foucault, the construction, identification, and confession of pleasure by both men and women is the nexus of sexuality in the twentieth century, and power is always the dominant infrastructure in the construction of pleasure: "The object . . . is to define the regime of power-knowledge-pleasure that sustains the discourse on human sexuality in our part of the world. . . . [I want to see] how it penetrates and controls everyday pleasure . . ." (*History of Sexuality*, 11). The woman's body, in particular, in the "scientific" discourse of twentieth-century sexology, has been nominated as the site of hidden "truths," and has therefore been construed as "an object of knowledge and an element in relations of power" (Foucault, 107).

All the sexologists of the turn of the century (and here we can momentarily group Freud with Havelock Ellis and Krafft-Ebing) put forth, in clinical and categorical terms, the "fact" of woman's pleasure as made evident by her body's confession of pleasure: "Through pedagogy, medicine, and economics, . . . sex became a matter that required . . . individuals, to place themselves under surveillance" (Foucault, *History of Sexuality,* 116). Confessions of the body, best captured by putting oneself and others "under surveillance," were privileged as inherently "true" because such confessions consisted of a silent, physical discourse seen as involuntary. By making confession "no longer . . . a test, but rather a sign, and by making sexuality something to be interpreted, the nineteenth century gave itself the possibility of causing the procedures of confession to operate within the regular formation of a scientific discourse" (Foucault, 67). When Gretta chastely kisses Gabriel, calling him "a generous person," he misinterprets this gesture as evidence that "the yielding mood had come upon her," and he seeks to convert her physical "confession" into a verbal one:

> —Gretta dear, what are you thinking about? . . .
> —Tell me what it is, Gretta. I think I know what is the matter. Do I know? (*D,* 218)

What follows is certainly a confession, but it is nothing like the one Gabriel was looking forward to interpreting.

What Gabriel wants is to be the erotic equivalent of Gretta's schoolmaster, teasing out the implication of her body's involuntary confession. His desire to serve as the master interpreter of her desire is in keeping with Foucault's general assertion that "[i]n the Christian confession . . . there was a whole series of methods that had much in common with an erotic art: guidance by the master along a path of initiation, the intensification of experiences extending down to their physical components, the optimization of effects by the discourse that accompanied them" (*History of Sexuality,* 70). In other words, "talking dirty." Gabriel is a would-be master of the erotic, a priest of love, taking the involuntary confessions of pleasure signaled by a woman's body as the discourse he wishes to interpret and optimize. Certainly the obsession that a male confessor has for the female body as a site of knowledge leads to a situation that Molly Bloom finds both puzzling and suspicious: "[H]e touched me father and what harm if he did where and I said on the canal bank like a fool" (*U,* 610). For the woman, allowing a man not one's husband to touch her body is a sin; this Molly knows or she would not think to confess it. But what surprises her is that the sin must be quantified according to what part of her body was touched. In this exchange, we can see an example of how the power implicit in the discourse of confession sets up erogenous zones on the female body where pleasure is intensified by a discourse that optimizes it.

Potentially, in her next encounter with an amorous male, Molly must allow or disallow touching in conscious correspondence with the prohibitive discourse produced by her confession. In other words, her confession inaugurates a configuration of power that will henceforth serve as the foundation for, or the destruction of, her scenario of pleasure. While the prohibitions so painstakingly reviewed during Molly's confession make clear the limits that must be observed by her if she is to feel innocent of sin, at the same time they make possible more deliberate and more conscious acts of transgression, acts that, by virtue of the fact they are sins, may now lead to an "intensification of pleasure" not possible before. Of course Molly's later question—"what did he want to know for when I had already confessed it to God"—shrewdly turns the tables on the priest as the master of the erotic who, like the archangel Gabriel, is able, by posing as an asexual go-between for God, to pretend to dispassionately question a woman concerning her body (*U*, 610).

Molly's suspicions that her confession has been directed and packaged in such a way in order to excite the priest are supported by Stephen's reaction to being asked if he has a vocation for the priesthood: "He would know the sins . . . hearing them murmured into his ears in the confessional under the shame of a darkened chapel by the lips of women and of girls . . ." (*P*, 159). Best of all, the priesthood will somehow allow him to experience this pleasure with no sense that to enjoy the confessions of women and young girls in this way is inappropriate: "[B]ut rendered immune mysteriously at his ordination by the imposition of hands his soul would pass again uncontaminated to the white peace of the altar" (*P*, 159). The mystery that purifies him is that which is provided by the magic of the commodity; once again, "Double your pleasure, Double your fun," by producing pleasure as a commodity devoid of all context, and therefore generating, to quote an ad for a breath mint "pure . . . sensation."

If any of this obsession with the "knowledge" about pleasure supposedly implicit in the female body is to make sense, women must be acknowledged as having a desire of their own; otherwise, what could they possibly have to confess? Once this point is made, however, there comes the much more difficult question, memorably expressed by Freud, but not only by him, "what does woman want?" The cryptic text of the "science of sexuality"—redefined by Freud as psychoanalysis—is the female body, seen as an object imbued with unconscious knowledge, which must be put into a power matrix that will allow it, encourage it, perhaps even coerce it into involuntarily confessing the "truth" about its experience of pleasure. The "science" of sexology, Foucault points out, "was in fact a science made up of evasions since, given its inability or refusal to speak of sex itself, it concerned itself primarily with aberrations, perversions, exceptional oddities, pathological abatements, and morbid aggravations" (*History of Sexuality,* 53). The situation of Molly, or any woman, in the confessional is similar; the pleasure inherent in sexuality must be as absent in the confessional as it is in Luke's version of Mary's "confession" to Gabriel in the story of the Annunciation.

Inside the Catholic confessional, sexual impulses must be confessed and discussed in order that they may be punished and forgiven. Or, to put this another way, scenarios that produce pleasure must be submitted for approval, and those who admit being moved by an unacceptable scenario must be reproved for having succumbed to a sinful, or "unnatural," impulse. The detailing of supposed perversions, however, either in the exhaustive catalogues of Havelock Ellis or in the anatomically specific confession elicited from Molly Bloom, while intended to protect and define behavior deemed as normal, can also have the opposite effect of broadening the definition of "normal" to include what was previously labeled as "perversion." Quite anxious to be seen as maintaining standards of normalcy, however, the sexologists themselves detailed an astonishing array of "perversions," and then, rather than normalizing them in any way, further stigmatized them as "strange pleasures . . . [that] would eventually result in nothing short of death: that of individuals, generations, the species itself" (Foucault, *History of Sexuality,* 54).

These "strange pleasures," never before clinically recognized, were "scientifically" organized in order that they might more definitively be marginalized—that is, removed from the "normal" register of sexuality—with the result that "normal" pleasures henceforth were off-limits to the otherwise obsessive surveillance of sexuality by twentieth-century discourses: "[H]eterosexual monogamy. . . . was spoken of less and less. . . . Efforts to find out its secrets were abandoned; nothing further was demanded of it than to define itself from day to day" (Foucault, *History of Sexuality,* 38). Pleasure, in other words, was exhaustively detailed if it was "strange," and left entirely unexamined if it was "normal." The result of this separation, if not consciously the purpose, was that the problem of pleasure—the fact that it could arise out of a disturbing matrix of pleasure, power, and knowledge—was effectively obscured.

In other words, some pleasures were invalidated as strange so that others could be viewed as normal, and thus the entire phenomenon of constructing pleasure could be misrecognized as a "natural impulse" that might be effortlessly enjoyed—but only if experienced within a "legitimate" context. Certainly Gabriel is well within this "legitimate" context when attempting to have sexual intercourse with his wife, but what his reverie highlights is the continued existence of the problem of pleasure, which is also, and always, the problem of power, within the unexamined relationship of heterosexual monogamy. Heterosexual monogamy is left unexamined by the sexologists not because it is "normal," but because such an examination would reveal tensions disturbingly similar to those found in the "strange pleasures" of "perversion." The heterosexual monogamous relationship, privileged as "legitimate," must remain largely unexamined by the new science of sexuality if pleasure is to be naturalized as a highly refined, and therefore rigorously controlled, "impulse," rather than conceptualized as a construction that involves, among other things, role-playing, costuming, dialogue, scenery, backdrops, and shifting epicenters of knowledge and power.

Even for the relatively more enlightened Freud, the fact that so many of his hysterical female patients were unmarried allowed him to believe, as he did with Dora, that their problems arose from resisting their "natural" status as objects of desire in the pleasure scenarios of men. In the twentieth century, women need a room of their own in order to discover a pleasure of their own—one that, while it may envision other people in different roles, nonetheless uses them as a supporting cast that permits and highlights their performance as the star; seen from this perspective, it is clear how power—which might be defined, most simply, as who gets to do what to whom—is an inextricable dimension in the construction of pleasure. The obvious difference between what Gretta is thinking and what Gabriel thinks she is thinking is that she remembers herself as the star of her own pleasure scenario, with Michael Furey as her leading man. Consequently, on this night of all nights, she does not have the energy to perform a subordinate role in his scenario.

What is interesting, relative to the burgeoning science of sexology, is that Joyce clearly explores the problem of pleasure *within marriage* in "The Dead." And in *Ulysses* he does so again, presenting in exhaustive detail a marriage in which "normal" intercourse has not occurred in ten years, and in which each partner in the marriage might be said to have an ongoing and active interest in constructing scenarios of pleasure—but not with each other. In giving us this detailed examination of the problem of pleasure, both within and beyond a "legitimate" context, Joyce seems to operate as a deliberately inverted sexologist; he invades the precise territory the others strategically left unexamined, and, in doing so, he problematizes the idea of pleasure in precisely the way their approach scrupulously avoided.

II

In contrast to this tendency of the sexologists to isolate an unexamined "normal" sexuality by constructing an exhaustive catalogue of the "perverse," those involved with commodity culture—whether in the area of design, marketing, advertising, or consumption—concerned themselves more and more with "discovering" what people want. As women were consumers too, understanding what they desire became potentially profitable and, therefore, too valuable to deny or ignore. In *Hard Core,* a study of twentieth-century heterosexual film pornography, Linda Williams notes her surprise at discovering that the "masculine" fantasies depicted in pornography, far from ignoring woman's pleasure, seem obsessed with discovering what it is. Even more surprising, the men portrayed in the films seem to view this discovery as an essential prerequisite for experiencing their own pleasure: "I expected to see the most unrelieved and unchallenged dominance of the phallus . . . I saw instead a remarkable uncertainty and instability" (x). Williams sees, as the central question of "masculine" fantasy, "how power and pleasure function in discourses in which women's bodies are the object of knowledge" (x). True to its patriarchal preoccupations, heterosexual pornography typically "discovers" that a woman wants what a man wishes she needed. Thus, in a psychic sleight of hand, the woman is acknowledged to be a sexual subject, with a desire of her own, but this unsettling recognition of a woman's sexual autonomy is then quickly obscured by the man's "discovery," confirmed by the "confession" of the woman's body, that her desire, as sexual subject, is to be a sexual object for the man.

From this perspective, Freud's analysis of Dora reads like a pornographic fantasy because he first grants the fact that she is a sexual subject, and then concludes that she has fallen ill because she is denying what he takes to be *her* desire to be a sexual object for a man. Also in this same sense, Gabriel Conroy, in his own erotic reverie, is recognizable as the quintessential twentieth-century "pornographic" hero because he raises the issue of Gretta's desire only to "discover" that she wants him to do to her whatever he feels he must. The expression of a woman's desire as nothing more than a need to be the object of a man's desire is admirably encapsulated in Mary's remarkably compliant request: "Be it unto me according to thy word."[8] Upon hearing this, the archangel Gabriel, not wanting to jeopardize this tableau of a happy ending, swiftly and silently departs: "And the angel departed from her" (Luke 1:38).

Williams notes that "the insecurity of all pornographic knowledge of the sexual 'other' . . . relies on the staging and inducing of involuntary confessions" (*Hard Core,* 278). Mary, like Gretta in Gabriel's reverie, but unlike her in reality, "looks up" upon hearing the angel speak, immediately recognizes "something" in his tone, and acquiesces to it with a suddenness and unqualified acceptance that approximates "involuntary confession." Mary's acceptance of God's will in the scene of the Annunciation has the briefness and exhilarating economy of gesture and expression that are featured in Gabriel's erotic reverie. Indeed, women acquiesce quickly and completely in most erotic postcard sets of the time (just as they continue to do so in contemporary heterosexual pornography). The angel Gabriel hardly explains himself at all; nevertheless, Mary's reaction is so swift and absolutely satisfactory that he then simply departs without further comment. Similarly, Gabriel's reverie trails off into an ellipsis of complete satisfaction, but the real encounter with Gretta leads to a sudden breakdown of all his treasured myths about himself and his marriage.[9]

In an astonishing feat of self-deception, Gabriel, after Gretta kisses him and calls him "a generous person," decides this is, finally, the required acquiescence that earlier he featured so prominently in his scenario of pleasure: "Perhaps she had felt the impetuous desire that was in him and then the yielding mood had come upon her. Now that she had fallen to him so easily he wondered why he had been so diffident" (*D*, 217–18). Again, Gabriel's word choice—"the yielding mood" and "she had fallen"—betrays his desire to dominate and subjugate, even as he tries to present Gretta, in theatrical terms, as giving in to *her* "desire" to have it done "unto [her] according to [Gabriel Conroy's] word."

Significantly, in what he imagines as his moment of impending triumph, Gabriel uses rhetoric that once again becomes biblical. Whereas the archangel Gabriel told Mary, "the Holy Ghost shall *come upon thee*," Gabriel Conroy conjectures that "the yielding mood had *come upon her*" (emphasis mine). And yet even before Gretta bursts into tears, Gabriel can feel that his scenario is once again about to founder on the unexpected rock of her contradictory desire, a desire he characterizes as alarmingly "other" by calling it her "strange mood," of which he "longs to be master." The scenario fails to be supported, in other words, by the very rock he intended to use as its cornerstone. In his erotic reverie, he imagines her body as "confessing" her desire to yield, and yet, in reality, it is her actual body—unmediated by his erotic reverie—that silently and involuntarily "confesses" precisely the opposite, her inability to subjugate her desire to his: "She did not answer *nor yield* wholly to his arm" (*D*, 218, emphasis mine).[10]

As with Freud (and his early mentor, Charcot), the male subject's fascination with "hysterical" women is that their bodies appear to "confess" what they are unable to say. This fascination with the physically visible symptoms of hysteria reflects the male subject's need to discover what women want—but to discover it in such a way that they "objectively" show that women need what men fantasize about giving them. Women who contradict this through word and action—women like Dora—are not exceptions, but rather the unfortunate rebels whose demonstrable suffering, easily photographed and thus made "scientific" and "objective," proves the necessity for a woman to recognize "her" desire. Since a symptom, by definition, defies the interpretation of the subject who suffers from it, psychoanalysis in its earliest stages often consisted of men free to interpret, in whatever manner they needed, the involuntary "confessions" of women about the "nature" of their desires. Quite often, Freud said to Dora, in not so many words, much the same thing the excited and expectant Gabriel says to Gretta: "I think I know what is the matter. Do I know?" Whereas Gretta bursts into tears when Gabriel asks this, thus offering a bodily "confession" of alien desire that causes Gabriel to stand "stockstill for a moment in astonishment," Dora, not having to puzzle through the added complexity of being married to her questioner, terminated the therapy. Freud's astonishment, also momentary, eventually gave way to his theory about transference and counter transference. It was this theory, more than any other, that problematized the supposed "nature" of both pleasure and desire by recognizing that power and pleasure are intertwined for the "masculine" subject when he approaches a woman's body as the object of knowledge.

Pleasure has a history, as Foucault demonstrated, and the conjunction of psychoanalysis and photography/cinema helped transform voyeurism and fetishism from a "perversion" to a "natural" scenario of pleasure. Linda Williams argues that psychoanalysis must be viewed in conjunction with the invention of photography and movies: "[I]t is not because men are naturally voyeurs and fetishists and that these perverse pleasures overwhelmed science. . . . Cinema implanted these perversions more firmly, normalizing them in technological and social 'ways of seeing'" (45–46). Indeed, she points out that Charcot photographed women in the throes of their physical symptoms, modeling his project on that of Edward Muybridge, the photographer who took pictures in rapid succession to study details of physical motion previously invisible to the naked eye: "[L]ike the cinema itself, [psychoanalysis] should be seen simply as another late-nineteenth-century discourse, another apparatus for aligning socially produced sexual desires with Oedipal and familial norms. . . . Neither institution actually reflects the 'confessional' truths they purport to record; rather, they produce these truths in their new forms of power and pleasure" (45). Charcot categorized his photographs in a way that purported to record objectively a woman's mounting awareness—from initial fear to eventual pleasure—that something she could not resist had, to paraphrase the angel Gabriel, "come upon her." In this case, what comes upon her is not the Holy Spirit but the projected desires of the analyst.

Charcot's categories—"threat," "appeal," "amorous supplication," "eroticism," "ecstasy"—amount to a Muybridge motion study of what is taken to be the bodily confession of a woman's desire. "As in most pornography," Linda Williams says about Charcot's photographic project, "the woman's body is solicited, questioned, and probed for secrets that are best revealed when she herself is not in control" (51). The symptoms photographed may have been real enough (although some commentators have questioned whether some of the women might not have performed, both for the camera and the authority figure who wielded it), but the narrative imposed on the photographic sequence—a narrative of a woman involuntarily "confessing," through body language, her desire to be the object of a man's desire—certainly is a pleasure production for the "masculine" subject similar both to Gabriel's reverie and sequences of erotic postcards in general.

Comparing the Annunciation with Gabriel's erotic reverie suggests both a similarity and a difference; they are both scenarios of female compliance leading to the satisfaction of male desire, but Luke's version is entirely rhetorical, with no mention of what she is doing, or who looks at whom. Gabriel Conroy's version, in contrast, casts him as the director, with lighting, costuming, expression, and even an all-important look from Gretta all featured in a precise configuration and sequence. Indeed, Gretta's overdetermined "look" at Gabriel probably would be featured as a close-up in an erotic postcard sequence (and, later, in cinema). Mary's verbal compliance is refigured by Gabriel Conroy's imagination into a confession by Gretta of equal compliance, but it is as purely visual and silent as erotic postcards or early cinema. As both Muybridge's photographic motion studies and Charcot's photographs of stages of hysteria suggest, the invention of photography, even well before the invention of movies, immediately led to a primitive cinematic narrative.

In Gabriel's reverie, it is Gretta's body that he must imagine as visually responding to his word with what he then misrecognizes as a confession of her desire, refigured as a photographic *tableau* constituting a particular "erotic organization of visibility." The particulars of the "organization," like pleasure itself, will have a material and narrative history, a history determined by a multitude of factors specific to a given culture, economy, and technology. Taken all together, such factors will produce a particular sexual zeitgeist that provides the construction of pleasure with a complex history. When Gabriel tries to actualize the fantasy in reality, it is indeed her body that confesses (she bursts into tears), but of course what it forces her to confess is not anything like what he needed to imagine. Readers of "The Dead" have taken it for granted that Gretta tells the story of Michael Furey because Gabriel asks her to do so. But is it really this simple? Growing rigid against his arm and bursting into tears amount to involuntary bodily confessions of her lack of desire for him at that moment, but her accompanying narrative is also a protest against years of having to playact what Gabriel wants her to be. Like Freud's Dora, she is saying, "Don't grant the fact of my desire in order to co-opt it for your own scenario of pleasure production." Or, put much less analytically, "Do you *really* want to know what I am thinking?"

Gretta, Molly Ivors, and Lily are all proof of why photographic and cinematic pornography was, and is, such an important part of the male production of what Foucault calls "everyday pleasure" in twentieth-century life. Once it was technologically possible, photographic and cinematic pornography then developed as a particular genre that, in turn, had a profound influence on the production of individual "pleasure scenarios." As Linda Williams points out, a "[g]enre . . . is not just a pattern of imagery, but the relation of this imagery to narrative structure" (247). The genre of heterosexual pornography—that is to say, the organizing principle of the visual images—involves "the posing, and 'solving,' of problems of sexuality within strictly limited parameters" (L. Williams, 247). Because the "solution" featured in the genre of pornography is so limited, and even fantastic, the organization of visual imagery highlights the problem of the very pleasure it encourages the viewer to produce, and it does so even while depicting the supposedly spontaneous eruption of it. Once a woman's body becomes the object of knowledge about the "truth" of female desire, then it is only in controlled scenarios such as Charcot's photographs, Gabriel's reverie, or Luke's version of the Annunciation that one can be certain that a woman's confession of her desire will result in a narrative that sustains the production of pleasure for a masculine subject.

Charcot's and Muybridge's sequence photography gave rise to a particular motion study of female desire as communicated by the female body, an encoded physical configuration that is also the basic formula for both pornographic depictions of the presumed female climax and the marketing of commodities. Turn-of-the-century manifestations of this formula included the erotic postcard, a technologically crafted scenario of "pleasure." Each picture builds pleasure slowly, just as in Gabriel's reverie and in Charcot's research, by charting—from "fear" to "ecstasy"—the gradual and involuntary bodily "confession" of a woman's desire to be the object of a man's desire.

Often, as in Gabriel's reverie, the initial photograph in the sequence shows a woman alone who is getting undressed, often preparatory to a bath. As with both Gabriel's reverie of Gretta undressing and his later painstaking and deliberate framing, or snapshot, of this moment of reality, the male viewer is invited to consider the sexual dimension of the woman's action. He is invited to do so with the understanding that the woman does not know she is being observed, and that in this initial moment she does not yet have any thoughts of a sexual nature. Next, a man enters the frame of the photograph and, gradually, "something" about him might be said to "strike her." The rest of the sequence typically shows her, through a body language of various looks and postures, "confessing" a desire identical to that which the man's annunciation of his desire has awakened in her. Since this is fantasy, the erotic postcard sequence presents her as doing this with a cheerful candor about which Gabriel Conroy can only dream, and with an easily photographed theatrical flair for which Charcot could only hope.

Although in the hotel room Gabriel is aware that he is looking at his wife, in the earlier scenario that awakened his desire, it is her anonymity that draws Gabriel's attention: "A woman was standing near the top of the first flight, in the shadow also. He could not see her face but he could see the terracotta and salmonpink panels of her skirt which the shadow made appear black and white" (*D*, 209). The tendency is to see this organization of visibility as that of a salon oil painting, one that he would call "*Distant Music.*" The odd quality of the light, however, also makes Gretta appear to be the living model of a black-and-white photograph.

While Gabriel's urge to come up with a title for Gretta's unconscious pose may be seen as an appropriate impulse given the resemblance of the scene to a painting, photographs in general, and erotic postcards in particular, almost always sported telltale labels to suggest the particular nature of the pleasure scenario, as this 1902 advertisement makes clear: "Suggestive Postcards for Art Lovers and Collectors" is the heading, followed by the more specific offer of "sets" with such titles as "Ardent Kisses," "The Cigarette," "In the Corn," "Alone at Last," and "Butterfly Hunting" (Hammond, 10). Dare we add to this suggestive compendium the titillating title "Distant Music"? Although there is no overt hint of eroticism in Gabriel's reverent description, Gretta's pose is nothing if not suggestive to Gabriel; he notes the quality of light that makes her skirt appear "black and white," and, in an odd echo of the postcard set entitled "Alone at Last," he anticipates, beginning with this "picture" of her, eventually being alone with her, actualizing his erotic reverie:

> When the others had gone away, when he and she were in their room in the hotel, then they would be alone together. He would call her softly:
>
> —Gretta! (*D*, 214)

As Hammond points out, the erotic postcard made explicit the eroticism that was implicit in the salon paintings: "The artisans who made postcards looked to Fine Art. The typical Salon painting, by Gerome, Bouguereau, Courtois, or Chocarne-Moreau, was created on an 'heroic' scale, photographically painted, and dignified in subject matter. . . . Just as the literary salon had given way to the cafe as the breeding ground of art, so Salon painting gave way to the picture postcard. . . . The eroticism in Salon painting was there, but never openly admitted. The postcard puts that eroticism in the limelight, so that it can't be missed" (11–12). Bram Dijkstra, in his book *Idols of Perversity,* notes, "Between 1875 and 1900 a wide range of new processes of photographic reproduction was making the world of contemporary painters accessible to millions of eager viewers all over the world. . . . The visual creations of the painters therefore came to occupy a position of international importance not unlike that occupied by television in our own time."[11] Paintings that were "photographically painted" were also, not coincidentally, intended to be photographically reproduced.

The mass production and dissemination of erotic postcards, then, were contemporaneous with the photographic reproduction of salon paintings. The relationship between these two forms concerned two different forms of erotic organizations of the visible, one implicit and one explicit. Also in this time frame, 1875–1900, the salon paintings were busily reinterpreting classical figures of women—from Venus to Ophelia to Salome—with much more overt erotic overtones. "Maurice Greiffenhagen," Dijkstra notes, "offered his admiring public an ecstatic version of the mystical, purified, feverishly sacrificial woman in a late Pre-Raphaelite-inspired 'The Annunciation'" (36).

If "Distant Music" is no more to Gabriel than a salon painting, the woman it depicted, in a static attitude of "grace and mystery," would be an object for "masculine" contemplation, devoid of sexual subjectivity. On the other hand, if "Distant Music" were the title for a set of erotic postcards, this pose would be followed by subsequent poses of the woman "awakening" to an awareness of her own pleasure—an awareness Gabriel imagines Gretta telegraphing to him via the look she will give him, after "something" in his voice "strikes her." My point is that salon paintings ideologically disallow the possibility of a woman's being a sexual subject ("Distant Music"), but pictorially they convey an exciting ambivalence. Despite the proper salon title that Gabriel gives to what he is seeing, it is this image of Gretta that begins his long, complex, and decidedly physical desire for her.

Ironically, it is erotic postcards that allow the possibility of a woman as a sexual subject because the depiction of her pleasure, while in line with patriarchal expectations, nonetheless is not contradicted by an ideology that promises pain and ruin were she to enjoy herself. Indeed, contrary to the received idea that pornography by definition oppresses women, Linda Williams points out that it is "[o]ne of the few popular genres in which women are not punished for knowing, pursuing, and finding their pleasure" (239). Of course, what they are "not punished for" is discovering they want what men want. In contrast, women in salon paintings show evidence of having grown "morally" through the experience of rejecting pleasure. Or, if they do seem to be physically enjoying themselves, they are depicted as treacherous and murderous femmes fatales who have moved beyond any configuration that could be regarded as human, and men can engage them only at the price of certain destruction to themselves.

"In 1910," one commentator tells us, "125 million cards were printed in France alone" (Farina, 11). Nor did such production go unnoticed by the authorities: "On August 22 1900 the gendarmerie raided shops all over Paris and seized 80,000 'objectionable' cards. It was to be the first of many such raids" (Farina, 11). Such cards were, of course, available to tourists, who in turn made them available to folks back home, and they could also be ordered through the mail. A possible working definition of *pornography*, then, one that would suggest its function as a product in commodity culture rather than simply lament its existence, might be to define it as any genre or system of representation that betrays an awareness that the presumably spontaneous and innate forces of pleasure, power, knowledge, and gender are in fact constructions.

Most pornography sets out to produce pleasure for some form of consumer, and its success at doing so determines its success as a product on the market. If the targeted market is the heterosexual "masculine" subject, the form that the production of pleasure takes may well offend, or at least generate boredom in, a consumer with differently perceived needs. Potentially, the reverse could be true; scenarios that produce pleasure for heterosexual women might puzzle, frighten, or enrage other people. Leopold Bloom, in his own pseudoscientific way, is, as I have suggested, as much an amateur sexologist as he is an amateur astronomer. His efforts to find material that will stimulate Molly show that he too is participating in the turn-of-the-century obsession to discover "what women want." Molly herself, while allowing the possibility that pornographic material might excite her, nonetheless dismisses books depicting the flagellation of women with her remark "theres nothing for a woman in all that" (*U*, 619).

Her remark has a certain prophetic ring relative to the marketing of pornography in our own time, when traditional X-rated videos now advertise "for viewing by couples." Sometimes they are more specific about what that means when they add, "no violence." In any event, this marketing maneuver has produced a new market; forty percent of X-rated films are now rented by women. In the scene from *Sweets of Sin* that catches Bloom's eye, it is the woman who arrives late (that is to say, at her own convenience). Clearly, she is still enjoying memories of her shopping expedition. Even though her "costliest frillies," paid for by her husband's money, are said to be "for Raoul," it is the woman in this scene who is the center of her own scenario of pleasure, and it is Raoul's growing awareness that he is merely playing a supporting role in her production that causes his annoyance and impatience (thus adding to her enjoyment of him as a rough, excitable fellow). While Bloom certainly finds this scene exciting, his decision to buy the book is motivated less by this than by his sense that Molly will be excited by it. Such a book nowadays, if acted out on video, would be labeled and marketed: "For viewing by couples, nonviolent."

Pornography for couples, to continue refining my deliberately nonpejorative definition, is the presentation, for the purposes of selling and making a profit, of staged scenarios, performed as if spontaneous, that optimize pleasure by obscuring the power that makes such pleasure possible. By this definition, a definition that does not include the graphic depiction of sex as a necessary ingredient, all advertising, and commodity culture in general, is pornographic. In both cases, pleasure is constructed and amplified by eliding its relationship to questions of power, and this elision is actualized for the strictly commercial purposes of engaging targetable desires—in both consumers and sexual subjects—and thus opening up a new market, either for a previously disorganized and unrecognized "perversion," or for a new and hitherto unknown product. The commodity, like the erotic reverie, constructs pleasure by obscuring power relations.

As Linda Williams points out, it is this common denominator that makes the concept of the fetish crucial to both Freud and Marx: "Although Marx and Freud define their fetishes very differently, they both share a common will to expose the processes by which individuals fall victim to an illusory belief in the exalted value of certain (fetish) objects" (104). Both the commodity and the erotic reverie operate like the fetish in that they offer "short-term, short-sighted solutions to more fundamental problems of power and pleasure in social relations" (L. Williams, 105). In *Love Story,* Erich Segal wrote: "Love means never having to say you're sorry." In pornography for couples, defined in this chapter as the production of pleasure scenarios for consumption and profit, love means never having to say "do this, or you'll be sorry." This form of pornography amplifies the problem of pleasure in heterosexual monogamy, a problem ignored by sexologists of Joyce's day.

III

Given that Paris had such a cheap, popular, and provocative export in the form of erotic postcards, it is perhaps now more clear why the timid and untraveled Little Chandler in "A Little Cloud" anxiously inquires of the cosmopolitan Gallaher, "is it true that Paris is so . . . immoral as they say?" (*D,* 77, Joyce's ellipsis). We do not know for sure, as we do with Stephen Dedalus and Leopold Bloom, whether or not Little Chandler possesses or has ever seen such postcards. I find it significant, however, that while his general dissatisfaction with the lack of passion in his wife may have been brought on by Gallaher's vague allusions to "immorality," his specific complaint focuses upon, and seems clarified by, her photograph.

Unlike the initial mental photograph in Gabriel's "sequentially photographed" reverie, Little Chandler's wife is not looking away, but staring straight at him: "He looked coldly into the eyes of the photograph and they answered coldly" (*D,* 83). While he grants aesthetic points to his wife's face and eyes ("Certainly they were pretty and the face itself was pretty"), there is no hope that her "defiant" and "repelling" facial expression might gradually be coaxed into "confessing" her desire to be the object of his desire: "Why was it so unconscious and lady-like? The composure of the eyes irritated him. They repelled and defied him: there was no passion in them, no rapture" (*D,* 83). Sequential movement that, through the female body, indicates the involuntary confession of pleasure—from lady-like composure to impassioned discomposure, from "normalcy" to "hysterical symptom," from "unconsciously" undressing to demonstrating "the yielding mood"—all figure in Gabriel's scenario, in erotic postcards, and in advertising in general. Annie's photograph, which has no hint of a performance along these lines, strikes Little Chandler as "cold."

Tellingly, just before critiquing the photograph, Little Chandler recalls a failed pleasure production of his own, in which he bought Annie a blouse in the hopes of eliciting a sexual response (that this is his intent is made clear by the acute discomfort he displays while buying the blouse). Just as Gabriel's hopeless, diversionary story of loaning Freddy Malins a pound earns him a dispassionate kiss, Little Chandler's indirect solicitation of Annie also leads to a perfunctory kiss. It is a kiss that is worse than no kiss at all because it betrays distance and aloofness rather than communicating the involuntary confession of pleasure: "At first she wanted to take it back but when she tried it on she was delighted with it, especially with the make of the sleeves, and kissed him and said he was very good to think of her" (*D,* 83). The make of the sleeves! His reaction, given a paragraph of its own, is an astonished and angry "Hm! . . ." (*D,* 83, Joyce's ellipses). Little Chandler, too, it seems, is regarded by his wife as merely a "generous" person when he intended to be—and, at least in fantasy, envisioned himself as—the Holy Ghost of passion, coming upon her, overshadowing her, striking her, and bringing to light, by interpreting and optimizing the involuntary confession of her body, that she has been chosen to be the handmaiden of his desire who must now express her desire to have it done to her according to his word. His wife's expression in the photograph, "unconscious and ladylike," might do very well as the first photo in a sequence of erotic postcards, but only by way of setting the tone for her subsequent ecstatic and involuntary discomposure brought on by "passion" and "rapture."

In order to find his wife's photograph so manifestly wanting in the specifics of desire, Little Chandler might well be comparing it to some other sort of photograph—an erotic postcard, I would suggest, of the sort that made him view Paris as an "immoral" city. "He thought of what Gallaher had said about rich Jewesses. Those dark Oriental eyes, he thought, how full they are of passion, of voluptuous longing!" (*D,* 83). But how does he know? What Gallaher said about rich Jewesses earlier in the evening never described their eyes: "There are . . . thousands of rich Germans and Jews, rotten with money, that'd only be too glad. . . ." (81, second ellipsis Joyce's). The implication of Gallaher's description, in complete contrast to Little Chandler's recollection, is that these women, who are "rotten with money," and "only too glad," are not likely to also have eyes of "passion" and "voluptuous longing." Furthermore, Little Chandler emphasizes "those dark Oriental eyes," a detail that also does not enter into Gallaher's discourse; in fact, all of Gallaher's allusions emphasize the general "immorality" of women's behavior, with nothing at all to say about facial expression. Once again, "voluptuousness" was a common label, promising a predictable pose. Likewise, "those dark Oriental eyes" were available as photographic images to Little Chandler in dozens of different incarnations. Thus, when Little Chandler laments, "Why had he married the eyes in the photograph," we might ask, what is his model for comparison? His wife's expression is "lacking" compared to what? It seems clear that he has seen these eyes, but improbable that "oriental" women in Dublin are in the habit of looking at him in this way—except through the medium of erotic postcards.

Indeed, relative to the erotic "otherness" implied in Little Chandler's detailed description of "Oriental eyes," historians of the erotic postcard note, "The nude pictures of primitive beauties who populated the colonies, portrayed on postcards using the excuse of anthropological documentation, were able to circulate freely because they were not considered outrageous or offensive" (Farina, 15). Given the expansive and grandiose nature of Gallaher's descriptions of women, he, too, may have made their acquaintance only through erotic postcards. How fitting that Little Chandler's most keenly felt disappointment about his sexual relationship with his wife should focus on a photograph of her. The fact that her "cold" expression defies his pleasure production, by refusing to confess "involuntarily" a corresponding pleasure, causes him to regret marrying "the eyes in the photograph." The entire strained dialogue of these two men earlier in the evening may have been produced and underwritten by "eyes in photographs." Eyes like Annie Chandler's are, it seems, disparaged in contrast to a mass-produced "erotic organization of visibility," configured by the eyes of women on erotic postcards. Thus, a problem with pleasure in the marital relationship is figured in the story by Little Chandler's complaint of the absence of any "erotic organization of visibility" in his wife's photograph. Such an absence is contrasted with a different photograph (or composite of many erotic postcards), depicting "dark Oriental eyes" full of "voluptuous longing."

In line with this, the ad jingle that runs like a thread through the patchwork of Bloom's day is a commodified erotic reverie/advertisement in which the commodity—Plumtree's Potted Meat—exercises that magical "something" that Gabriel hoped to convey when he said his wife's name. As this ad asks you to picture it, the inhabitants of a given home will be going about their duties. They will not hear at first. Then, "something will strike them"; they will turn, and look . . . "BLISS!" A Marxist analysis of this can of potted meat as a commodity fetish would emphasize how all connection between its existence and the human beings who produced it has been elided. But the jingle, which serves to make this product more valuable than its intrinsic value as a can of meat, does so by operating (in terms of itsfunction,not in terms of its depiction of sexuality) as a "pornographic" reverie that produces "spontaneous" pleasure by eliding the presence of power relations that are always present, and that always make pleasure problematic.

In this respect, it was not only Freud who wanted to know exactly what it is a twentieth-century woman wants; retailers, advertising executives, and department store managers ask themselves the same question. The objective, of course, is not to heal the psyche but to move merchandise out of their stores by offering a scenario of pleasure that elides the very power relations that make the "pure sensation" of such a pleasure impossible to experience as anything but fantasy. Such business people, of course, would rather interview Joyce's Gerty MacDowell than Freud's Dora because Gerty consumes in order to feel like a "woman," and Dora has stopped trying to achieve this same status. Even Freud's immediate precursors, Havelock Ellis and Krafft-Ebing, can be seen as primitive (albeit unwitting) market researchers, mapping out the dark continent of human sexuality in order that it might be more accessible to those who construct pleasure scenarios for profit. Indeed, as Thomas Richards points out in *The Commodity Culture of Victorian England,* the increasingly detailed definition of "adolescence" as a psychosexual state of being spawned a plethora of products designed to offer pleasure scenarios that attempted to produce pleasure by appearing to transcend inequities of power in social relations.

Although the questions of what a woman wants sexually and what she wants when she goes shopping were not recognized as similar, Molly Bloom's erotic reveries, laced as they are with recollections of shopping (and hopes for future shopping), often seem to collapse any imagined distinction. That the distinction for men had been collapsed for some time is evident both by the practice of including photographs of scantily clad women in packages of cigarettes, and by Bloom's as yet unrealized idea to sell stationery by putting attractive women in a transparent showcase. The fact is, a consumer—whether male or female—once recognized as capable of desiring one thing, henceforth must be considered an individual who might desire anything. Lacan describes the human subject as "thinking with one's objects" (*Four Fundamentals,* 53), which suggests we may never so much be ourselves as when we go shopping, or when we are in the presence of an advertisement that exhibits, to paraphrase Ellis, the power to concentrate (the consumer's) attention on a point "outside the natural path of instinct," a point that then opens up new markets by permitting "ways to form new mental constructions around that point."

Stephen Dedalus's "den of monstrous images" is (and was becoming) the stock and trade of advertising in twentieth-century commodity culture. If the word "*Foetus*" carved into a desk "shocked him" because it represented, in the "outer world a trace of what he had deemed till then a brutish and individual malady of his own mind," what would he think in today's world after watching thirty seconds of MTV? The contemporary ad campaign for the perfume Obsession operates on the dynamic of mainstreaming "monstrous images" in such a way that they suggest new ways to form pleasure scenarios ("mental constructions"); significantly, the photographs of this ad campaign often are featured as a sequence of images that might be regarded as the postmodern incarnation of the erotic postcard.[12] Foucault maintains, "Power operated as a mechanism of attraction; it drew out those peculiarities over which it kept watch. Pleasure spread to the power that harried it; power anchored the pleasure it uncovered" (*History of Sexuality*, 45).

The commodity, accompanied by the "optimizing discourse" of advertising, also provides the consumer with an erotic reverie (an erotic organization of visibility) in which pleasure scenarios are constructed and amplified in proportion to the degree that implicit power relations are muted. The essence of consumer seduction, after all, is to coerce someone into feeling a certain way, thus creating an interest in a given product, by persuading them such a desire originates in their own "den of monstrous images." But in the twentieth century there are few "individual maladies" and "the den of monstrous images" is called a newsstand or a television. The images inviting and affording pleasure production are part—not of our collective unconscious—but of our collective consciousness. When Stephen agonizes, "By his monstrous way of life he seemed to have put himself beyond the limits of reality," he could not yet have any idea how the "limits of reality," or what Ellis calls "the natural path of instinct," could give way to the imaginative and profitable expansions of commodity culture's semerotic pleasure machine.

4

The Virgin Mary and the Urge in Gerty

Praying, Buying, and the Packaging of Desire

I. The female body as investment portfolio

Some early critics of the "Nausicaa" chapter saw Gerty MacDowell as another virgin temptress—not unlike the young women who made Stephen Dedalus so restless in *A Portrait of the Artist as a Young Man.*[1] Another approach, put forth most notably by Hugh Kenner, is to view the chapter primarily in terms of what it says about Bloom, and then show how this relates to his activities in other chapters.[2] Suzette Henke's essay in 1982 considerably widened the possible interpretations of this chapter when she focused almost exclusively on the portrayal of Gerty MacDowell and asked: "Does Joyce intend to ridicule his character for playing the seductive nymph? Or is he presenting her as the pathetic victim of social and religious enculturation . . . ?"[3] Henke goes on to make a convincing case that the American romance novel *The Lamplighter,* which Gerty consciously recalls at one point, is the text that Joyce is parodying.[4]

In an essay published in 1985, Kimberly Devlin qualifies Henke's point by arguing that Gerty MacDowell, rather than being a straightforward reincarnation and parody of Gertrude Flint, actually "stands in ironic contrast" to the heroine of *The Lamplighter:* "An exemplary text such as *The Lamplighter* may strive to 'brainwash' its audience, but in Gerty's case the mission has not been totally successful. . . ."[5] Cummins's novel stresses that a young girl must learn to control her temper at all times, and that she must never consciously cultivate the attention of a man either through any artifice of conversation or through deliberate posturing. As Devlin makes clear, this lack of calculation is hardly a trademark of Gerty MacDowell, descriptions of whom "give the reader the distinct impression that she is highly self-conscious of her 'winsome' appearance and actively cultivates it" ("Romance Heroine," 388).

Thomas Richards offers a more specific explanation of why Gerty MacDowell is more "modern" than Gertrude Flint: "'Nausicaa' marks the capacity of manufactured objects to become dominant images for the self, to take on, as we say, 'personality'."[6] I would go further and suggest it is not that products have "personality," but that Gerty's "personality" is a product. More than that, she carefully advertises and packages her sexuality as a complex masquerade of femininity designed to attract a male consumer—in this case, Leopold Bloom. Far from being sexually naive and one-dimensional, Gerty has a keener understanding of sexuality than Bloom does because she understands that the anatomical act of sex is as irrelevant as whatever is inside a carefully advertised package.

The fact that Gerty's sense of self is almost entirely formulated by what she imagines she looks like to men only emphasizes the fact that Bloom does not see her as a person, but only as a guarantor of the truth of his own fantasies—that is to say, as "feminine." Gerty does not cultivate the question of her own existence because to do so would make it impossible to market herself as "feminine," which, after all, is a male-defined concept. My thesis about "Nausicaa" is that Joyce chooses to modernize Cummins's portrait of an adolescent female by showing how Gerty must, as a survival technique, market herself as "more feminine" than other girls (Cissy and Edy, in particular, since they are there on the beach with her). In essence, Gerty packages her body in a manner that advertises the culturally accepted norm of femininity. Joyce's heroine does stand in ironic contrast to the heroine of *The Lamplighter,* as Devlin makes clear, but the reason this is so is that Joyce modernizes the romance heroine by showing her as a self-conscious image manipulator who views herself as a commodity that must be carefully packaged and advertised, in accordance with a media representation of what is feminine, in order to attract a male consumer. Advertisers of cosmetics, after all, would be aghast at the stringently modest sensibility of someone like Gertrude Flint in *The Lamplighter.* How could she be persuaded to buy eyebrow liner when to use such a product would violate every principle of "femininity" in America in 1850?[7]

Gerty is anxious to be properly put together because, as she phrases it, "there was just a might that he might be out" (*U,* 287). She has done everything that has been required of her by the advertising copy and beauty columns of magazines: "She did it up all by herself and what joy was hers when she tried it on then, smiling at the lovely reflection which the mirror gave back to her!" (*U,* 287). Her reward, which acts as a guarantee of her authenticity, is that the reflection smiling back at her from the mirror is not her at all but rather a manufactured likeness of a culturally defined standard of what is feminine—a standard that can be met only by regularly using a variety of highly advertised products. This male-defined standard of femininity is what Lacan calls "The Woman." He crosses out the article *the* to indicate that this male-constructed idea does not exist outside of the masculine subject's need to believe that "The Woman" is capable of verifying the myth of his own sexual identity. A woman masquerades as what she is not, so that a man can better imagine who he believes himself to be. The subject, according to Lacan, first begins to believe in the fictional unity of his consciousness by observing the coherence of his own reflection—literally, in a mirror, as well as figuratively, through other people, who "reflect back to him the image of himself he has come to believe in: The subject is only ever supposed. It is its condition to be only supposable. If it knows anything, it is only by being itself a subject caused by an object. . . ."[8] Advertisements echo this original mirror in the way they provide an assured sexual identity to the consumer who buys the featured product.[9]

Thus, the masculine subject looks to "The Woman" to confirm his identity, and that is why women compete, aided by the images and products featured in advertisements, to give the best approximation of this mythical beast the masculine subject needs in order to believe in what he in fact only imagines himself to be. "The Woman," Lacan tells us, "will reject an essential part of her femininity, notably all its attributes, through masquerade. It is for what she is not that she expects to be desired as well as loved" ("Seminar," 84). Gerty is wearing blue, for example, because "it was expected in the *Lady's Pictorial* that electric blue would be worn" (*U*, 287). In other words, the gender construction urged by advertisements plays a crucial role in the formation of fantasies by which the male and female reach each other.

Gerty knows she must buy an image of herself as "feminine" in order to be visible to a masculine subject. She must view her face as having a certain amount of currency, as much as if it were a coin. She worries about how her body can best advertise its worthiness to be placed inside a lovely home. In essence, throughout this chapter, Gerty is an obsessive witness to her own commodification. The advertisements swirling around Gerty not only pitch a particular product, they help generate her conscious subjectivity by insisting their products will make her sufficiently feminine to attract a masculine gaze. In effect, she advertises herself to Bloom as a product he must have to complete himself, and she does so in order to imagine herself as complete. The advertisements that preoccupy Gerty all insist that their products will provide her with the latest version of a culture's definition of what is "truly feminine." Paradoxically, these advertisements assure Gerty that femininity is innate, even as they inform her of what she must buy to construct it. It is through advertising pitches that Gerty is able to imagine herself as looking like what men want to see. Far from being a narcissist, Gerty divorces herself from whatever her actual reflection might be in order to masquerade as an image that excites male desire.

II. Dreaming who we are: Gender construction in advertisements

Advertisements offer to sell the consumer a coherent image of him- or herself; they are successful only to the degree to which they are able to present their product as a necessary component for the consumer's unified sense of self. According to Lacan, subjectivity is based on lack. Quite simply, advertisements present their product as the thing that will absolve the inevitable incertitude of subjectivity and gender, which Lacan calls a "want-in-being." The coherent sense of self offered by the ad is either "masculine" or "feminine," and the ad often promises that the product will make the user more "masculine" or more "feminine." For example, by purchasing Secret or Brut, the modern consumer is not choosing one version of deodorant over another (they are virtually all the same), but is actually selecting a fantasy package that offers confirmation of either masculinity or femininity. A man is self-evident, phallic, free standing, centered: a brute. A woman is mysterious, inscrutable, skilled at suggestion: a secret. As Judith Williamson has said: "Ads create an 'alreadyness' of 'facts' about ourselves as individuals: that we are consumers, that we have certain values. . . . We are trapped in the illusion of choice. . . . they invite us 'freely' to create ourselves in accordance with the way in which they have already created us" (42). Simply by leafing through *Cosmopolitan* and then through *Esquire,* we can see the perfume ads in *Cosmopolitan* dancing in step with the cologne ads in *Esquire* in a highly stylized waltz of "masculinity" and "femininity" that is not all that different from the "feminine" and "masculine" masquerade that Gerty and Bloom perform for each other on Sandymount Strand.

The primary myth of the advertising jargon surrounding Gerty is that masculinity and femininity are innate qualities in the male and female, which, when properly accentuated and brought together, perfectly complement each other to form a partnership in which the private fantasies of each person, however different from each other, will be perfectly and completely satisfied. The psychoanalytic theory of Jacques Lacan offers powerful (if occasionally obscure) insights into how gender is constructed by the individual to form a fictional sense of unity. "To be human," writes one explicator of Lacan's theory, "is to be subjected to a law which decenters and divides. . . . the subject is split; but an ideological world conceals this from the conscious subject" (Mitchell, 26). Lacan insists that the "opposition masculine-feminine" is "in an entirely different register from the biological . . . there is nothing corresponding to the terms masculine and feminine which can be directly grasped as such in our experience" ("Seminar," 107).

And yet, in advertisements, as in the "Nausicaa" chapter itself, the "masculine" and "feminine" genders come together in a mutual orgasm of pyrotechnic phantasmagoria. Significantly, Gerty's "orgasm," presented as simultaneous with Bloom's, is not at all biological. Her mounting excitement is brought on by the fact that Bloom's increasingly ardent gaze is responding to the combination of products that announce her femininity. While Bloom's orgasm has an obvious biological component, nonetheless, he himself recognizes it never would have occurred had he known about her limp: "A defect is ten times worse in a woman. . . . Glad I didn't know it when she was on show" (*U*, 301). His allusion to her limp as a "defect" characterizes her as a damaged product, and this characterization is further strengthened by his conclusion that it must be this defect that has caused her to be "left on the shelf." His orgasm, in other words, is directly predicated on his belief in her masquerade of femininity—and her realization of this about him provides her own climax.[10]

If we look at Gerty's fantasy of serving breakfast to an ideal husband, we can see that the primary assumption of the fantasy is that she must be intensely "feminine" in order to attract someone intensely "masculine." The fusing of genders produces a satiation of desire so intense that the narrative tone devolves into the warm, embryonic bliss of baby talk:

> No prince charming is her beau ideal to lay a rare and wondrous love at her feet but rather a manly man with a strong quiet face who had not found his ideal. . . .
>
> She would care for him with creature comforts too for Gerty was womanly wise. . . . then, when they settled down in a nice snug and cosy little homely house, every morning they would both have brekky, simple but perfectly served, for their own two selves and before he went out to business he would give his dear little wifey a good hearty hug. . . . (*U*, 288–89)

I wish to emphasize the compulsive pairing up that is described, as if she and her "beau ideal" were two halves of a complete and ideal personality. What authenticates this fantasy match is not anything unique or interpersonal in the relationship, but simply the fact that her dream breakfast partner is authenticated as a "manly man" and she is authenticated as "womanly wise." Lacan asserts the idea that a complete and assured sexual identity belongs in the realm of fantasy, and what we have in this passage is precisely that fantasy. Certainly the passage has strong sexual overtones—with everything slipping into its natural and proper space, and the encounter ending in "a good hearty hug"—but more importantly, at least to my reading, is the way "perfect femininity" and "perfect masculinity" come together to form a bond of permanent bliss that is completely outside the biological and physical register.

This fact underlies my assertion that Gerty is not as repressed about sexuality as is commonly assumed. Rather, she knows, quite correctly, that the sexual act is insignificant—impossible even—except in as much as it is correctly packaged and advertised for a targeted member of the opposite sex. Certainly Bloom seems aware of this when he recalls an encounter with a woman in which he could not get her to perform properly the fantasy role he needed her to play: "Girl on Meath Street that night. All the dirty things I made her say. All wrong of course. My arks she called it. Hard to find one who" (*U*, 303). The sentence breaks off here, just as Bloom's sentence intended for Gerty will never be fully written in the sand; if a man cannot "find one who—," then he is unable to go beyond the words "I am a—." Gerty MacDowell's masquerade of femininity is the rest of Bloom's sentence, but since her femininity is a masquerade, his masculinity remains an incomplete sentence. A woman masquerades as feminine, and the man worships her as his savior, thereby forgetting that he is the one who has constructed her as an imaginary end point to the fantasy of himself.

What Lacan says about sexual relations being impossible except in the realm of fantasy holds equally true, I would argue, for the relationship of a consumer to a product: "the intervention of an 'appearing' . . . gets substituted for the 'having' so as to protect it on one side and to mask its lack on the other, with the effect that the ideal of typical manifestations of behaviour in both sexes, up to and including the act of sexual copulation, are entirely propelled into comedy" ("Seminar," 84). When you buy Brut or Secret, you are allowing what you buy to substitute for who you imagine yourself to be. It is easy to get impatient with Gerty's dreamy interpretations and sentimental sublimations of physical desire until we factor in Lacan's point that we cannot reach our partner at all without fantasy and dreams—or, in the parlance of our consumer society, without packaging and advertising. "*Lingerie* does it," Bloom muses (*U*, 302, Joyce's italics). "Say a woman loses a charm with every pin she takes out" (*U*, 302). What Gerty subscribes to in the breakfast passage quoted above is the myth of absolute heterosexual gender complementarity.

Of course, if this redemptive complementarity of "innate" masculine and feminine qualities were as natural as advertisements insist it is, then the effectiveness of advertisements would be negligible, and we would see rampant consumerism as a silly impulse to buy what we don't need. However, because absolute gender complementarity, as well as coherent sexual identity, is a myth, the vision of a "manly man" making her "womanly wise" has an orgasmic fantasy quotient for Gerty that is at least the equivalent of whatever her underpants are able to do for Bloom. "How do neurotics make love?" Lacan asks. "Neurosis is dream rather than perversion. Neurotics have none of the characteristics of the pervert. *They simply dream that they have.* Which is natural since how else could they reach their partner?" ("Seminar," 156, my emphasis). Advertisements allow us to dream who we are; they institutionalize fantasy in a manner that helps us reach our partners. By telling us what is "feminine" and what is "masculine"—and how best to become one or the other—they help program our desire until it runs a course as precise and proscribed as the arc of a firecracker. "My fireworks," thinks Bloom ruefully. "Up like a rocket, down like a stick" (*U*, 304).

III. Consumers and other lovers

Gerty refuses to dwell on the anatomical intertwining of the sexual act because she has been instructed and persuaded that the packaging and advertising of her sexuality are what direct the arc of masculine desire (and, besides, sexual thoughts are sinful). The question of her own sexuality has been completely elided because, as with any marketed product, her desire is to be desired. And so we learn that: "As for undies they were Gerty's chief care. . . . she had a brickbat to keep the iron on because she wouldn't trust those washerwomen as far as she'd see them scorching the things" (*U*, 288). Doesn't this sound a little like the manager in charge of quality control at a factory? One can almost hear the voice-over: "Here at Fantasy Drawers, quality control is job number one; we know how scorched undies can be the fatal defect that reveals femininity as a masquerade, exposes the labor behind an apparently natural female sexuality, and exposes the would-be bride to fatal accusations of being a conniving, overdetermined femme fatale, who is not what she seems." Indeed, Gerty's ability to imagine herself as seventeen and eminently marriageable is dependent upon the color of her underwear, how well-pressed it is, and what sort of extra ribbon she has attached to it. We learn that how she puts the underwear on—accidentally putting it on inside out, for example—means she might meet her lover; if the ribbon comes untied, then "he" is thinking about her. How the day will turn out depends on the manner in which she puts herself together. The most significant part of Gerty's day—which allows her to glimpse the future—is that moment when she prepares her appearance in accordance with a media representation of what a "feminine" girl should look and feel like.[11]

But if this emphasis on her underwear makes her frivolous, shallow, and pathetically sentimental, how do we characterize the scene in the background of a group of men praying to a virgin for relief from the urge to drink themselves into a stupor every night? Faith, hope, and charity, as presented by advertisements, attract and direct unhappy consumers as much as the joyful, sorrowful, and glorious mysteries of the Virgin Mary attract and direct unhappy alcoholics. Indeed, when Gerty hears the ongoing devotions, she does not wish that her father were there with the other men, praying for relief from the dissatisfaction in their lives that makes sobriety impossible; instead, she recalls something she takes to be a more powerful curative because it is advertised in a magazine: "Had her father only avoided the clutches of the demon drink, by taking the pledge or those powders the drink habit cured in Pearson's Weekly . . ." (*U*, 290). Gifford quotes a typical advertisement of this sort, seen in 1904: "TO CURE DRUNKARDS . . . with or without their knowledge. . . . a wonderful powdered remedy that has saved homes" (319). In other words, one buys the product and prays for a miracle.

Bloom seems to understand that the relationship of the praying men to the infinitely capable and sympathetic Virgin Mary is similar to the relationship of hope and belief that exists between a consumer and a well-phrased advertisement: "Mass seems to be over. Could hear them all at it. Pray for us. And pray for us. And pray for us. Good idea the repetition. Same thing with ads. Buy from us. And buy from us" (*U*, 309). His phrase "all at it" recalls his earlier reference to his own masturbation as "at it again," and so the consumer is a masturbator pleading for the intercession of a carefully packaged woman like the Virgin Mary to make his ideal self real. The relationship is summed up in a favorite poem of Gerty's (she can remember only the first line): "Art thou real, my ideal?" In the background, Gerty can hear: "Queen of angels, queen of patriarchs, queen of prophets"; this litany is counterposed with her own litany, which begins, "Queen of ointments" (*U*, 286).

Gerty is more desperate than many to market herself as sufficiently feminine because she does not come from "a nice snug and cosy little homely house"; instead, "that vile decoction which has ruined so many hearths and homes had cast its shadow over her childhood days. Nay, she had even witnessed in the home circle deeds of violence caused by intemperance and had seen her own father, a prey to the fumes of intoxication, forget himself completely . . ." (*U*, 290). The "self" that she presumes her father "forgets" is the manly man of advertising lore that she hopes to attract by being sufficiently "feminine." Both Gerty's figure and complexion are described as something created and maintained by advertised beauty products: "Her figure was slight and graceful, inclining even to fragility but those iron jelloids she had been taking of late had done her a world of good much better than the Widow Welch's female pills . . ." (*U*, 286). One reason Gerty may have switched brands (which might be akin to switching saints when praying to one doesn't work) is that the image conveyed by the brand name "Widow Welch" is that of an older woman who has passed the difficult task of getting married. This does not correspond to the "winsome spectacle" Gerty wishes to be seen as. "Her fine hands," we are told, "were of finely veined alabaster with tapering fingers and as white as lemonjuice and queen of ointments could make them . . ." (*U*, 286).

"Queen of Ointments," according to Gifford, was the slogan of a product called Beetham's Larola, which "Makes the skin as soft as velvet, Removes all Roughness, Redness, Heat Irritation, Tan and Keeps the Skin Soft, Smooth and White all the year round" (385). Gerty's sense of her posture as "queenly" in the next passage is actually dependent upon the fact that she uses a product advertised as the "queen of ointments": "There was an innate refinement, a languid queenly *hauteur* about Gerty which was unmistakably evidenced in her delicate hands . . . (*U*, 286). The narrator of this chapter occupies Gerty's head like an omniscient adman who is able to perfectly tailor his descriptions of Gerty to what she imagines a man would like to see. The major feature of this voice-over is that it is easily able to drown out the strains of any other discourse in her mind. In fact, the tone of the narration follows the basic strategy of advertising copy in that it obsessively describes Gerty's physical being in terms of how "feminine" various products will make her appear to any "manly man" who chances to see her. Consumer discourse in "Nausicaa" is a marauding discourse that superficially connects itself to almost any verbal cue, and then diverts the language into breathless descriptions of what products have done, or will do, for the otherwise useless Gerty MacDowell.

All the genuinely unpleasant emotion Gerty experiences is subsumed by the consumer discourse that dispels anger, regret, and sadness by placing them under the general advertising rubric of "that tired feeling." All the possible dissatisfactions in Gerty's life are transformed into beauty problems of the kind that Madame Vera Verity might discuss on the Woman Beautiful page of the *Princess Novelette*. Gerty's face, which is drawn with anxiety as a result of her home life and her fear of the future, is described as "lovely" because the anxiety would appear as charmingly mysterious to a male observer: "Mayhap it was this, the love that might have been, that lent to her softlyfeatured face at whiles a look, tense with suppressed meaning, that imparted a strange yearning tendency to the beautiful eyes, a charm few could resist" (*U*, 286). The narrator praises her for looking as if she desires something, but the point is clear that what makes this look "charming" is that it is all attitude with no content. She should look as if she were yearning for something, but she must only desire to be desired. Any active questioning of her sexual identity would mar her "feminine" image. Likewise, the fact that she looks as if she is "lost in thought" is represented by the narrator as being effective only if she is not thinking anything.

De Lauretis has stated: "The ideological effect of commodity logic on a large scale is . . . the deflection of any dissatisfaction with one's life or any critique of the social system onto an intensified concern with a body which is in some way guaranteed to be at fault."[12] There is a complete absence of social criticism or plan of action throughout the detailed description of Gerty. Beauty columns seem to provide the only philosophy she needs because, as de Lauretis suggests, advertising rhetoric, like that attributed to Madame Vera Verity, encourages the displacement of all dissatisfactions onto a concern with the body and one's status as a spectacle. "Then there was blushing scientifically cured," Gerty thinks, "and how to be tall increase your height and you have a beautiful face but your nose?" (*U*, 286). The curious cycle I am describing here is that advertisements present products as necessary to the woman who wishes to turn herself into a commodity that is recognizable to the masculine subject as "feminine" (that is to say, as a representation capable of verifying and completing the myth of himself).

Although the beauty columns make a token attempt to praise what is already there, they only do so as a justification for urging extensive (and expensive) improvements. This is part of the illusion of "alreadyness" that Williamson refers to. "You already have a beautiful face," runs the logic of the beauty column, "but all is lost if you fail to do something about your nose." The body is always defective, but this is presented by the advertisement as being its source of endless potential; unlike one's emotional state, all the flaws and lacks of physical appearance, however numerous, can be corrected given products enough and time. If one's appearance is properly attended to, then emotions can be treated as merely the dynamo that runs the beauty machine. Gerty thinks about crying, for example, and quickly she represses the cause of her sorrow and concentrates instead on how the act of crying might best be transformed into a gesture that would not repel the male gaze: "she would give worlds to be in the privacy of her own familiar chamber where, giving way to tears, she could have a good cry and relieve her pentup feelings though not too much because she knew how to cry nicely before the mirror" (*U*, 288).

Much later in the chapter, after Edy has asked about her boyfriend Reggy Wylie, Gerty again transforms her emotion into static posing by concentrating on how she must look: "Gerty's lips parted swiftly to frame the word but she fought back the sob that rose to her throat, *so slim, so flawless, so beautifully moulded it seemed one an artist might have dreamed of*" (*U*, 297, my emphasis). We can hear the advertising voice kick in for the latter half of this sentence. Instead of answering back, we are told, Gerty "glanced at her new conquest for them to see" (*U*, 297). Her response, in other words, is to try to get them to see that she is being seen. By proving she has attracted a masculine gaze, Gerty can feel sure she has transcended all her dissatisfactions by occupying the cultural space designated as feminine. "[T]hey both knew," she continues, "that she was something aloof, apart, in another sphere, that she was not of them and never would be and there was somebody else too that knew it and saw it so they could put that in their pipe and smoke it" (*U*, 297). This verification by "somebody else" is crucial to Gerty. She does not lean back because she is sexually promiscuous; she does so because she has found a worthy consumer with whom she is conducting a marketing test in order to determine the desirability of her product. As Gerty covertly watches Bloom watching her, she is in the odd position of envisioning her own underwear, through the medium of his gaze, as something magical and irresistible. This, I would argue, is the pure self-referentiality of the commodity, which has no existence beyond its effect on the subjectivity of the consumer.

IV. Product loyalty and the fictional unity of subjectivity

The mystery of Gerty's identity and the incertitude of her femininity can only be solved and authenticated by attracting the gaze of that "manly man" for whom she serves a fantasy breakfast. This "manly man" achieves yet another incarnation in a picture she keeps in the outhouse: "the picture of halcyon days where a young gentleman in the costume they used to wear then with a threecornered hat was offering a bunch of flowers to his ladylove with oldtime chivalry through her lattice window" (*U*, 291). Lowly Bloom becomes the avatar of all these men for her: "he would embrace her gently like a real man, crushing her soft body to him" (*U*, 294). So strong is her fantasy of absolute gender complementarity that it allows her to be crushed and gently embraced at the same time. "She must have been thinking of someone else all the time," Bloom thinks. "What harm? Must since she came to the use of reason, he, he and he" (*U*, 303–4). Bloom is both right and wrong. She has not been thinking specifically of "someone else" while leaning back for him to see, instead she has been imagining him as nothing less than the masculine gaze in her head, for whom she is always posing, which might be described, using the repetitious effect so basic to advertising, as "he, he, and he."

The male gaze she dreams of attracting is like a lighthouse beam casting this way and that across the sea. If she is not a sufficiently arresting spectacle of femininity, it will sweep past her and leave her in darkness. The idea of the male gaze as a lighthouse that might guide women who are lost at sea to the safe harbor of a "snug and cosy little homely house" is further suggested by Gerty's attitude toward the lighthouses out on the bay: "And she could see far away the lights of the lighthouses so picturesque she would have loved to do with a box of paints because it was easier than to make a man" (*U*, 298). From this notion, she thinks of the male lamplighter who will soon light the lamp that used to show her Reggy Wylie outside her window. Finally, from that thought she recalls the Cummins's book about a kindly lamplighter who takes pity on a poor girl and brings her to a cozy home. The same metaphor holds through each of these associations: a woman will be lost at sea or wrecked on the rocks in the absence of a male gaze to guide her home. The advertising pitch that if we do not use a product, we will miss out on something wonderful is a particularly persuasive one because there is no way to verify whether it is true. This pitch not only helps to sell a particular product, it also aggravates our general anxiety about the vagaries of fate. In this way, it creates a reliable consumer who feels a loyalty toward a particular product that is akin to what a superstitious person feels for a good-luck charm.

This description of the "strange yearning tendency" in Gerty's "beautiful eyes" is concluded with a question: "Why have women such eyes of witchery?" (*U*, 286). This is the sort of rhetorical question advertisements feature all the time because it produces a quality of "alreadyness." The question merely calls attention to its answer, which is always the product. "Why have women such eyes of witchery?" such an ad might begin; "because they use xyz eyebrowleine" would be a typical conclusion. Sure enough, as if Gerty were being featured in "before" and "after" pictures for eyebrow liner, she loyally reveals, as though she were giving a testimonial, what gives her "such eyes of witchery": "Time was when those brows were not so silkily seductive. It was Madame Vera Verity, directress of the Woman Beautiful page of the Princess Novelette, who had first advised her to try eyebrowleine which gave that haunting expression to the eyes, so becoming in leaders of fashion, and she had never regretted it" (*U*, 286). We see that "the love that might have been" is something she could miss and then regret forever unless she uses the product for which she will never have any regrets. In fact, to say "she had never regretted it" seems a strong statement to make about the use of eyebrow liner unless we understand it as confirmation of that other frequent advertising claim: "Use it. You'll never regret it." Just as ads assure Gerty she is beautiful—but not beautiful enough—they also inform her she has always wanted what they wish to provide.

In the way Leopold Bloom reacts to Gerty's limp, he demonstrates his need for the masquerade of femininity in order to excite masculine desire. As he thinks of the spectacle of her legs, the phrase "a dream of wellfilled hose" flits through his mind. "Where was that?" he questions, trying to place the source of this phrase. "Ah, yes," he concludes, "Mutoscope pictures in Capel street: for men only" (*U*, 301). The phrase, it turns out, is a slogan advertising a peep show. In promising a dream of wellfilled hose, the advertisement announces a display of what Lacan calls "The Woman." Here we begin to see that Gerty's compulsion to advertise and package herself as a commodity labeled "feminine" is also an urge to compete with other media representations of female sexuality. Lacan insists that, in a patriarchal culture, the way female sexuality is represented determines how it comes into play. The "reality" of female desire has no more relationship to how a woman displays her sexuality than a product does to the way it is packaged and marketed. If Gerty did not self-consciously display herself to Bloom, it would not mean that he would get a "more real" sense of female sexuality in looking at her; it would mean that he would not "really" see her, since he is looking for a representation of "The Woman"—not a woman—to complete himself.

This odd interfacing of the commercial with the fantastic, acted out along conventional ideas of what is "masculine" and what is "feminine," illuminates the deeper implications of Bloom's statement that what occurred between them was "like a language." "Man has only to dream," says Lacan, "to see re-emerging before him that vast jumble, that lumber room he has to get by with" ("Seminar," 159). When man is not dreaming, he prays for reasons to believe in the unity and coherence of his identity, since this belief will help him forget that lumber room where he first combined discordant images to form the myth of himself. The construction in the advertising media of what is "already" masculine and what is "already" feminine supplies the conventions needed to translate Gerty's and Bloom's insulated fantasies into a communication. On this day, Gerty and Bloom constitute themselves for each other. Each one prays, buys, and masturbates to their own ideal image, which is in fact a cultural construct that seems to "already" verify the authenticity of their gender and identity. Their relationship to their now ideal image is summed up by Gerty's favorite poem, "art thou real, my ideal?"[13]

V. Beauty and the marketplace: Calling female sexuality into play

In a world where "femininity" is male-defined, Lacan compares a woman seeking to determine her value as "The Woman" to pieces of furniture jumbled in an antique store trying to determine—for themselves—their authenticity and market value. In this situation, subjective experience is disallowed as a source of authentication because competitive value is determined by something in the marketplace that is "Other"—the masculine subject's need to believe in the fantasy of himself: "no piece of furniture can guarantee its own authenticity. Imagine now a piece of furniture which struck by this inability to certify its own authenticity, lights on the idea of the stamp, which the other pieces of furniture seem equally deprived of. . . . But it would need only one piece of furniture to bear the stamp for the situation of all the others to change completely. Each one would rig itself out with the same stamp and . . . . sing out its own exchange value, its use value" ("Seminar," 133). Magazine advertisements offer their products to Gerty as a way for her to stamp the authenticity of her masquerade.

The paradox of masquerading as some mythical species, the existence of which a man believes in as a way to confirm the myth of himself, is that a woman becomes, like Tinkerbell, dependent on the regard of men to assure her she exists. Gerty's competitiveness toward Edy and Cissy causes her to critique their masquerade and try to judge its effect on Bloom. At one point, Gerty resentfully interprets Cissy's smoothing the twins' hair as an attempt to look attractive to Bloom: "Cissy took off the twins' caps and tidied their hair to make herself attractive of course" (*U*, 296–97). And then there is Cissy's running; this is particularly painful to the lame Gerty because this is one way Cissy is clearly superior to her. Not surprisingly then, her most severe critique is reserved for the way Cissy's energetic motion makes any static conveyance of an image of "The Woman" impossible: "Cissy came up along the strand . . . and she did look a streel tugging the two kids along with the flimsy blouse she bought only a fortnight before like a rag on her back and a bit of her petticoat hanging like a caricature" (*U*, 295).

Lacan's assertion that it is representations of feminine sexuality that condition how it comes into play would seem to illuminate Bloom's insistence that women need to be theatrically posed, in a manner that recalls media representations of desirable women, if they are to excite men: "Must have the stage setting, the rouge, costume, position, music. The name too. *Amours* of actresses. Nell Gwynn, Mrs Bracegirdle, Maud Branscombe. Curtain up" (*U*, 303, Joyce's italics). Gifford tells us that in 1877, at the height of her fame, 28,000 photographs of Maud Branscombe were sold (325). In other words, she was a popular product, bearing the stamp of feminine beauty. Other women then evaluated themselves in relationship to this stamp, and turned to advertising for tips on how to most closely approximate it. Significantly, what Bloom does not recall is Maud Branscombe's highly publicized divorce from her husband in 1895 on the grounds of physical violence. The private life behind the carefully composed face in the commercially reproduced photograph of Maud Branscombe is irrelevant; what she is must not mar what she looks like. Suffering—the emotional equivalent of Gerty's limp—acts as a deterrent to masculine desire, and thus is elided when a woman is subjected to the male gaze.

Gerty's apparent orgasm is as commercial a reproduction of her desire as Maud Branscombe's photograph is a commercial reproduction of her face. Her cry of joy is simultaneous with her discovery that the multiplicity of products producing her appearance have bestowed upon her the grace that she requires to represent something "feminine," and to thereby bring her sexuality into play. The various items she is wearing have been successfully combined to form a well-phrased sentence, and Bloom is the exclamation point. In essence, she imagines herself as a living advertisement for "The Woman" that is overwhelmingly persuasive to Bloom. After his passion for her image is spent, Bloom, too, sees Gerty as a packaged product, advertising herself as a marriageable woman. "No reasonable offer refused," he thinks. "Out on spec probably" (*U*, 302). There is a certain product consistency in the "masquerade of femininity" that allows women to have a fluctuating value (like currency) in a marketplace where they must judge their worth in relationship to a "stamp," such as the Maud Branscombe photograph.

The setting aside of questions of sexual identity in favor of the masquerade of femininity is heralded as self-discovery by advertisements: "what joy was hers when she tried it on . . . smiling at the lovely reflection which the mirror gave back to her!" (*U*, 287). And yet, there is something cruel in the fact that Gerty's masquerade is so successful with Bloom that his typical sensitivity to suffering is lulled to sleep by her performance. While wondering about her attitude toward being lusted after by him, he thinks: "They don't care. Complimented perhaps. Go home to nicey bread and milky and say night prayers with the kiddies" (*U*, 303). We know this is not the domestic scene Gerty is returning to, though it is the one she fantasizes about. He assumes she already has what she is in fact trying to attract. This lack points out the other unfortunate paradox of a woman who is posing as "The Woman." As Irigaray has stated it, "the masquerade . . . is what women do . . . in order to participate in man's desire, but at the cost of giving up theirs."[14] Because she effectively poses as the object of his desire, he presumes all her simple desires have already been met (as does Gabriel with Gretta).

The goal, put most simply, is to perform the masquerade of femininity more convincingly than other women. Of course, the woman who does it the best of all, and who fills rooms with men who gaze at her and pray she will enter their homes, is the Virgin Mary. The narrator's description of the huddled and prayerful men highlights their need to believe in something that believes in them: "And careworn hearts were there and toilers for their daily bread and many who had erred and wandered, their eyes wet with contrition but for all that bright with hope for the reverend Father Hughes had told them . . . that it was not recorded in any age that those who implored her powerful protection were ever abandoned by her" (*U*, 292). Pray to her and you will never regret it. Buy from us and you will never regret it. We can recognize in this passage the hyperbole of advertising slogans, which consistently use absolute terms such as "never" and "always." Whosoever buys the ideal image of themselves offered by advertisements can take solace that it is not recorded in any age that those who implored the powerful protection of a product were ever abandoned. More than this, we are later told, "whosoever prays to her *with faith and constancy* can never be lost or cast away" (*U*, 294, my emphasis). Here is a liturgical version of the sort of advertising rhetoric that reinforces brand name loyalty and an aptitude for buying in the consumer. The pitch here is that you cannot simply use the product once, you must use it forever. Failure to do so means a loss of grace or gracefulness.

Bloom's and Gerty's ability to meet sexually is monitored and directed by the institutionalized fantasy of absolute gender complementarity that is presented, with effective repetitiveness, in advertisements. Bloom wishes to unwrap Gerty in order to discover the gift inside that will complete him. He has faith that she will answer his prayer. She poses as someone eternal—"The Woman"—an avatar of the Virgin Mary, "who is in her pure radiance a beacon ever to the stormtossed heart of man" (*U*, 284). For Gerty, the only way to make this ideal seem real is to appear as something she is not. This paradox short-circuits Freud's question "what does woman want?" by presenting a dynamic in which all she can want is a man to want her; she can then authenticate her value as something she is not—as something "feminine"—announcing her identity the way she does in this chapter as a "womanly woman." The "simultaneous orgasm" experienced by Gerty and Bloom, though they never actually touch, is brought about by the fact that their discourses have intercourse.

VI. Girl watching as window shopping

As my Lacanian approach to "Nausicaa" suggests thus far, coating everything in the "Nausicaa" chapter of *Ulysses* is the sticky sweet essence (both rhetorical and actual) produced by Gerty MacDowell's and Leopold Bloom's lascivious indulgence in the deliciously prolonged frustration of desire. But now I wish to examine this chapter from the more historicized point of view of cultural materialism. Gerty and Bloom are able to look at one another as much as they want, but only because they both know that actually touching what they so enjoy gazing upon is out of the question. This is a similar dynamic to that experienced by the consumer in the modern marketplace, who is invited to gaze wantonly upon objects deliberately arranged so as to titillate all who pass by.

Merchandise in shop windows is put in plain view of all who pass in the street, but the plate glass assures that only those who make the commitment to purchase what has attracted their gaze will actually get to touch it. The pastime of "just looking" is cruelly democratic in that the poor have equal visual access with the rich to desirable objects. The emotions stirred by merchandise displays, therefore, can bring about economic epiphanies whereby the helplessness caused by poverty is experienced in a keenly personal way: "Stephen looked at his thinly clad mother and remembered that a few days before he had seen a mantle priced at twenty guineas in the windows of Barnardo's" (*P*, 97).

In the song "Those Lovely Seaside Girls," the suggestion is made that women, like merchandise, learn to exhibit themselves to all male viewers in the hopes that one man among the many will step forward and pledge whatever is necessary for the singular privilege of unwrapping and handling them in the privacy of his own home: "Down at Margate looking very charming you are sure to meet / Those girls, dear girls, those lovely seaside girls, / With sticks they steer and promenade the pier to give the boys a treat" (Gifford, 76). Indeed, Fritz Senn's description of how Gerty exhibits herself sounds very much like a description of objects artfully arranged in the department store for the purpose of attracting the consumer's attention: "Gerty, injured and slighted, presents herself to her best advantage for one short span, at the proper distance, with just the right degree of illumination to increase her glamour."[15] Bloom, ever the cautious consumer, views her from a safe distance. When he later perceives her limp, his sympathy for Gerty is expressed solely in commercial terms. The male singer of "Those Lovely Seaside Girls" also makes the point that these "dear girls," although they have a bewildering variety of names, essentially all look alike: "Lace and grace and lots of face, those pretty little seaside girls."

Indeed, these "girls" wear the same mass-produced items as an essential accompaniment to their equally uniform style of flirtation: "in pique silks and lace, they tip you quite a playful wink." The result of this extreme uniformity is that women themselves become the equivalent of mass-produced commodities who must learn to exhibit themselves to the male observer/consumer: "You fall in love of course upon the spot, / But not with one girl, *always with the lot*" (emphasis added). A *lot,* in this context, is a commercial term for a large quantity of identically produced commodities.

"Once we learn of Gerty's lameness," Henke writes, "we have to admire the bravado of her self-assertion in the competitive sexual market of 1904" ("Gerty," 134). What a closer look at the lyrics of "Those Lovely Seaside Girls" suggests is that we also have to mourn its futility. In a world where women are packaged commodities, with every woman vying against every other for the attention of the jaded male consumer, even something as subtle as misapplied make-up must stand out as a "defect." Gerty's extraordinary attention to dressing in the style dictated by fashion magazines is not, as has often been suggested, an indication of simple-mindedness, but rather a strategy of increasingly desperate shrewdness whereby she hopes to decisively defeat other women in terms of her appearance. And she does so not out of vanity, but out of self-preservation. We have only to think of the "life in death" quality of the unmarried Maria, the slavey in "Two Gallants," or Corley's previous girlfriend, now a prostitute, to see that Gerty's concerns and preoccupation are anything but frivolous.

Indeed, she must surpass other women in appearance if she is to offset the "defect" of her limp: "she felt that the years were slipping by for her, one by one, and *but for that one shortcoming* she knew she need fear no competition and that was an accident coming down Dalkey hill and she always tried to conceal it" (*U,* 298, emphasis added). In the social and economic climate of 1904 Dublin, Gerty's appearance is her career; if her obsessive attention to every detail of this appearance seems pathetic or trivial, we need to understand this pathos in the wider context of the ruthless sexual marketplace that sprang into being as advertisements (and other media phenomena such as women's magazines and beauty columns) helped disseminate a rigid standard of "femininity" that women were then taught to approximate as their one viable strategy for securing financial security (theoretically, at least) and social respectability as someone's wife. It is this context, and not some "natural" law, that produces the competitive atmosphere where a "defect" is "ten times worse in a woman."

As a male consumer in the sexual marketplace, Bloom is overwhelmed by Gerty's display: "Lord! It was all things combined. Excitement. When she leaned back felt an ache at the butt of my tongue. Your head it simply swirls. He's right" (*U*, 305). But also, as a professional advertiser, he is able to view her as a product endowed with consciousness: "Dressed up to the nines for somebody. Fashion part of their charm. . . . No reasonable offer refused" (*U*, 302). Nowadays, of course, the spectacle of male and female bodies congregating and cavorting upon Fort Lauderdale beach in the springtime has given rise to the expression "meat market," but a similar dynamic is occurring at Margate Beach and, in "virtual" terms, at Sandymount Strand.

The "meat" in this "market," however, is anything but raw.[16] In the case of "lovely seaside girls" (such as Gerty MacDowell), a woman's carefully layered style of dressing operates as a sort of reverse striptease in which what she has so slowly and carefully put on is more exciting to the male consumer than anything he might imagine a woman taking off: "In bloomers smart they captivate the heart, when cycling down the prom. / At wheels and heels and hose, you must not look 'tis understood, / But ev'ry Johnnie knows, it does your eyesight good." Of course, Sandymount Strand is not very much like the British seaside resort of Margate. There is no promenade for pedestrians and bicycles, and no ever-present crowd of young men to judge the sartorial strategies of the young women. The austerity of Sandymount Strand, however, actually serves to emphasize the degree to which eroticism and gender construction are constructed outside and beyond the actual circumstances that put desire into play. Bloom and Gerty desire one another, as I hope to show, in strict conformity to media representations of "feminine" and "masculine" sexuality. Although practically alone on a deserted strip of sand, they conduct themselves, in every detail, in accordance with the heavily mediated atmosphere of the British beach resort on the other side of the Irish Sea.[17]

The presence of the other young women (Cissy and Edy, and the babies they are supervising) sets in motion an even more complex scenario of voyeurism and exhibitionism. Each woman is shown as advertising her body to Bloom according to competing strategies; in an interconnected geometry of gazing, each woman eyes not only Bloom but also the other women on the beach, and even herself, in an effort to gauge her success at capturing the attention of the male "customer" Bloom. Kimberly Devlin notes, "The young women who appear to be keeping an eye on the three children are in fact keeping an eye on everything else, surveying each other, surveying themselves, and surveying the mysterious gentleman who in turn surveys them, intensifying the self-consciousness of their deportment" ("Female Eye," 135). What Devlin calls "deportment," I would call striking a commercial pose. "Madcap Ciss with her golliwog curls" represents a type, also featured in advertisements of the time, of the impetuous, athletic older girl who has not yet awakened to the more thoughtful pose of dawning womanhood. Gerty's limp, of course, forbids her from imitating this style, and besides, at twenty-two years of age, she is too old for the part.

Gerty is nonetheless very concerned that Cissy's active performance, also designed to display her body to commercial advantage in relation to Bloom's gaze, might prove more attractive to him. As if to mentally forestall this possibility, Gerty critiques Cissy's exhibition of her hair, legs, and petticoat in a sarcastic tone that ridicules her effectiveness and impugns her morals:

> She [Cissy] jumped up and called them [Jacky and Tommy] and she ran down the slope past him [Bloom], tossing her hair behind her which had a good enough colour if there had been more of it but with all the thingamerry she was always rubbing into it she couldn't get it to grow long because it wasn't natural so she could just go and throw her hat at it. She ran with long gandery strides it was a wonder she didn't rip up her skirt at the side that was too tight on her because there was a lot of the tomboy about Cissy Caffrey and she was a forward piece whenever she thought she had a good opportunity to show off and just because she was a good runner she ran like that so that he could see all the end of her petticoat running and her skinny shanks up as far as possible. It would have served her just right if she had tripped up over something accidentally on purpose with her high crooked French heels on her to make her look tall and got a fine tumble. *Tableau!* That would have been a very charming exposé for a gentleman like that to witness. (*U*, 294–95)

Despite the fact that Gerty's withering assessment of Cissy's attempt to attract Bloom's attention is so ungenerous and disapproving (we might also note her perhaps deliberate borrowing from the "Seaside Girls" song for the sake of irony: "Down at Margate looking *very charming*," in contrast with Gerty's sarcastic phrase "a very charming exposé"), we should not miss the fact that she faults Cissy specifically for using some of the very strategies she currently employs in her efforts to enhance the effect of her own performance as "feminine."

Gerty, for example, uses a wide variety of cosmetics, and, as we have seen, she carefully blends their brand names and advertising slogans into a flattering description of herself. And yet, when referring to the fact that Cissy uses something in her hair, she presents this information as crudely as possible by omitting any mention of a brand name: "all the thingamerry she was always rubbing into it." *Thingamerry* is a nonsense term that vaguely denotes "something one does not wish to or cannot specify" (Gifford, 391); the phrase "rubbing into it," which Gerty uses to describe how Cissy applies this generic product, hardly matches the royal Gerty's much more noble application of her queenly (and trademarked) ointment. The betrayal of cosmetic secrets and the belittlement of beauty tips were presented even earlier in "Nausicaa" as the major sources of friction among the girls: "it was not true that she used to wear kid gloves in bed or take a milk footbath either. Bertha Supple told that once to Edy Boardman, a deliberate lie, when she was black out at daggers drawn with Gerty (the girl chums had of course their little tiffs from time to time like the rest of mortals)" (*U*, 286).

Women are taught, at an early age, to demean the masquerade of femininity as performed by other women in order to strengthen the illusion of reality in their own performance. The stakes are both competitive and high since the "girls" are competing for the limited financial resources of a limited number of legitimate male consumers. Next, Gerty scorns Cissy's run down the beach as a vulgar attempt to display her legs, even though moments earlier she converted the opportunity of kicking the ball to Bloom into a strategy for giving him a better look at her legs without betraying any consciousness of doing so: "He was looking up so intently, so still, and he saw her kick the ball and perhaps he could see the bright steel buckles of her shoes if she swung them like that thoughtfully with the toes down. She was glad that something told her to put on the transparent stockings" (*U*, 293).[18]

As for the possibility that Cissy might trip "accidentally on purpose with her high crooked French heels on her to make her look tall," this is, again, simply Cissy's different, more active, strategy for performing the final tableau that only Gerty achieves: "and her face was suffused with a divine, an entrancing blush from straining back" (*U*, 300). According to Gerty, if Cissy were to tumble, the result would be a discreditable exposé, and yet Gerty describes her own tableau as a "wondrous revealment" (*U*, 300). We can see, having examined Gerty's critique of Cissy, that the fierce competition among women for male attention serves to alienate women from one another. This alienation, in turn, perpetuates the phenomenon of the sexual marketplace since it persuades each woman to pursue a male-defined standard of "femininity" without ever seeking to demythologize this pursuit in dialogues with other women. Women socialize with one another often enough, Bloom muses, "Till Mr Right comes along, then meet once in a blue moon" (U, 302). Gerty's uncharitable account of Cissy running down the beach shows the extent to which women have been taught to see other women strictly from the imagined perspective of a male consumer.

From this alienated perspective, other women's strategies are critiqued as vulgar and immoral, while one's own devices are thought to bring about a "wondrous revealment." Significantly, when Bloom ruminates on how vicious women can be to other women ("wouldn't lend each other a pinch of salt"), he envisions one woman meeting another woman on the street in what he describes as a tableau: "*Tableau!* O, look who it is for the love of God! How are you at all? . . . Picking holes in each other's appearance. You're looking splendid. Sister souls. Showing their teeth at one another. How many have you left?" (*U*, 302). Contained in Bloom's description are both the savage countenance of animals contending for limited sustenance ("showing their teeth") and the more "civilized" strategy of gauging one's competitor in the same way a prospective buyer determines the market value of a horse: "How many have you left?" In imagining women surreptitiously examining the welcoming smile of another woman in order to count her teeth, Bloom presents women as cruelly trapped in a competitive mode where the only value they have is whatever value they represent to a male consumer.

What is astonishing about Bloom's analogy of women and horses is that he figures a scene in which one "horse" examines the teeth of another "horse" in order to arrive at an estimation of their own value before they trot off to the market to be sold. Accordingly, Gerty's "self"-esteem is completely dependent upon the value she imagines Bloom has fixed upon her (a value further enhanced by the fact that he has chosen not to stare at Cissy): "If ever there was undisguised admiration in a man's passionate gaze it was there plain to be seen on that man's face. It is for you, Gertrude MacDowell, and you know it" (*U*, 296). There is little hope of breaking this cycle of dependence on the male gaze because Gerty, like all "those lovely seaside girls," views her fellow victims as vulgar and conniving rivals whose masquerade of femininity must be scorned and degraded if the prospective worth of her own performance is to be exalted (at least in her own mind).

When Bloom reflects on the performance of the young women, his detached assessments of their various qualities and demerits is, in fact, that of a consumer reflecting on products that look good at first glance, but that may prove to be of poor quality once they are tried out: "That squinty one is delicate" (*U*, 301). Bloom's various musings on how the young women fall short of the "standard" of "femininity" further illustrate my assertion that Gerty's keen interest in fashioning her image according to magazines is not an idle and vain pursuit. Instead, we must understand it as an extremely serious endeavor upon which her economic survival hinges. Of Madame Vera Verity, Henke writes, "the aim of Madame Verity's cosmetic art is not truth, as her name would imply, but a simpering obfuscation of reality" ("Gerty MacDowell," 135). I would like to suggest the opposite; although Madame Verity's prose style appears to be an "obfuscation," its economic message is quite direct: without this product, your eyebrows will fail to attract male attention, and you will be left on the shelf in the sexual marketplace.

"Reality" is constantly revealed as a social construct in *Ulysses* generally, and in "Nausicaa" in particular. It would be comforting to dismiss Madame Vera Verity's precious pronouncements as so much fluff because then we could reassure ourselves that Gerty's fear concerning her own future is just so much adolescent melodrama, and she won't really come to any harm. Gerty makes this point of view an easy one to maintain because she describes her future in high-blown phrases and hyperbolic daydreams. But I would like to suggest that the information in women's magazines is presented in an aggressively trivial style precisely because the actual economic message the magazines contain is so grim: "throughout the first third of the twentieth century, the marriage rate in Ireland ran less than half that of England and Wales and of Denmark, a country of comparable size and type on the continent."[19] Gerty's superficially absurd obsession with her appearance is in fact a crucial "self"-defense in which she seeks to overdramatize serious events to such an extent that she will not have to take them seriously.

"Such conditions," Walzl goes on to note, "were more serious for women because women's vocational choices were so much more limited than men's" (37). To realize this, one has only to think of the difference in lifestyle between the unmarried James Duffy of "A Painful Case" and the unmarried Maria of "Clay"; Duffy has the independence that goes with a steady job, while Maria works as a laundress in a "charitable" business designed to employ former prostitutes.[20] However unlikely an eventual marriage with Reggy Wylie might appear to the reader, for example, the fact that he no longer pays attention to Gerty has very real implications for her future economic security. It is all very well to see Gerty as a regrettably prefeminist woman who is overly concerned with clothes and boys, but Joyce sketches out, in "a style of scrupulous meanness," the economic impossibility of female autonomy in Ireland (*D*, 269). If we accept my rereading of Gerty as crafty, hard-working, persistent, and resilient, perhaps it is less difficult to imagine how successful and independent she might well be in a different cultural and economic climate. Her intelligence and resourcefulness must be judged in relation to how appallingly few alternatives she has.

What Henke calls "a whirlpool of commercial fantasy" ("Gerty," 134) is in fact the relentlessly real "owner's manual" that an Irish woman in Joyce's time must scrupulously consult if she hopes to maximize her limited opportunities in the overcrowded sexual marketplace. She must improve her chances of being taken off the shelf by molding herself as persuasively as possible into an approximation of the current standard of femininity, as presented in magazines such as the *Lady's Pictorial*. The commercial world outlined in its pages is all too real, and it is in fact Gerty who must become a fantasy if she is to secure a modicum of financial security by making a man's head swirl. For Gerty, marriage is the Scylla and spinsterhood is the Charybdis through which she must pilot her body. She is a "product" in the sense that how well she packages her "femininity" will most likely determine whether or not a "manly man" purchases her for his home.

Henke claims, "Gerty serves as a herald of the twentieth-century goddesses staring from the covers of *Cosmopolitan, Women's Day,* and *Playboy*" ("Gerty MacDowell," 147). What is instructive about Henke's assertion (with which I concur) is that *Women's Day* is a magazine designed for a female audience, and *Playboy* is a magazine designed for a male audience. And yet a similar type of woman stares out from the covers of all three. *Playboy* encourages men to consume the image of a woman, while magazines such as *Cosmopolitan* and *Mademoiselle* teach their female audience how to consume products that will make them an attractive package to the male gaze. The commercial equation is clear: A female must become a consumer in order to package herself as a "woman"—in order to appear as "real" and "valuable" to a male consumer. What she spends on various products is frequently presented as an investment toward making her"self" a valuable object in the sexual marketplace.

Women's Day and *Lady's Pictorial* are "how-to" books, or instruction manuals, on how best to compile the finished product of "femininity." This same product is directly presented to male consumers as the essence of "womanhood" by magazines such as *Playboy*. "Men's" magazines such as *Playboy, Penthouse,* and *Esquire* operate as a sort of mail-order catalogue of "femininity" for the viewing pleasure of the male consumer. The detailed instructions on how a woman must construct her "femininity" through preapproved strategies of consumption, everywhere present in magazines such as *Lady's Pictorial* and *Cosmopolitan,* are completely elided in the "natural" representations of "femininity" found in *Playboy* and the Mutoscope located somewhere on Capel Street.

To put this another way, women know they must submit themselves to the instruction of magazines like *Women's Day* and *Cosmopolitan* because men are already consuming this artificial construction as something "natural," in magazines such as *Playboy* and *Penthouse.* For Bloom, the equivalent of *Playboy* is the Mutoscope pictures. Later, Bloom recalls the decisive motion of Gerty leaning back using the Mutoscope picture title "A Dream of Wellfilled Hose" as an unconscious reference point: "Lord, I am wet. Devil you are. Swell of her calf. Transparent stockings, stretched to breaking point. Not like that frump today. A. E. Rumpled stockings" (*U,* 304–5). Clearly the woman he has seen riding the bicycle with A. E. is not a viable product on the sexual marketplace because her "rumpled stockings" do not even begin to approximate the "dream of wellfilled hose" that Bloom values so highly.

The difference between depictions of "femininity" in the *Lady's Pictorial* and in the Mutoscope picture is one of degree and not of kind. Gerty, who I am insisting is much more of a realist than has generally been allowed, seems to understand this fact perfectly well:

> His hands and face were working and a tremour went over her. She leaned back far to look up where the fireworks were and she caught her knee in her hands so as not to fall back looking up and there was no-one to see only him and her when she revealed all her graceful beautifully shaped legs like that, supply soft and delicately rounded, . . . she knew too about the passion of men like that, hotblooded, because Bertha Supple told her once in dead secret and made her swear she'd never about the gentleman lodger . . . that had pictures cut out of papers of those skirtdancers and highkickers and she said he used to do something not very nice that you could imagine sometimes in the bed. But this was altogether different from a thing like that because there was all the difference. . . . (*U,* 299–300)

Gerty's attempt to distance herself from these images of "highkickers," which are overtly intended to fuel a man's masturbatory fantasies, collapses into a vague and circular logic: "this was altogether different from a thing like that because there was all the difference." She deliberately approximates these "highkickers" in order to monopolize Bloom's gaze, and yet we also see the extent to which she relies on the absurdly lighthearted rhetoric of the lady's magazine to protect her "self" from too keen an awareness into the carefully unacknowledged source of her masquerade. Subtle (that is, "romantic") depictions of the male-defined standard of femininity are carefully presented in magazines designed for women, while cruder images (that is, "pornographic") of this same standard are to be found in the Mutoscope pictures in Capel Street.

In "Wandering Rocks," Joyce presents the differing reactions of Miss Dunne and the young Master Paddy Dignam. In doing so, he again makes the point (of which Gerty MacDowell is timidly aware) that the exact same representation of "femininity" may be taken as an instruction manual on how to be a "woman" to a woman, and as a crass exhibition of sexual availability to a man:

> Then she stared at the large poster of Marie Kendall, charming soubrette. . . . She's not nicelooking, is she? The way she's holding up her bit of a skirt. Wonder will that fellow be at the band tonight. If I could get that dressmaker to make a concertina skirt like Susy Nagle's. They kick out grand. Shannon and all the boatclub swells never took his eyes off her. (*U*, 189)

> [H]e saw the image of Marie Kendall, charming soubrette. . . . One of them mots that do be in the packets of fags Stoer smokes that his old fellow welted hell out of him for one time he found out. (*U*, 206)[21]

A *soubrette* was a term that typically referred to the saucy maid, or other minor female characters in a play, whose primary role was to display the latest style of coquetry. If magazines gave the reader a sense of what an up-to-the-minute static image of femininity should look like, the soubrette offered playgoers a glimpse at current strategies of flirtation. Not surprisingly, then, Miss Dunne's evaluation of Marie Kendall's pose ("holding up her bit of a skirt") uses the same ungenerous tone that Gerty uses in her critique of Cissy. And yet, Miss Dunne then segues immediately into a reverie about the sort of skirt she needs to wear ("a concertina skirt like Susy Nagle's") if she is to successfully attract the male gaze with a "forbidden" glimpse of her legs ("they kick out grand"). This glimpse must be presented in a manner that appears to absolve her of any awareness of what she is doing.

Once again, the unacknowledged standard for Miss Dunne's imagined performance is the "skirtdancers" (as opposed to the "highkickers") that Bertha Supple saw hanging on a man's walls. We can see clearly the imputations that Gerty and Miss Dunne seek to avoid when we witness young

Dignam's reaction to Marie Kendall's image as one of "them mots" (showgirls, popular actresses) that men are invited to collect when they buy cigarettes. The marketing idea of hiding a provocative image of an attractive woman inside a package so that one must purchase the cigarettes in order to open the package and look at it is merely a more commercial example of Gerty MacDowell's unwrapping herself for Bloom. The fact that *Playboy* magazine is usually taped shut on the newsstand suggests that the phenomenon of "the centerfold" is simply a contemporary version of the cigarette girl. The poses of women on the cigarette cards, like the highkickers or the women in the mutoscopes on Capel Street, were somewhat more suggestive than the "dauby smile" of Marie Kendall, "charming soubrette," but, significantly, young Master Dignam fails to see any difference.

Indeed, Miss Dunne also seems to be uncharitably miffed that Marie Kendall has developed, and consequently perfected, a commercially effective way of showing her legs to large nightly audiences of male consumers who pay to see her perform. Her next thought, which she does not experience as contradictory, is that she had better obtain a style of skirt that will allow her to do the same thing. In the "Circe" chapter, when Bello Cohen is dressing up Bloom in order to auction him to the highest bidder, it is the likeness of Marie Kendall (or rather her pose as a "charming soubrette") that he instantly adopts: "(*charming soubrette with dauby cheeks, mustard hair and large male hands and nose, leering mouth*)" (*U*, 437). In addition to dressing like a woman, Bloom is told by Bello that he is going to have to be educated in various "feminine" calisthenics: "Learn the smooth mincing walk on four inch Louis Quinze heels" (*U*, 441). This is the same style of shoe that Gerty has already belittled because it is worn by the fleet-footed Cissy: "It would have served her just right if she had tripped up over something . . . with her high crooked French heels on her to make her look tall" (*U*, 295).

The media-produced and male-defined standard of femininity may be presented with varying degrees of subtlety, and it may encompass a wide range of styles and strategies, but its central purpose is to instruct a woman on how best to market herself to the male consumer. This is never so apparent in *Ulysses* as when Bello Cohen puts the newly "feminized" Bloom on the auction block: "Swell the bust. Smile. Droop shoulders. What offers? (*he points*) For that lot. Trained by owner to fetch and carry, basket in mouth. (*he bares his arm and plunges it elbowdeep in Bloom's vulva*) There's fine depth for you! What, boys? That give you a hardon? (*he shoves his arm in a bidder's face*) Here wet the deck and wipe it round!" (*U*, 440, Joyce's italics). "Femininity," then, is indistinguishable from the marketing of the female body. "You fall in love . . . not with one girl, always with *the lot,*" croons the male singer of "Those Lovely Seaside Girls." Bello Cohen, somewhat less dandily, bellows out to the gathered crowd of male consumers, "What offers? . . . *For that lot*" (emphasis added). If, as the myth of Circe insists, women reduce men to pigs by the skillful use of their "charms," they do so by first submitting themselves to a profoundly commercial process of measurement, standardization, and artificial enhancement of physical attributes.[22]

VII. Through the looking glass: The physical as fiscal

Appropriately, it is in the "Circe" chapter that Joyce powerfully presents this "beautification" process as analogous to the commercial process that livestock undergo as they are readied for market: "Whoa, my jewel! Beg up! Whoa! (*he brands his initial C on Bloom's croup*) So! Warranted Cohen! What advance on two bob, gentlemen?" (*U*, 440, Joyce's italics). What Joyce's presentation emphasizes is the sheer physicality of this process—the pushing, squeezing, and branding of flesh that eventually produces the hallucinogenic vision of "those lovely seaside girls." Significantly, this lighthearted music-hall song is also called to mind by Bloom when he is standing in Glasnevin cemetery, pondering the morbid vision of hundreds of bodies decomposing in the earth beneath his feet: "But they must breed a devil of a lot of maggots. Soil must be simply swirling with them. Your head it simply swurls. Those pretty little seaside gurls" (*U*, 89). Ashes to ashes, dust to dust; but in between there is the tremendous sound and fury of cosmetics, flirtation, the *Lady's Pictorial*, pornography, music-hall vamps and swells, corsets, transparent stockings, and myriad other cultural forces that make the human body a semiotic clearinghouse of inconceivable complexity.

One phenomenon that commercialized what we might call this "semerotic" sign system is the advent of a commodity culture in which countless articles began to be manufactured and advertised with reference to the human body. Even the "Nymph of the Bath," whom Bloom praises in "Circe" as "beautiful immortal," protests that he found her "in evil company" with "highkickers" and "immoral panto boys in fleshtights":

> I was hidden in cheap pink paper that smelt of rock oil. . . . ads for transparencies, truedup dice and bustpads. . . .
>
> Rubber goods. Neverrip brand as supplied to the aristocracy. Corsets for men. I cure fits or money refunded. Unsolicited testimonials for Professor Waldmann's wonderful chest exuber. My bust developed four inches in three weeks, reports Mrs Gus Rublin with photo. (*U*, 444–45)

When Master Paddy Dignam devalues Marie Kendall as "one of them mots" on cigarette cards, we might initially see this as the imposition of a vulgar mindset on a perfectly "charming soubrette"; in fact, the boy's lack of education permits the unintentionally astute observation that media representations of femininity always answer to a style of male-defined female sexuality—whether or not the particular context of the image invites one to characterize it as "charming" or "arousing." Of course, the misogynistic point of view that "all women are sexual objects" would seem to be the underlying impetus of Master Dignam's comment. Likewise, this is certainly the implication of the urbane male observer in "Those Lovely Seaside Girls"; but what Joyce intricately demonstrates throughout *Ulysses* is that in the sexual marketplace of Dublin, where there are few vocational outlets for a woman, women are forced either to market their sexuality in accordance with a male-defined standard or to wander the dismal path illustrated by someone like the elderly Maria (in Joyce's story "Clay"), who finally, because it is impossible to determine "what sort of a woman" she might be, is placed incongruously in a laundry established for reformed prostitutes.

As wondrously packaged products, women promenading the sexual marketplace are initially greeted with delirious approval by the singer of "Those Lovely Seaside Girls." Eventually, however, the fact that these pretty objects are not readily available for "handling" irks the singer to the point where, in the closing verse, the "dear girls" are taken on a boat ride. Once on the boat, the seaside girls get seasick. In describing their discomfort and public humiliation, the singer articulates his revenge; whereas these "girls" previously made his head swirl with unrequited lust, now their heads swirl with the effects of nausea. Furthermore, the sorry spectacle they present at the close of the song is represented solely in terms of the way their seasickness has stripped them of all the cosmetics and fashion accoutrements that previously made them "lovely." Their complexions, formerly described as "pink and white," now appear "green and white." Their hats (which Gerty has shown to be a valuable fashion prop for coquetry) "fly off," and even their beautiful hair is revealed to be something bought in London's most fashionable shopping district: "at your feet falls golden hair from Regent Street." And, in the final line of the song, even the most trivial cosmetic products that the "lovely girls" used suddenly spill out into the plain view of the disenchanted male consumer: "Rouge and puffs slip down the cuffs of pretty little seaside girls."

The "girls," initially hailed as wonders of nature in the opening of the song, are now presented as shamefully artificial creatures who have caused a man's head to "swirl" in a crass effort to secure their financial futures.

This shift on the male voyeur's part from worship to desecration is similar to the resentment consumers often feel when they discover they cannot afford to purchase what has already fascinated their gaze.[23] Surprisingly enough, this perspective is most succinctly expressed by the singularly inarticulate Corley (in the *Dubliners* story "Two Gallants"):

> —First I used to go with girls, you know, said Corley, unbosoming; . . . I used to spend money on them right enough, he added, in a convincing tone, as if he were conscious of being disbelieved.
>
> But Lenehan could well believe it; he nodded gravely.
>
> —I know that game, he said, and it's a mug's game.
>
> —And damn the thing I ever got out of it, said Corley. (*D*, 52)

This analysis gives the impression that "girls" practice a profitable game in relation to men (or, to grant Lenehan's term, "mugs") with few risks to themselves. But, with no consciousness of contradiction, Corley goes on to summarize the history of the one "girl" on whom he once spent money: "She was . . . a bit of all right, he said regretfully. . . . She's on the turf now. I saw her driving down Earl Street one night with two fellows with her on a car" (*D*, 53). Having failed to attract a more permanent buyer (and we know her final mistake was expecting something permanent from Corley), Corley's former love has been forced to offer herself for rent.

When Joyce presents us with a glimpse of Corley's latest conquest, he telegraphs to the reader, in his description of her clothing, that she, too, is in imminent danger of falling off the shelf of the marriage market and onto "the turf" of the prostitute market: "She had her Sunday finery on. . . . She wore a short black jacket with mother-of-pearl buttons and a ragged black boa. The ends of her tulle collarette had been carefully disordered and *a big bunch of red flowers was pinned in her bosom, stems upwards*" (*D*, 55, emphasis added). What this anonymous woman represents is a sort of "bargain basement" Gerty MacDowell. The fact that even her "Sunday finery" features a "ragged" boa and also that her sense of a sophisticated appearance does not extend to making sure the stems of her corsage point downward combine to offer a semiotic portrait of the prostitute as a young woman. In this same context, Gabriel's decision to "thrust" a coin into Lily's hand might be his startled recognition that she may be on the verge of being forced into downgrading the terms of her availability on the sexual marketplace.

The women's magazines that Gerty reads are in fact rather grim economic manuals; the sugary sweet rantings about "true love" and domestic bliss serve to mitigate the dire warning, contained in some form in every column and every advertisement, that a woman who fails to successfully masquerade as a "woman" may be forced to submit to public auction in the sexual marketplace. In a star illustration of this fate, Gerty's "coquettish little love of a [straw] hat" goes through a degrading metempsychosis and reemerges into the view of the recently united Stephen and Leopold:

> The face of a streetwalker glazed and haggard under a black straw hat peered askew round the door of the shelter palpably reconnoitring on her own with the object of bringing more grist to her mill. . . .
>
> Stephen had not noticed her and shrugged his shoulders, merely remarking:
>
> —In this country people sell much more than she ever had and do a roaring trade. . . . She is a bad merchant. She buys dear and sells cheap. (*U*, 517)

The cliché "grist to her mill" connotes something material employed by someone for the purpose of turning a profit. This woman, however, has set up business "on her own" by utilizing her actual body as the grist in her own "mill"; thus, she is "a bad merchant," slowly grinding herself into oblivion.

To reiterate my principal theme, there is no "real" world of "womanhood" that is obfuscated by the advertisements in the *Princess Novelette;* femininity itself is a cultural construct, designed with reference to male desire. It serves as a standard in relation to which women are "ticketed" and perhaps "purchased" on the sexual marketplace. A woman who marries well has managed to buy cheap and sell dear, while a woman who fails in courtship and winds up on the turf will henceforth buy dear and sell cheap. Luce Irigaray sums up this equation by asking an unsettling question that I have been posing, in one form or another, throughout this chapter: "How . . . can the analysis of women's exploitation be dissociated from the analysis of modes of appropriation?" (83). Joyce juxtaposes those "charming" images of "femininity" deliberately marketed for women with those "pornographic" images of "femininity" deliberately marketed for men in order to show that the way female sexuality is depicted (as a packaged commodity) determines the way it comes into play (as the male-defined standard of "femininity").

Indeed, male-defined "femininity" is the gold standard that authenticates the currency of erotic feeling that flows back and forth between Gerty and Bloom. While Gerty voraciously consumes the syrupy prose of the women's magazines, her central purpose in adhering so closely to their dictates is that she wishes to be a "good" merchant—that is, one who buys cheap and sells dear:

> Gerty could see without looking that he never took his eyes off of her . . . and she just swung her foot in and out in time as the music rose and fell. . . . Three and eleven she paid for those stockings in Sparrow's of George's street on the Tuesday, no the Monday before Easter and there wasn't a brack on them and that was what he was looking at, transparent, and not at her insignificant ones that had neither shape nor form (the cheek of her!) because he had eyes in his head to see the difference for himself. (*U*, 294)

We know from Bloom's ruminations about "rumpled" stocking versus "wellfilled hose" that Gerty's point of view here is not the least bit naive. Indeed, as we learn in the exceptionally uninhibited "Circe" chapter, Bloom was sensitized to the erotic currency of "femininity" at a very young age: "A little then sufficed, . . . even a pricelist of their hosiery" (*U*, 447).[24]

When Bloom reflects that his encounter with Gerty featured "a kind of language between us" (*U*, 305), he is displaying a vague awareness of the extent to which his "simple" sexual climax has been mediated by such erotic catalogues as advertisements, "pornographic" flicks like "A Dream of Wellfilled Hose," the bargain bin of Clery's department store, and popular songs such as "Those Lovely Seaside Girls." As Irigaray puts it, women are commodities and "commodities speak. To be sure, mostly dialects and patois, languages hard for 'subjects' to understand. The important thing is that they be preoccupied with their respective values, that their remarks confirm the exchangers' plans for them" (179). Gerty's limp is her one physical attribute that mars the syntax of her conversation as a commodity. Because it remains unrepresented by beauty tip columnists like Madame Vera Verity, her limp, quite simply, is not "feminine" and therefore it is not legal tender. Not surprisingly, then, Bloom as a consumer, responding to the language of the "semerotics" of the sexual marketplace, is relieved that he was not forced to "read" this syntactical glitch in the otherwise well-formed sentence of Gerty's appearance. Such an obvious "stutter" on her part might have interfered—or rendered ungrammatical—the exclamation point of his orgasm.

And yet, his further musings on this point make an even more subtle point; given enough time for mental preparation, even Gerty's limp might be infused with enough erotic connotations to stimulate him to a climax: "Curiosity like a nun or a negress or a girl with glasses" (*U*, 301). In the case of glasses, the device that both announces and corrects a "defect" becomes, if properly marketed, a "curiosity" that might be as erotically charged as garters or underwear. If Gerty's limp disqualifies her as a "seaside girl," then she becomes salable as a "curiosity"; that is to say, as someone who is an exciting "bargain" because she is "damaged" or "irregular." Although Bloom acknowledges that a defect is ten times worse in a woman, speaking as an adman, he knows how to present this defect as an advantage: "But makes them polite" (*U*, 301). We might translate "polite" as describing the deferential and forthcoming behavior likely to be exhibited by a woman who, in terms of her "feminine" market value, cannot afford to pose as something very expensive. Bloom's new sense of Gerty as a "curiosity"—a sort of "cheap" thrill—has caused her to be "marked down" in his mind. "You won't get a virgin in the flash houses," he is told by "the Bawd" just before Gerty approaches: "(Leering, Gerty MacDowell limps forward. She draws from behind, ogling, and shows coyly her bloodied clout.) GERTY: *With all my worldly goods* I thee and thou" (*U*, 361, emphasis added). Since the "flash houses" were "higher-class houses of prostitution where the women wore evening dresses," we can see that in the more straightforward economic structure of prostitution, as in the marmalade-like prose of "Nausicaa," Gerty presents herself to Bloom as a bargain (Gifford, 458).

The prim and proper Madame Vera Verity, whose precious prose style coyly introduced Gerty's charms in "Nausicaa," has metempsychosed into a much coarser "Madame," referred to as "the Bawd," who crudely recites what makes Gerty valuable to the steady stream of anonymous men walking through nighttown in search of just such a bargain. A "clout" is "any worthless piece of cloth" or "a cloth used to mend something." Gerty brandishes it before Bloom to prove he has taken something from her—her virginity—for which he now must pay. But its soiled condition identifies it as a reincarnation of a fashion accessory so dear to the Gerty of "Nausicaa." In that commercially "pure" context, the department store equivalent of her "bloody clout" was "on sale" at Clery's department store, and Gerty was able to buy it cheaply as a consequence of its having been unpacked, used, soiled—in other words, deprived of its virginity and put in the "marked down" bin: "All Tuesday week afternoon she was hunting to match that chenille but at last she found what she wanted at Clery's summer sales, the very it, slightly shopsoiled but you would never notice . . ." (*U*, 287).[25] In "Circe," both Gerty and the cloth are "slightly shopsoiled."

Also in the "Circe" passage quoted above, Gerty appropriates what is supposed to be the groom's wedding pledge in the Catholic marriage vow.

This vow reads in part, "this gold and silver I thee give: and with all my worldly goods I thee endow" (Gifford, 458). Gerty's "worldly goods" are, to name a few, her carefully shopped for stockings, her underwear, her hat, and her body, which serves as the semerotic intersection of all these "feminine" signifiers. As the bride, the way she packages her sexuality as "feminine" determines the apparent value of the "product" that she brings to the bargaining table to match the groom's silver and gold. If we glance back to "Nausicaa," we can see that Gerty misquotes another portion of the vow from the Catholic marriage service. Instead of the phrase "for richer, for poorer," she thinks, "for riches for poor" (*U*, 289). This again suggests that underneath all the breathless hyperbole about "true love," Gerty is painfully aware of the grim truth that she is both an aging beauty and a damaged commodity still hoping to be taken down from the shelf in the ruthlessly competitive sexual marketplace.

Gerty's status as a "marked down" virgin allows Joyce to explore the full range of marketing and consumer strategies in the sexual marketplace. His relentlessly commercial depiction of heterosexual attraction richly undermines the fantastic idea—insisted upon by the fantastic rhetoric of women's magazines—that sexuality is a "natural" urge that runs its course independent of the mediation of gender representation and economic exigencies. "Heterosexuality is nothing but the assignment of economic roles," Irigaray asserts. "[T]here are producer subjects and agents of exchange (male) on the one hand, productive earth and commodities (female) on the other" (192). The sentimental myth of "true love" overlays the economic reality that women must package their female sexuality into the easily advertised commodity of "femininity." Foucault makes the general point that "sexuality must not be described as a stubborn drive, by nature alien and of necessity disobedient to a power which exhausts itself trying to subdue it and often fails to control it entirely. It appears rather as an especially dense transfer point for relations of power" (*History of Sexuality*, 103). Foucault is notoriously vague about what he means by "power," but in my discussion of "Nausicaa," I am talking about economic coercion, the conforming force of limited marketing strategies, and the competitive modes of appropriation that occur in heterosexual lust between the man as a consumer and the woman as product (as well as the constant pressure for a woman in the sexual marketplace to avoid becoming "a bad merchant" and to learn how to buy cheap and sell dear).

According to his brother Stanislaus, the youthful Joyce was exquisitely aware of how the "taking" of a woman's virginity must be viewed as an especially dense transfer point for relations of power: "Jim began to describe in minute detail all the preparations, physical, spiritual, and financial that would be necessary before beginning to lay siege to her virtue. . . . The denouement, the comments of all the members of both families, including the cooks, were very funny" (*My Brother's Keeper,* 131). What Joyce's performance illustrates is that at the center of this hurricane of voices there is nothing like "true love" magically transcending the mediating forces of the marketplace; romance becomes, to borrow Donald Trump's humble phrase, "the art of the deal." And yet it is true love—that many-mediated thing—in which Gerty struggles to believe (even as she knows enough to pay careful heed to the commercial advice just beneath the surface of the syrupy imagery and prose).

VIII. Popular culture and the performance of gender: Learning (how) to look

Toward the end of her essay on "Nausicaa," Henke speculates, "Joyce may be suggesting that, in some way, we all are conditioned by the popular culture that surrounds us" ("Gerty MacDowell," 147). I would make her speculation more assertive by arguing that the "way" popular culture conditions gender is to instruct women on how to masquerade as "women," thus reaffirming and granting authority to a semerotic economy of the sexual marketplace that allows men to act like "men" (that is to say, as male consumers of the commodity "femininity"). The images of "women" represented in magazines and advertisements (both in Joyce's time and our own) are so persistently and effectively identified as "natural" that the woman who fails to accept them as a "natural" phenomenon appears as "unnatural"—as someone who is "not a woman." As Gabriel walks away from his disconcerting encounter with the "unfeminine" Molly Ivors, he thinks of her as "the girl or woman, or whatever she was" (*D,* 190).

When Bloom reflects on some of the married women he has met (women who are no longer "out on spec," as he says of Gerty), he also is at a loss to describe them; he finds that women become startlingly "nondescript" after they are no longer competing for the male gaze: "Wife locked up at home, skeleton in the cupboard. Allow me to introduce my. Then they trot you out some kind of a nondescript, wouldn't know what to call her" (*U,* 305).[26] Whereas a virgin like Gerty is at least still on the shelf, the married woman is even more out of reach, in the cupboard (bought and paid for, no longer on display); the commodity that once advertised its "femininity" does not seem to exhibit this "essential" quality once it is "locked up at home."

Gerty is on the beach to offset her dread that she is no longer a viable product on the marriage market. The British seaside resort, such as Brighton or Margate, was, as Thomas Richards describes, "a site of fantasy and a primary locus of Victorian sexual politics. . . . the male consumer could become, like Nabokov's Humbert Humbert, a connoisseur of nymphets. . . . seaside resorts successfully integrated sexual practice into the practice of consumption" (*Commodity Culture*, 227–28). Sandymount Strand is nothing like Margate in terms of pageantry, and this tends to underline Joyce's more subtle point that commodification is so integrated into the presentation and consumption of sexuality that one does not need all the trappings in order to conduct oneself according to its dictates. Richards goes on to say that "Gerty is herself the seaside girl, looking at passersby from within the frame of an advertised fiction by which she is wholly circumscribed, looking out at a scene over which she reigns as the queen of ointments" (234). But as I have been trying to demonstrate, she is not "wholly circumscribed"; rather, she is painfully balanced between a wholehearted effort to believe in the "old time chivalry" of "natural" attraction between "men" and "women" and a shrewder attempt to maintain her competitive edge in the sexual marketplace based on the male-defined "feminine" model of the seaside girl.

The singer in "Those Lovely Seaside Girls" confidently addresses a uniformly "masculine" audience ("*you* are sure to meet"), and "the girls" are also referred to as though they were interchangeable units of "femininity." Heterosexuality is indeed "the assignment of economic roles" in this song. The girls are clearly on display as "they steer and promenade the pier." The detailed description of their fashionable dresses ("in pique silks and lace") parallels Gerty's careful attention to wearing only the latest styles that she knows her competitors (other "girls") will be wearing: "A neat blouse of electric blue selftinted by dolly dyes (because it was expected in the *Lady's Pictorial* that electric blue would be worn)" (*U*, 287). Even in this ecstatic and self-confident description, the fact that this "electric blue" is produced as cheaply as possible ("selftinted by dolly dyes") reminds us that Gerty spends an enormous amount of her time trying to reproduce an image she cannot afford to buy outright: "All Tuesday week afternoon she was hunting to match that chenille" (*U*, 287). Irigaray maintains that "woman has value on the market by virtue of one single quality: that of being a product of man's 'labor'" (175). This would appear to be true of the "lovely seaside girls," who "steer and promenade" in mass-produced "pique silks and lace." But, once again, Joyce complicates this scenario by showing us an Irish woman who must struggle to imitate an invention of British advertising agencies by piecing together the image she cannot afford to buy. Instead of breezing into a fashionable shop in Regent Street to be expensively outfitted, she spends the entire afternoon looking for a scrap of cloth in various bargain bins.

In essence, Gerty, by virtue of long and intensive labor, is trying to increase her market value beyond what her economic status can easily maintain: "she looked so lovely in her sweet girlish shyness that of a surety God's fair land of Ireland did not hold her equal" (*U*, 286). This is "shopping" as a desperate and crafty tactic for survival and not as the vain pursuit of a simpleminded girl.[27] The cruel irony, however, is that in striving to imitate a mass-produced image, Gerty merely succeeds in looking like every other woman who attempts to imitate the same standard. As I have already pointed out, Bloom compares Gerty's "wellfilled hose" with other representations of "the same thing." He maintains, for example, that the "transparent stockings" Gerty has shown him have "made up for that tramdriver this morning" (the one who inadvertently deprived him of a glimpse of stocking). In a subsequent image, just a few lines down from this, women become for Bloom as bewilderingly numerous and identical as a school of fish: "Shoals of them every evening poured out of offices" (*U*, 301). Products in the marketplace are also designed to look exactly like every other unit in "the lot," and a detail in one package that is not reproduced in all the others will emerge as a "defect."

In this sort of marketplace, where women "promenade" the pier before the watchful eyes of male consumers, an individuating characteristic—such as Gerty's limp—becomes an exceptionally unfortunate liability. Any undeniable revelation of physical existence disconcertingly undermines (from a male consumer's point of view) the purely artificial construct of femininity. When a woman's body is subordinated to a male-defined cultural ideal of femininity, however, then what a "man" is becomes equally abstract: "[B]y submitting women's bodies to a general equivalent, to a transcendent, super-natural value, men have drawn the social structure into an ever greater process of abstraction, to the point where they themselves are produced in it as pure concepts" (Irigaray, 190). This curious balance is similar to what Baudrillard calls the "hyperreal," where media simulations of a "natural" phenomenon (in this case sexuality) become the only knowable reality (the standard by which we evaluate our"selves"), and thus the subject is the "fantasy" that tries to simulate the "reality" represented in the media.

Women who successfully mimic the advertising trope of "the seaside girl" become as anonymous and interchangeable as a "trademark" product: "These two labors are interdependent and unequal. Male identity exists prior to and during the act of consumption; female identity gets effaced in the process. Bloom remains Bloom but Gerty must become the seaside girl" (Richards, *Commodity Culture,* 246).[28] I agree that these labors are "interdependent and unequal," as Richards asserts, but I do not agree that Bloom has an a priori existence and that he "remains" Bloom during this exchange. Richards argues in this same paragraph, "women and men had different domains of response mapped out for them. Women were taught to identify with the seaside girl image while men were encouraged to desire it. These gendered variants are illustrated simply and directly in 'Nausicaa,' where Gerty consumes the seaside girl while Bloom consumes Gerty" (*Commodity Culture,* 246). On the contrary, the illustration in "Nausicaa" is neither simple nor direct; more accurately, Gerty and Bloom constitute "reality" for one another in their mutual masquerade. In terms of the semerotics that operates as "a sort of language" in this chapter, Gerty is the signifier and Bloom is the signified.

Male hostility, as I have noted, creeps into the chorus of the song "Those Lovely Seaside girls" when the male singer details the artificial quality of their manufactured image, especially their dyed "golden hair from Regent Street." The reference to "Regent Street" brings in the complex panoply of that district in London, which is devoted to women who can afford to shop for the latest fashion image. The following description of Regent Street is from the *Illustrated London News* of 1866: "[A]ll is bustle and gaiety. . . . The brilliant ever-shifting scene presented daily in Regent Street during the season is dizzying in confusion. On days of court ceremonial strings of carriages filled with beauty, rank and fashion, creep at a snail's pace. . . . At other times, the fireflies of fashion glance rapidly hither and thither."[29] This "dizzying . . . confusion" produces the au courant "feminine" image for which the male consumer's head "simply whirls."

In the competitive sexual market, how is one woman to determine that her feet are more "dainty" than another woman's? Once again, commodity sizing supplies Gerty with the qualitative standard she needs to evaluate her worth relative to other "products" (the "lot" of other women) on the marketplace: "Her shoes were the newest thing in footwear (Edy Boardman prided herself that she was very *petite* but she never had a foot like Gerty MacDowell, a five, and never would" (*U,* 287).[30] Because women's bodies persist in coming in all shapes and sizes, the corset came to be invented, manufactured, and advertised as the product that could standardize a woman's "unnatural" body proportions(!) until they approximate the same dimensions as "feminine" luminaries of the day; these luminaries (Lily Langtry, for example) endorsed corsets the way modern athletes endorse sneakers and basketballs (and also the way contemporary women, such as Elizabeth Taylor, endorse perfume).

The relationship between the latest desire manufactured for (and experienced by) the "boys" and the latest fashion produced for (and displayed by) the "girls" is also sketched out in the second verse of "Those Lovely Seaside Girls": "The boys observe the latest thing in socks, / They learn the time by looking at the clocks." A "clock," in addition to its obvious meaning, is "a short embroidered or woven ornament on each side or on the outer side of a stocking." Here, once again, is a "kind of language" between "boys and girls." It is a semerotic system mediated by the complex media machine of fashion, mass production, and advertising. "Boys" are as much an abstraction as "girls" in this equation because they "learn the time" by learning how to consume the latest images of femininity. Women using fashion to masquerade as "women" are the clocks by which men wind the watch of their own eroticism. The manufactured items women are taught to exhibit ("the latest thing in socks") become the signifiers of what the boys are taught to desire ("they learn the time by looking at the clocks"). The point to be made here is that both the woman's appearance and the man's desire have been produced in reference to a simulated gender construct that generates a semerotic system of hyperreal erotic impulses.

Because the lyrics of the music-hall songs were typically reprinted in advertisements and posters, their ideology circulated beyond actual performances. In videos on MTV (which seems to be an electronic equivalent of the music hall so popular in Joyce's day), the misogynistic sentiments of the male singer in "Those Lovely Seaside Girls" seem very much alive (and even more effectively disseminated). Brilliantly made-up women (in both senses of this phrase) are frequently splashed with mud, abandoned on dirt roads, or sprayed with hoses, all to the frustrated squeal and grind of "heavy metal" guitar. One of the theater posters (circa 1898) reproduced in Cheryl Herr's book *Joyce's Anatomy of Culture* has sentiments rather similar to "Those Lovely Seaside Girls," and suggests that the advertising trope of "the seaside girl" spawned a genre of frustrated male consumer songs, in which the men contrive to sneak free peeks at the promenading "women":

> I also am a modest man,
> And when at the seaside,
> I hate to see men stare while girls,
> Are bathing in the tide;
> Oh, no! I'm not a hypocrite,
> I practice what I preach,
> And whilst the girls are bathing, I
> Am never on the beach

But I'm, near it, nice and near it,
I seek a nice secluded spot
And thro' my glasses see a lot,
Quite near it, oh, so near it,
Not near enough to get run in—but near it! (203).[31]

IX. Legal tender: The blooming of Milly

Bloom also thinks about his daughter, Milly, in the context of "Those Lovely Seaside Girls" (in fact, the first appearance of this song in *Ulysses* occurs in her letter, which Bloom reads in "Calypso"). At the age of fifteen, she is entering the same period of "feminine" adolescence to which Gerty, at the age of twenty-two, is still trying to cling. Richards notes, "The seaside girl eulogized adolescence and signaled the formation of what we now call 'youth culture'. At one and the same time she marked off the adolescent female body as an object of commodity culture and changed the shape of women's anatomy by making that body normative and compulsory" (*Commodity Culture,* 241). One reason Bloom is so sensitive to Milly's adolescence is that he understands she is leaving girlhood behind and entering the sexual marketplace of womanhood: "A wild piece of goods. Her slim legs running up the staircase. Destiny. Ripening now. Vain: very" (*U,* 293). As Richards makes clear, the "ripening" female body was the primary focus of almost all advertisements targeted toward women. "Every patent medicine advertiser's dream," Richards writes, is to have "every act of consumption . . . become an act of rejuvenation" (241).

Bloom recalls that Milly already possessed, while only a young girl, a sense that her own complexion lacked the "rejuvenating" effect supplied by rouge: "He smiled with troubled affection at the kitchen window. Day I caught her in the street pinching her cheeks to make them red. Anemic a little. Was given milk too long" (*U,* 293). In trying to explain, with reference to her feeding habits as an infant, why Milly pinches her cheeks to make them red, Bloom misses the point; he unwittingly accepts as normative the "pink and white" complexion endorsed by advertisements designed to sell rouge. In effect, he nominates a biological cause to explain why Milly has failed to meet what is in fact the artificial "pink and white" complexion of the rouged seaside girl. Thus Milly's complexion is seen, both by her and her father, as being in need of an "act of rejuvenation" that can only be brought about by an "act of consumption." Milly's pinching of her cheeks indicates she is already conditioned to be a reliable consumer of "feminine" cosmetic products as soon as she is allowed to do so.

In Bloom's phrase "day I caught her" there is a clear implication that he has scolded her for trying at too young an age to reproduce a cosmetic effect permissible only when she is older. On the one hand, Bloom reasons that the coloring supplied by rouge is more "healthy" and "natural" than Milly's pale ("anemic") complexion, and yet it is also perfectly clear to him that she is (at least on the day he "caught her") still too young to sport this "natural" look. But Bloom also knows that cosmetics, like lingerie, are synonymous with "product enhancement." The woman who uses rouge and eyeliner is understood to be a competitor in the sexual marketplace, and even though the "feminine" look she exhibits is trumpeted as that of a young girl, anyone who is in fact a young girl is forbidden to implicate herself in the semerotic network designed to attract the attention of the male consumer.

Indeed, advertisements featuring the trope of "the seaside girl" deliberately exploit the tension of this paradox because, as Richards makes clear, they instruct mature women on how to look and act like a young girl: "Many seaside girls were in fact seaside women. A 1928 advertising handbook called *Advertising for Women* makes it clear that what mattered was not actual youth but the appearance of what was uniformly called 'youthfulness,' defined as the 'desire to remain attractive—young—in the eyes of man'. . . . The ideal type of womanhood has become prolonged girlhood" (*Commodity Culture,* 244). Thus, girls are forbidden to use the very cosmetics they will later use as women in their effort to look like (seaside) "girls." The unacknowledged reason that young girls are forbidden by their elders to use products designed to prolong "girlhood" is that, in the sexual marketplace, "women" posing as "girls" present a semerotic message that no one is comfortable seeing if it emanates from someone who is in fact still a girl.

Significantly, Bloom's very next recollection of Milly amounts to a proud parent's debunking of the final verse in "Those Lovely Seaside Girls"; whereas the "girls" in the song lose their "pink and white" complexions in a manner delightful to the male singer, Bloom recalls that when Milly went out on a boat in rough weather, she struck a picturesque pose that refutes the pathetic image of the seasick seaside girls: "On the Erin's King that day round the Kish. Damned old tub pitching about. *Not a bit funky.* Her pale blue scarf loose in the wind with her hair" (*U,* 54, emphasis added). In addition, his recollection makes it clear that it is Milly's own hair—and not "golden hair from Regent Street"—that is blown back along with her "pale blue scarf" in a forthright image of autonomy and resiliency. In his typically anecdotal yet nominally scientific manner, Bloom is rejecting the rather cruel final verse of "Those Lovely Seaside Girls."

And yet Bloom will "consume" the image of the seaside girl in "Nausicaa" even though, in "Calypso," he regrets that his own daughter will inevitably enter this same marketplace: "A soft qualm, regret, flowed down his backbone, increasing. Will happen, yes. Prevent. Useless: can't move. Girl's sweet light lips" (*U*, 294). As a businessman and an advertiser, however, and not as a parent, Bloom is fascinated by how women learn to market themselves. When thinking along these lines, he seems to accept the necessity of Milly's somehow learning the tricks of the trade: "Neat way she carries parcels too. Attract men, small thing like that. Holding up her hand, shaking it, to let the blood flow back when it was red. Who did you learn that from: Nobody. Something the nurse taught me. O, don't they know!" (*U*, 304). Once in this mood of professionally evaluating Milly's increasingly sophisticated marketing techniques, Bloom is able to move to a concise comparison of his daughter and Gerty: "Straight on her pins anyway not like the other" (*U*, 305). This sort of cool comparative glance again approximates the gaze of someone comparing two similar items in the competitive atmosphere of a department store.

Ironically, it is the manner in which Milly conducts herself while shopping ("neat way she carries parcels") that Bloom sees as having a direct bearing on how attractively her sexuality is packaged: "Attract men, small thing like that." The system in which women promenade and men stare frames even the most subtle gestures of a woman. As Foucault maintains, "Sexuality is not the most intractable element in power relations, but rather one of those endowed with the greatest instrumentality: useful for the greatest number of maneuvers and capable of serving as a point of support, as a linchpin, for the most varied strategies" (*History of Sexuality*, 103). But Foucault implies that these "power relations" somehow take place on a level playing field where everyone competes for personal gain. It is here that Irigaray's economic and psychoanalytic theory of "women on the market" offers a compelling explanation of what organizes the instrumental quality of sexuality, what monitors the production and consumption of "the greatest number of maneuvers," and why women must occupy a position as salable objects.

To put the case as simply as possible, female sexuality is transformed into the standardized commodity of "femininity" so that it may serve as the commodified standard by which the relative worth of "varied strategies" in the economic system of semerotics will be evaluated: "Commodities can only enter into relationships under the watchful eyes of their 'guardians'. It is out of the question for them to go to 'market' on their own, enjoy their own worth among themselves, speak to each other, desire each other, free from the control of seller-buyer-consumer subjects. And the interests of businessmen require that commodities relate to each other as rivals" (Irigaray, 196).[32] This atmosphere of desperate contention produces the behavior among women that Bloom takes as a "natural" exhibit of a woman's "essential" dislike for other women.

Gerty is equally scornful of a "new" marketing strategy that only women who are "straight on their pins" can employ:

> In bloomers smart, they captivate the heart, when cycling down the prom. ("Those Lovely Seaside Girls")
>
> She was a womanly woman not like other flighty girls unfeminine he had known, those cyclists showing off what they hadn't got. (*U*, 293)

She presumes that Bloom has probably noticed the way the new invention of cycling, and the ad campaign that succeeded in making it acceptable for a woman to cycle, has brought about a new way to show off a woman's leg, a way that also meets the requirement of appearing to be unselfconscious (he certainly has, as has the lyricist of "Seaside Girls"!). Nevertheless, she consoles herself that, as he has a rather old-fashioned appearance, perhaps he has not accepted this latest permutation of what is deemed "feminine"; perhaps he rejects the new (improved!) kinetic display of "femininity" and longs instead for last year's model of static perfection.

So what does it mean, finally, that the seaside girls get seasick? The song "Those Lovely Seaside Girls" is one of the most omnipresent allusions in *Ulysses*. At various times, the refrain of this song is closely associated with Bloom, Blazes Boylan, Milly, Molly, and Gerty. Indeed, the full dimensions of Blazes and Molly's love tryst cannot be understood without detailed reference to the complex commercial interactions that underlie their affair. Blazes Boylan, for example, takes care that a present comes before he does; Molly muses that gifts of lingerie are in order if the affair is to continue; and Bloom himself takes a good deal of comfort in what he sees as the unemotional, economic dimension of his wife's semerotic intercourse with Blazes: "And they like dressing one another for the sacrifice. Milly delighted with Molly's new blouse. At first. Put them all on to take them all off. . . . Us too: the tie he wore, his lovely socks and turnedup trousers" (*U*, 302). In this context, Molly's affair takes on the erotic charge of a shopping spree with Blazes Boylan as her big "spender."

Indeed, the entire stock market of the male-defined sexual economy depends on women's masquerading as "feminine," that is to say, as the objects of transaction in all symbolic exchange operations (erotic, economic, and cultural):

> For, without the exploitation of the body-matter of women, what would become of the symbolic process that governs society? What modification would this process, this society, undergo, if women, who have been only objects of consumption or exchange, necessarily aphasic, were to become a "speaking subject" as well? . . .
>
> That would not fail to challenge the discourse that lays down the law today, that legislates on everything, including sexual difference, to such an extent that the existence of another sex, of an other, that would be woman, still seems, in its terms, unimaginable. (Irigaray, 85)

No wonder the confidence of the male singer swells as he reports the final image of the seasick seaside girls "hanging o'er the vessel's side."

What this image inadvertently acknowledges, however, is that beneath all the frills of "femininity," the body of a woman is still left unaccounted for. Eveline (in Joyce's story "Eveline") is an unsentimentalized seaside girl frozen in a posture of nightmarish exclusion:

> —Come!
>
> No! No! No! It was impossible. Her hands clutched the iron in frenzy. Amid the seas she sent a cry of anguish!
>
> . . . . She set her white face to him, passive, like a helpless animal. Her eyes gave him no sign of love or farewell or recognition. (*D*, 41)

Her inarticulate cry and her frantic yet unspoken exclamation "No!" both combine to form a different sort of nausea, one in which familiar landmarks of the semerotic system—such as "love," "farewell," and "recognition"—are wholly absent.

The implication of the song "Those Lovely Seaside Girls" is that, once back on solid ground, the "girls" will set their wigs straight, smooth their stockings, and reapply their rouge. Having once experienced the severely debilitating vertigo that results from being forced to abandon the masquerade of femininity, they will cling to it more absolutely as they gratefully resume their promenade along the pier (a disappointed bridge, as Stephen instructs his class). The final verse of the song acts as a preemptive punishment and humiliation for any woman who refuses to become a "woman." What says the patriarchal order to the idea of a new (improved!) social order in which women cease to function as objects of exchange? As the male singer says to his exclusively "masculine" audience (through the medium of a woman's passive body), "your head it simply swirls."

5

Molly Bloom's "Lifestyle"

The Performative as Normative

Consumption is not a passive mode of assimilation. . . . [It] is an active mode of relations (not only to objects, but to the collectivity and to the world), a systematic mode of activity and a global response on which our whole cultural system is founded.[1]

[S]ure you cant get on in this world without style.

(*U*, 618)

Money don't buy everything, it's true.
But what it don't buy, I can't use.

(Barry Gordy)

Life-style, according to the *Oxford English Dictionary,* was "a term originally used by Alfred Adler (1870–1937) to denote a person's basic character as established early in childhood which governs his reactions and behaviour." The idea that *lifestyle* (the word was hyphenated for a few decades, but appears now as one word) once designated something as organic and precultural as "a person's basic character" must strike us as odd, given the word's current usage, where it indicates an individual's or a group's established pattern of consumption. On the front page of the *New York Times* on March 30, 1991, for example, we read: "If you look at the records you find that on one of her trips Imelda [Marcos] was able to spend $6,000 on the first day for chocolates. That is the kind of *lifestyle* that used up the money" (emphasis added). Of course, Ms. Marcos's astonishing shoe collection is better known to the public than her prodigious sweet tooth, but her conspicuous pattern of excess consumption is consistently described and vilified as a "lifestyle." When this style of consumption is directly compared to the poverty of the rural people of the Philippines—people who are understood to represent "real" life, rather than a "lifestyle"—pejorative adjectives such as *obscene* are added. Such nomenclature is intended to reflect a general moral outrage that one individual should aggressively consume so many luxury items while her country's people subsist on nothing more than their daily bread.

In another example of the contemporary usage of the word *lifestyle,* the popular American television show entitled *Lifestyles of the Rich and Famous* presents various homes as showcases of spectacular abundance. In this show, the "rich and famous" people are considerably less interesting to the viewer than the spectacular and detailed pattern of consumption (a "systematic mode of activity," to use Baudrillard's term). Put another way, the people are no more and no less to the viewer than the signifying constellation of objects with which they surround themselves.

The point I want to make relative to the word *lifestyle* and Molly's complex ruminations in the final chapter of *Ulysses* is that although the word *lifestyle* is not available to her in 1904 (nor was it available to Joyce in 1922), her use of the word *style* to denote "a way of being" ("sure you cant get on in this world without style") clearly forecasts the intricate integration of identity and commodity objects currently celebrated or denigrated as a "lifestyle."[2] Whereas a "style" may refer to the cut of a hat, or a mode of speaking and writing, "lifestyle" necessarily involves the transformation of commodities into a theatrical spectacle within which the consumer performs his or her "life" through the presentation of "style":

> The consumer is not (just) an active appropriator of objects for sale. His or her entire identity, the constitution of the self as a social subject, a "citizen of consumer society," depends on the acquisition of appropriate objects: appropriate for the time (the seasons of fashion) and for the image which s/he is to project via the nuances of codes in dress and possessions—all the appurtenances of a "lifestyle" that can be recognized by other members of the society.[3]

The consumer's interior aspirations are approximately signified in a careful display likewise intended for consumption by a mass audience.

When Molly complains that "sure you cant get on in this world without style all going in food and rent when I get it Ill lash it around I tell you in fine style," we can see in her juxtaposition of ideas, as well as in her awkward repetition of the word *style,* that she is trying to articulate an urge to be a modern consumer with a "lifestyle" (and not merely a woman able to dress in the latest "style"). Her phrase "you cant get on in this world," for example, indicates that in "this world"—that is to say, Molly's contemporary world—an individual whose money is "all going in food and rent" lacks what we now call the "discretionary income" needed to support a lifestyle that solicits the gaze of others. As Wicke points out, a lifestyle, even though privately manufactured by a consumer, still must be made visible to others or it cannot be said to exist at all.[4]

Ireland's colonial position relative to the British Empire makes the adoption of a "lifestyle" particularly problematic. Developing a "lifestyle" is simply not possible for a citizen in any economy where it is presumed one's income must "all go in food and rent"; and yet, with absentee landlords and economic restrictions on Catholics, this is essentially the sort of economy Ireland had up until the early twentieth century. In the *New York Times,* an advertising executive had this to say about the difficulty of introducing western advertising into recently liberated Eastern Europe: "It would be a major mistake to try lifestyle advertising, because their lifestyles are just beginning. . . . They must develop their own style by drawing from their own heritage." Another executive stated, "At the moment, what our Western clients are looking for is not advertising; it's understanding of their markets."[5] The goal of "understanding their markets" is to learn how to commodify their "heritage" so that life can be recast into the marketable commodity "lifestyle." I would suggest that the situation of the West vis-à-vis Eastern Europe is not unlike that of nineteenth-century England looking for a new market for commodities in relatively rural Ireland.

Significantly, the so-called Celtic Twilight—championed by Yeats and rejected by Joyce—resisted this commercial colonization by going in search of the perfectly uncommodified peasant—one whose "own style" would in no way reflect a British "lifestyle," and one whose "heritage" would be incapable of being translated into a "market" by England. But as the project by Haines demonstrates, even the clever sayings of those Irish folk who have never heard of Plumtree's Potted Meat, are, if marketed correctly, a salable commodity. The search for the Irish peasant that Haines is conducting is the commercial equivalent of Yeats's and Lady Gregory's more nationalistic project (and I sense a deliberate juxtaposition of the two projects on Joyce's part). Where Yeats would hold back the introduction of commodity culture into Ireland, Joyce sees such a plan as impossible, self-delusional, and even selfish, given that Yeats has no use for the sort of "trinkets" mass marketing and mass production make possible for the lower classes. And yet, if Yeats has no patience with the vulgar trinkets of mass production, clearly, as I discussed earlier, trivial items such as souvenir purses delight and sustain a character like Maria in Joyce's short story "Clay."

Baudrillard has defined consumption in the twentieth century not as the quantity of one's possessions, or the insatiable urge to gratify specific desires with specific commodities, but rather *the organization* of all these commodities—both inside the home and outside in the street—into a complex semiotic message that signifies the "life" we imagine we are living (*Selected Writings,* 71). Although Baudrillard's theory of desire bears some resemblance to that of Lacan, he speaks of the "language" of *things* as well as words. For Baudrillard, the objects and desires strategically integrated by a consumer are signifiers that constitute a language of commodities that can be understood—by oneself in conjunction with others—as a "lifestyle." The language of things is further publicized and made sacred by the ceremony of advertising, and this permits the "personalization" of commodities into the private prayer of an individual's immediate environment (an environment that, paradoxically, seeks to elicit a global response even while claiming to be personal).

The "world" that results from this interpenetration of the global and the personal is a simulacrum within which the consumer experiences life as a style of consumption: "[I]n consumption objects become a vast paradigm designating another language through which something else speaks. . . . The flight from one signifier to another is no more than the surface reality of a desire, which is insatiable because it is founded on a lack. And this desire, which can never be satisfied, signifies itself locally in a succession of objects and needs" (Baudrillard, *Selected Writings,* 45). As long as this flight from one signifier to another is possible, then desire is a language that, like the best advertising, promises "complete satisfaction" in the near future (provided one continually "takes flight" to the "new" object).

When Gallaher refers to Little Chandler's act of marrying as "putting your head in a sack," he is attacking Little Chandler's lifestyle, and belittling it in relation to his own apparently boundless ability to consume and be consumed: "Everything in Paris is gay. . . . They believe in enjoying life. . . . they've a great feeling for the Irish there. When they heard I was from Ireland they were ready to eat me, man. . . . There's no woman like the Parisienne—*for style, for go*" (*D,* 77, emphasis added). Both Molly and Gallaher link the word *style* to a verb phrase in an attempt to show the relationship of "style" to the dynamic, theatrical, and increasingly spectacular process of "life" and not merely to the static image of unstylish consumption, where "all" goes "for food and rent." Gallaher struggles just as much as Molly does to describe something not adequately designated in the outmoded word *style.*

I. Performing the normative: Dramatizing the everyday

By the turn of the century, advertising had gone well beyond merely announcing the price and availability of a product. Instead, both advertising copy and magazine articles operated together to formulate what we might call "a philosophy of things." Countless ads suggested that what one buys, where and when one buys it, the manner in which one chooses to display it, and the imagined audience that is expected to see it all combine to produce a stable identity where a performative structure is tacitly (mis)construed as a "normative personality." In Lacanian parlance, the clothes we wear and the things we arrange around us can function as our construction of the benevolent gaze of the Other who can "see" that we are who we can only imagine ourselves to be.

In an "article" (really an advertisement) published in the July 1904 *Weldon's Ladies' Journal,* the latest fashion is actually presented not merely as a "style," but as a style of living, and the private act of shopping becomes an off-stage endeavor that must be meticulously prosecuted if one is to be a success when the curtain rises:

> Fashions for July
>
> What is Worn. THE halcyon days of an English summer encourage us to don the prettiest raiment we possess. Our frothiest muslin frocks and smartest of cool linen suits are none too bright and gay to grace the golden period of the year. The prospect of holidays, and necessary outfits, are subject meet for enthusiastic discussion at the present moment, and the pros and cons of washing frocks, muslin robes, and lovely millinery usurp all our attention. . . . Exquisite mercerised sateens and lawns, with all the appearance of the best foulard silks, make up into inexpensive yet elegant little gowns.

As a first step in presenting the style of living, the article (which, of course, functions as an advertisement) puts the scenery in place in a manner that also sets the consumer's mood ("the halcyon days of an English summer"). From there, the costumes appropriate to such a setting are detailed ("our frothiest muslin frocks"); after this, the ad establishes the need to carefully synchronize this display with the imagined audience. We can assume our imagined audience has read the same ad we are reading, and that they will applaud "style" or hiss at unauthorized deviations, just like the well-primed audience of a melodrama. Phrases such as "necessary outfits . . . enthusiastic discussion . . . pros and cons" constitute the central paradox of fashion discourse: the ephemeral is imperative, at least for now.

The woman who buys in accordance with this multi-layered scenario consumes, as Baudrillard has phrased it, in "an active mode of relations (not only to objects, but to the collectivity and to the world.)" A "systematic mode of activity" is exercised in the pursuit of a hoped-for "global response." This sense of others seeing us as we wish to see ourselves may be likened to Lacan's theory of the gaze, "which circumscribes us, and which in the first instance makes us beings who are looked at."[6]

Henri Lefebvre, as Jules David Law notes, designated June 16, 1904, as the "momentous eruption of everyday life into literature." Law examines this concept further and asks: "The history and the culture of everyday life: are these parodic oxymorons, or modernist ideologies par excellence? And if it is possible to write the history and the culture of everyday life, is Joyce's work an authentic—or even, perhaps, a unique—contribution to that project?"[7] Law goes on to suggest that the quotidian, or the "everyday," is the realm of the unintentional: "Freudian everyday life is defined precisely as the realm of experience in which our actions and expressions are so habitual and un-thought-out at the conscious level that their disruption by unconscious intentions is all the more likely to be noticed" ("Simulation," 202). But the effect of pursuing a "lifestyle" is that the unintentional (the Freudian everyday) is what commodity culture converts into the intention to consume (the commodification of the everyday).

In a current commercial for the candy Skittles, a group of visibly bored people is shown viewing artwork in a museum and listening to a lecture. The lecturer drones on in self-satisfied ignorance of their detachment, and the people stand listless, their thoughts wandering, until the action of popping a Skittle into one's mouth causes a flood of noise and color to escalate the moment into one of spectacle and sensation (waves of brightly colored water come crashing through the room, silencing the stunned lecturer and delighting the somnolent crowd). The quotidian is equated with boredom and sensory deprivation, and countless products with a varying degree of sophistication (candy, handheld video games, walkman radios) puncture and punctuate the "unintentional" world (coded as aimless and undifferentiated) with intentions to buy, sell, and "have fun."

The obsession with spectacle in nineteenth-century theater is a curious prototype of modern television advertising. As M. R. Booth suggests, Victorian theater companies were obsessed with presenting on stage a spectacular display of materials, fashions, and commodities: "The very existence of new materials, new stage machinery, and new methods of lighting impelled them into a dramatic structure which in part existed to display the ingenuity of machinist, gasman, head carpenter, costume designer, and stage manager."[8] In nineteenth-century popular theater (especially pantomime and melodrama), a major consideration of a production became "how large numbers of actors and quantities of expensive fabrics could best be deployed" (Booth, 64).[9] Indeed, a humorous contemporary poem describing the "Cave Scene" of the pantomime *Ali Baba and the Forty Thieves* suggests that the attitude of the audience for Victorian spectacular theater became not simply that of a playgoer, but that of a shopper as well: "Whilst ladies, who with awe this sight regard, / Whisper, 'I'm sure it costs four pounds a yard'" (qtd. in Booth, 88–89).

Like a clever lighting director or costume designer, the writer of the *Weldon's* article quoted above also offers tips to the would-be actress/consumer on how to design a wardrobe that looks expensive—but isn't. John Mercer was only one of several textile manufacturers who invented ways to treat ordinary cloth to make it appear extraordinary, and fabric that had been submitted to the process he invented was referred to as "mercerised": "*Exquisite mercerised sateens* and lawns, with all the appearance of the best foulard silks, make up into *inexpensive yet elegant* little gowns." Part of the fun—as well as the drama—of developing and critiquing lifestyles is trying to see past someone's appearance directly to the theatrical process that has enhanced that appearance. At the same time, however, one must struggle to hide from one's own spectators the "mercerised" quality of one's own public performance.

There is little wonder that theater audiences translated the appearance of costumes into estimates of what they were worth per yard; department stores at this time also benefited enormously from, and were completely transformed by, "the very existence" of "new materials, new stage machinery, and new methods of lighting." As Rachel Bowlby has said of the modern department store window that faces out into the street, "[g]lass and lighting . . . created a spectacular effect, a sense of theatrical excess coexisting with the simple availability of individual items for purchase. Commodities were put on show in an attractive guise, becoming unreal in that they were images set apart from everyday things, and real in that they were there to be bought and taken home to enhance the ordinary environment" (2). As Kim Devlin has noted, Molly "perceptively recognizes in the seemingly real the paradox of the genuinely fraudulent."[10] And she does so, I would add, not out of some Hamlet-like "Nay, madam, I know not seems" disgust with the playacting of emotions, but rather as part of her constant effort to enhance the quotient of "genuine fraudulence" in her own performance. The idea of the home as a combination of onstage and offstage, where Molly can either successfully perform or be caught between acts, is illustrated further by her aversion to answering the door for someone whom she is not expecting: "[Y]ou think its the vegetables then its somebody and you all undressed or the door of the filthy sloppy kitchen blows open the day old frosty face Goodwin called about the concert in Lombard street and I just after dinner all flushed and tossed with boiling old stew dont look at me professor I had to say Im a fright yet" (*U*, 613).

The scene played with Goodwin is painfully awkward for Molly because it is unexpectedly real; she is caught backstage in two different ways: first, she is not prepared to step into the footlights of Goodwin's gaze ("dont look at me"); and second, the house itself is not ready to have the curtain raised ("the door of the filthy sloppy kitchen blows open"). Furthermore, these first two exposures are aggravated by the fact that Goodwin is there to discuss an even more public performance: the concert in Lombard street. As Leopold Bloom has noted to himself, there is a mirror in place by the door so that Molly can glance at her reflection before she opens it. It is also worth noting in this context that Molly's fondest memories (and erotic memories, as I discuss later in this chapter) all showcase her clear belief that for the duration of the recalled moment in which she appeared to the other person—in terms of her style, her strategy of consumption, and her posture—she exhibited herself exactly according to the theatrical tableau she had planned: "[T]here I was leaning over him with my white ricestraw hat to take the newness out of it the left side of my face the best my blouse open for his last day . . ." (*U*, 625). This memory is the fruit of the work of consumption. Molly experiences the newness of sex even as she is "taking the newness" out of her hat in a manner that keeps her best profile on display. The "everyday" is made dramatic by Molly's posture, her new hat, and the special style of her blouse (designed, like Gallaher's Parisienne women, "for go") (Law, 2).

Molly's feelings about being surprised at home also indicate that she stages and performs her lifestyle for an imagined audience that is of a particular social class: "You think its the vegetables and then its somebody." If someone from a different class were to observe her (the man who delivers vegetables, for example), she would not feel she had been caught unaware because he is not part of the imagined audience for which she performs. Like the popular actresses of her time, Molly knows that an individual's persuasive presentation of a manner and an attitude—whether in the theater or in the home—requires good costuming and appropriate set design. When Molly thinks about the possibility of taking Stephen as a lover, her first thought is that the pre-publicity photo Bloom has already shown him puts the specifics of her drama of seduction into peril: "[S]howing him my photo its not good of me I ought to have got it taken in drapery that never looks out of fashion" (*U*, 637). Molly's momentary regret that she is not "in drapery" reflects the particular plot she has in mind with Stephen—a plot that involves her being cast as "the immortal woman" of his poetry. Such a woman, destined for immortality, should not be sporting this or that fashion; instead, her costume should call eternity to the audience's mind with a style that seems impervious to the crude vagaries of time.

By contrast, when Molly imagines the particulars of her wardrobe in reference to the gaze of Blazes Boylan, "drapery" and classical posing are the last things on her mind: "I wonder what kind of underwear he likes none at all I think" (*U*, 626). Certainly one could argue Molly exhibits some phallocentrism in this passage, and that she appears to be more of a male fantasy than a woman, but I would suggest instead that Molly thinks of the men with whom she is involved (or with whom she might yet be involved) in the way an actress thinks of her leading man; she is willing to cater to the needs of their performance, but only as a way to assure a more dramatic role for herself.

In this regard, Blazes Boylan has already proved a partial disappointment as a leading man for Molly because the second act of her imagined scenario with him calls for him to write her passionate love letters: "I wish somebody would write me a loveletter his wasnt much and *I told him he could write what he liked* yours ever Hugh Boylan" (*U*, 624, emphasis added). Like Annie Chandler or Bartell D'Arcy, Boylan has missed his cue. Furthermore, Molly's deliberate prompting makes it clear that she is expecting an involved performance from Boylan that is not supposed to open and close on the same night. Significantly, she is not worried about the veracity of the letters, but only about their ability to make the everyday dramatic: "[T]rue or no it fills up your whole day and life always something to think about every moment and see it all round you like a new world" (*U*, 624). Likewise, in the first act of her imagined tryst with Stephen Dedalus, she makes him faint with appreciation for the display of herself (a genuine form of applause that, unlike clapping, is not easily feigned). But in return, in the second act, he makes her the sole subject of his poetry. Molly, in other words, dresses to please, but not without the expectation of producing pleasure for herself.

Indeed, by casting herself as a performer in her own productions of pleasure, she performs not merely as an actress but as a director as well: "Ill read and study all I can find or learn a bit off by heart if I knew who he likes so he wont think me stupid . . . and I can teach him the other part Ill make him feel all over him till he half faints under me then hell write about me lover and mistress publicly too with our 2 photographs in all the papers when he becomes famous" (*U*, 638). The favorite technique employed by both Gabriel and Molly within the fantasy staging of their own erotic melodramas is the tableau—a "device of dramaturgy," Peter Brooks tells us, where "we grasp melodrama's primordial concern to make its signs clear, unambiguous, and impressive."[11] As in the structure of melodrama, Molly envisions a mute tableau that reveals a "moment of truth" ("till he half faints under me") followed by the public and blatantly triumphant achievement of all her long-thwarted goals ("our 2 photographs in all the papers"). As Brooks has argued, melodrama is a genre where "'life' has become wholly 'drama,' and . . . this offers the actor *an unrivalled opportunity for the uninhibited play with style*" (48, emphasis added). Or, "lashing it around," as Molly would have it. Molly's urge to "play with style" leads her to wonder what style of underwear Boylan yearns to see and what style of poetry Stephen hopes to write. While she is willing to wear the one and recite the other, it is still her style she hopes to "lash around" in a production that features her own pleasure in a final tableau of impressive proportions.

II. "Oh! I'm spending!": The erotics of shopping

As Jennifer Wicke has argued, "eros itself arises out of the matrix of consumptive strategies . . . shopping is both a terrifying labor of scrutiny and frustration, as well as the site of the dream of satisfaction" (Wicke, *JJQ*, 18). In theatrical terms, the "work of consumption" is a behind-the-scenes endeavor that eventually, and hopefully invisibly, makes possible the public spectacle of a lifestyle performed before a live audience. When we are shopping, we imagine other people looking at what we are looking at, and from this vantage point try to imagine "what we will look like" when we are wearing it. In the passage from *Sweets of Sin* that catches Bloom's eye, the erotic triangle of "husband," "lover," and "the beautiful woman" is augmented by a different "site of the dream of satisfaction"—the department store: "*—All the dollarbills her husband gave her were spent in the stores on wondrous gowns and costliest frillies*" (*U*, 194, Joyce's emphasis). Here we need to recall that "spending" is Victorian slang for orgasm (Molly uses the term this way twice), and then we can see that "the beautiful woman" is causing her husband to "spend" dollar bills, which she, through the act of shopping, converts into "costliest frillies," which in turn will cause her lover, Raoul, to "spend."

Indeed, having been to the department store en route to meeting her lover, "the beautiful woman" is utterly confident that the silent tableau of her appearance—not unlike that of a mannequin in a department store window, or an actress doing a tried and true "star turn" on stage—will vanquish the "suspicious glare" with which Raoul initially greets her: "*—You are late, he spoke hoarsely, eying her with a suspicious glare. The beautiful woman threw off her sabletrimmed wrap, displaying her queenly* *shoulders and heaving embonpoint. An imperceptible smile played round her perfect lips as she turned to him calmly*" (*U*, 194, Joyce's italics). If her smile is in fact "imperceptible" (as opposed to the more widely used cliché "barely perceptible"), then Raoul can't even see it, and this description of a woman "displaying" her fur coat, queenly shoulders, and "heaving embonpoint" should be read as a private expression of satisfaction and confidence that is emanating from a beautiful consumer who is well pleased as a result of her own "spending." Indeed, fresh from the Bon Marché department store, sporting her "imperceptible smile," she is the Mona Lisa of commodity culture.[12]

Embonpoint means excessive plumpness or stoutness, but it also carries the literal translation of "in good condition," which suggests that "the beautiful woman's" physical excess is also figured as a sort of perfectly maintained material abundance. One of the phrases that stays in Bloom's mind after his initial reading of the passage is "(*her heaving embonpoint!*)." This image of an abundant and spectacular excess deliciously threatening to overspill its confines (heaving!) is also, as I have already suggested, a basic feature of set design in Victorian spectacular theater. It is, as well, a basic strategy of merchandise display in the newly illuminated department store windows. Inside the store, bins were filled to "overflowing," and products were stacked in giant pyramids in an effort to overwhelm the shopper with the visual equivalent of luxury, pleasure, and satisfaction. Abundance, in other words, and excess as well, is an integral part of the seductive dynamic of spectacle, display, and "lifestyle."

As Veblen's famous phrase "conspicuous consumption" (coined in 1900) makes clear, a modern lifestyle is nothing if not visible, and the socially successful consumer must display a pattern of consumption as a visible "style." The idea of a stout woman's body as a metaphor for commodity excess and spectacular display is suggested by the description of how Raoul reacts to what "the beautiful woman" shows him: "*Her mouth glued on his in a luscious voluptuous kiss while his hands felt for the opulent curves inside her deshabille*" (*U*, 194, Joyce's italics). "Luscious" has the connotation of "sweet to excess," and "voluptuous" implies "full of . . . indulgence in luxury." Her "simple" kiss, then, overwhelms Raoul with the sensual equivalent of a "spectacle of excess." Furthermore, "opulent" denotes physical stoutness, but it is also used, especially in turn-of-the-century economic discussions, to characterize either a lavish display of merchandise or an abundance of "natural" (that is, undeveloped) resources.

In this context, Raoul's invasive and appropriating gesture ("his hands felt for the opulent curves") might additionally be read as a psychological echo of the foreign policy of an imperialist economy that is attracted to the luscious, voluptuous, opulent, and untouched resources of a land like India, Africa, or Ireland. Stephen Dedalus, in the "Proteus" episode, has already associated the image of one mouth "glued" to another mouth with vampirism, and so "the beautiful woman" has "her mouth glued on his" even as her natural resources are appropriated ("felt for"). She also poses—in the form of a seductively packaged object—as the sort of sensual and spectacular commodity that imperialism makes possible. My primary point, then, is that the scenario that stimulates Bloom at the turn of the century contains images of both commodity abundance and spectacular excess where the act of sex mirrors the act of consumption to the point that both foreplay and shopping lead to a climax of "spending."[13] Erotic experience for Molly and Leopold Bloom—in separate but equal ways—relates to a new form of market economy, a new style of merchandise display, and a new pattern of "individual" consumption. But this consumption is always collective in nature and in search of a global response. It is a "lifestyle," conducted within a social "reality" that permits the dramatization of the everyday.

Bloom, of course, is not a wealthy imperialist, and Ireland is still a colonized country. Accordingly, Bloom's erotic reverie is shattered by the intrusion of the profoundly unerotic shopkeeper:

> The shopman's uncombed grey head came out and his unshaven reddened face, coughing. He raked his throat rudely, puked phlegm on the floor. . . . and bent, showing a rawskinned crown, scantily haired.
>
> Mr Bloom beheld it.
>
> Mastering his troubled breath, he said:
>
> —I'll take this one.
>
> The shopman lifted eyes bleared with old rheum.
>
> —*Sweets of Sin,* he said tapping on it. That's a good one. (*U,* 194)

Aging and balding flesh, frank ill-health, disgusting secretion of body fluids—this shopman is as physical an anticlimax as "the beautiful woman" is a climax. The stimulating scenario of healthy, aggressive "masculine" imperialism and corresponding submission and opulent display is replaced by the unspectacular fact of an old (perhaps dying) shopkeeper making a few shillings by selling used books from a street cart. The most crucial strategy of seductive display—a strategy employed equally by the spectacular theater, the modern department store, and the "individual" consumer's attractive "lifestyle"—is to hide the unmediated reality that continues to exist behind the displayed illusion of reality. When this unmediated reality comes to the fore in the form of the shopkeeper, Bloom is able to "master his troubled breath" all too easily.

In the "halcyon days" of British imperialism, it is Lily Langtry, with her famous and opulent curves, who becomes the enviable standard for the "perfect" female form. Appropriately enough, it was widely understood that she was the lover of Prince Edward—the reigning symbol of Empire—(a relationship Molly ruminates upon). In "Ivy Day in the Committee Room," King Edward is cast as a dubious character by Mr. Lyons, but Mr. Henchy quickly defends him as "an ordinary knockabout like you and me. He's fond of his glass of grog and he's a bit of a rake, perhaps, and he's a good sportsman. Damn it, can't we Irish play fair?" (*D,* 132). The British imperialist figure feeling for opulent curves is merely "a bit of a rake," while Parnell, the colonialist politician, is characterized by Mr. Lyons as "[not] a fit man to lead us." Clearly Henchy supports implicitly the idea that imperialism is never having to say you're sorry. Bloom's hesitant fascination with Raoul's aggressive and unapologetic consumption of "the beautiful woman" suggests the complex ambivalence that a colonialist like Bloom feels—both anger and awe—for the institutionalized indifference with which imperial leaders "spend" at his expense.

The intersection of the Langtry/King Edward relationship with marketing is quite explicit in that Lily Langtry gave her name to a heavily advertised corset that promised to give all women similarly "opulent" curves. Approaching this from a different angle, there is another article in the July 1904 *Weldon's Ladies' Journal* entitled "Beauty for Women" and subtitled "There is no Power like the Magnetism of Curves":

> Beauty rules the world. . . . In every circle . . . there is a woman who is ruler—and there is also a secret of her power.
>
> This question is of vital interest to every girl or woman in England. When a little silent struggle takes place between two or three women for supremacy in their set, or for the place of queen in the heart of some man, who wins? Always the woman of beautiful figure, of attractive curves—and who realises her power. . . . For those who lack the natural development of bust, a new and remarkable treatment has been devised. It is called "Diano." . . . This treatment will quickly develop the bust six inches, and any woman can use it at home. (xxiii)

Women of Empire who wish to "rule the world" with a "secret power," and who compete for unrivaled "supremacy," must first develop their bust six inches more; that is to say, they must increase the attractiveness of their "natural" resources from a "masculine"/imperialist point of view. Indeed, a contemporary translation of "heaving embonpoint" might be "well-endowed," which indicates that a woman's bust—those "opulent curves" that make "a woman a ruler"—is also viewed, in a patriarchal economy, as her permanent fund or source of income.

The corset ad that Molly recalls, in addition to promising profitable curves, also promises to "obviate" ("eliminate disadvantages by effective measures") unprofitable ones.[14] This optimization of natural resources (the application of Diano), we are told, may be accomplished in a "personal" and "individual" act of consumption performed in the "privacy" of the home. But the collective nature of this act is apparent when we see, in a widely published advertisement, the "[opulent] curves" of a woman's breasts represented as the source of a secret and indomitable global power. "[H]e caressed them outside," Molly says when recalling the attention Mulvey paid to her breasts, "they love doing that its the roundness" (*U*, 625). Thus, in keeping with the metaphor of a woman's body as a colonized country, the product Diano urges "the women of England" to "develop" their natural resources and capitalize on the result.

The only way for women to capitalize on their resources is to pose successfully as a physical metaphor for the luxuriant and voluptuous excess of masculine imperialism; and, by doing so, seduce a man into spending some of his appropriated wealth on her. Or, as Molly Bloom states in her succinct summation of this same equation, "he's not a marrying man so somebody better get it out of him" (*U*, 617). Behind this act of seduction, as the *Sweets of Sin* excerpt suggests, there is a prior seduction to which the woman succumbs: "[T]he making of willing consumers readily fitted into the available ideological paradigm of a seduction of women by men, in which women would be addressed as yielding objects to the powerful male subject forming, and informing them of, their desires" (Bowlby, 22). Raoul's suspicious accusation ("You're late") indicates his fear that he has been kept waiting while "the beautiful woman" satisfied herself elsewhere. Her "imperceptible smile" of "private and individual" pleasure (it is, in fact, social and collective) indicates to him that she must have been spending without him. His suspicions are well founded—except that she has been seduced by the marketing techniques of a department store, and it is this—not another lover—that has caused her to spend.

When Molly recalls a purchase *not* made, she describes this lost moment with the same nostalgic yearning that characterizes her recollections of Mulvey: "[A] peachblossom dressing jacket *like the one long ago* in Walpoles *only* 8/6 or 18/6" (*U*, 641, my emphasis). One dimension of the "dear dead days beyond recall" is a nostalgia for a missed shopping opportunity. "I was thinking about a person *long ago*," Gretta tells Gabriel, in reference to Michael Furey (*D*, 218, my emphasis). But "the one long ago" may also be a peachblossom dressing jacket! Coupled with Molly's regret is the vague recollection that, at the time, it seemed too much to spend ("8/6 or 18/6"). The actual price has faded from memory, but the color of the dressing jacket—"peachblossom"—a term invented by the designer or the advertiser for marketing purposes, is nearly as vivid to her as the eyes of Michael Furey are to Gretta.

The cycle of seduction in the bedroom and the department store finally comes full circle when we learn, in the closing moments of *Ulysses,* that the most powerfully seductive line Leopold Bloom has ever spoken to her—the one that prompts her to ask him with her eyes to ask again—is "you are a flower of the mountain yes so we are flowers all a womans body yes that was one true thing he said in his life" (*U*, 643). His observation that her body is a flower is as unforgettable and seductive to her as the peachblossom jacket. Both Leopold Bloom and the department store retailer seduce Molly because they formulate a slogan about her body that she considers to be a "true thing."

When Bloom happens upon this floral metaphor, a metaphor that is at the "normative" center of Molly's pleasure construction (which is to say she does not view it as a role performed solely for the benefit of a man's excitement), she pays him the sort of compliment that any manager of a department store would love to hear: "I saw he understood or felt what woman is" (*U*, 643). At the turn of the century, it is the department stores, not men in general, who are most anxious to discover what makes a woman spend. It is significant, therefore, that Molly's "normative" idea of pleasure echoes a marketer's "performative" advertising strategy: "Wear this peachblossom jacket because your body is a flower."

We can better appreciate the department store marketer as someone unusually motivated to discover what a woman wants (as opposed to what he wants her to do for him) by imagining what Corley would have come up with if asked to describe the color of the dressing jacket—"orange tart" is one possibility. Even Freud's famous query "what does woman want?" sounds like the crucial question of a department store board meeting. Indeed, a saying made famous by the founder of the Marshall Field's department store, which later was used as the title of a book recounting the history of the store, was "Give the lady what she wants." Freud, of course, in line with the grasping Raoul, thought a woman's body was not a flower but "a dark continent"—which suggests to me that it is a good thing he never went into retail sales. His suggestion for naming the color of Molly's fondly recalled dressing jacket might have been "savage sunset." Such an item, even with identical styling, certainly would have remained on the shelf and out of Molly's mind.

Leopold Bloom, in keeping with his general sensitivity about marketing technique, rejects the novel *Fair Tyrants* in favor of *Sweets of Sin.* The purchase is a highly erotic interlude for him, but this should not blind us to the fact that he is a consumer making a "choice" in the (sexual) marketplace: "No. She wouldn't like that much. Got her it once. . . . *Sweets of Sin.* More in her line" (*U*, 194). Granted, this purchase has a more demonstrable physical effect on Bloom than his earlier purchase of lemon soap, but buying in a contemporary commodity culture, as the boy in "Araby" also demonstrates, frequently has an erotic dimension. Nor is Bloom's production of pleasure individual; it is collective in that he imagines its effect on Molly even as he experiences its effect on himself. Bloom's phrase about *Sweets of Sin* ("more in her line") is really a marketing term normally used to suggest the particular "line" of goods a merchant specializes in selling.

Bloom is correct that purchasing the book will not be an inducement for Molly to spend: "he brought me that twice I remember when I came to page 50 the part about where she hangs him up out of a hook with a cord flagellate sure theres nothing for a woman in that all invention made up" (*U*, 619). Molly objects to this scene as too staged—too obviously a performance. Like the excitement of watching a good play, eroticism depends on a suspension of disbelief. One must at least pretend that the performative is normative. We see from Molly's recollection that Bloom has tried to sell her on this idea not once, but twice. Given that the female body/flower metaphor strikes her as a "true thing," it is hardly surprising that she finds unstimulating the role of whipping the fanny of someone who is hanging from a hook ("there's nothing for a woman in that"). The dressing jacket that so attracted her, after all, was called "peachblossom" not "pink bottom."

Indeed, one of her central complaints about men (and Bloom in particular) is that they excessively gaze at her buttocks, where there is no possibility for a woman to stimulate herself by doing a "star turn": "[A]ny man thatd kiss a womans bottom Id throw my hat at him . . . where we havent 1 atom of any kind of expression in us all of us the same 2 lumps of lard" (*U*, 639). Molly wishes, like "the beautiful woman," to display herself in such a way that she can see from her lover's expression that her performance has that necessary erotic component of genuine fraudulence, like the look that made Blazes spend: "I gave my eyes that look with my hair a bit loose from the tumbling and my tongue between my lips up to him the savage brute" (*U*, 621). "Savage brute" is not so much what Boylan is; it is *the role* she has assigned to him as her leading man, to facilitate his acting as a foil to heighten the brilliance of her own performance. Blazes's pleasure consists of an involuntary spasm, while Molly's is a sustained tableau; a "star turn" is what turns her on.

III. Satisfaction guaranteed: Consumption and pleasure production

The act of sex in a commodity culture, like the act of consumption, is not motivated by "natural" and "individual" desire, but instead is a collective endeavor that produces pleasure as part of a collective enterprise:

> The truth about consumption is that it is a function of production and not a function of pleasure, and therefore, like material production, is not an individual function but one that is directly and totally collective. . . . Pleasure would define consumption for itself, as autonomous and final. But consumption is never thus. Although we experience pleasure for ourselves, when we consume we never do it on our own (the isolated consumer is the carefully maintained illusion of the ideological discourse on consumption). (Baudrillard, *Selected Writings,* 46)

In a commodity culture, to wear is to be aware; to live is to have a visible and collectively affirmed "lifestyle." Likewise, what one buys to put in the room of a home also makes that room a stage.

Dialogue between a husband and wife, against the backdrop of modern furnishings, is a popular advertising technique at the turn of the century. In one advertisement, for example, the wife's purchase of inferior "ladder tapes" for window blinds is cited as "The Cause of Their First Quarrel." In the first drawing, the wrecked blinds serve as the background for the husband's denunciation of his wife's shoddy pattern of consumption: "'Didn't I tell you to get Carr's Stamped Quality Ladder Tapes? Instead of which you get these wretched things, and'—(gives way to despair)." The drawing next to it is titled "Happy Reunion"; the blinds are nicely shut behind them, and, as we are told by the ad copy printed beneath the second picture: "They Lived Happy Ever Afterwards."

This two-act melodrama (the script even has stage directions) exclusively features the dramaturgical effect of the tableau, and thus converts the home into a stage. The inferior product serves as the backdrop against which the couple quarrels, and the advertised product provides the improved backdrop before which they enact their "Happy Reunion." The husband's ire has been aroused because he feels his wife has failed to observe the connection between a strategic pattern of consumption and the carefully maintained display of an enviable lifestyle. The couple's quarrel is a "private" drama brought about by the husband's concern that their "normative" performance, produced for an imagined audience, will instantly reveal itself as contrived if their props are in disrepair; after all, nothing more quickly reminds a spectator that he is watching a performance than to have part of the scenery fall down. The resolution of domestic strife by the timely intervention of a product is so endemic to turn-of-the-century advertising that one might well view the final tableau of "A Little Cloud" as the first panel of an advertisement for a product that fails to materialize. To turn "A Little Cloud" into an advertisement scenario, we need only imagine a subsequent panel saying, "Never run out of tea," superimposed on a picture of the happy couple, while the baby sleeps peacefully in the background.

In a different two-act melodrama, one that also uses two contrasting scenes, this time to advertise Monkey Brand soap, the first panel shows a husband shooting a pistol while he brandishes a decree of divorce before the tear-stricken and horrified face of his wife. The man and woman are drawn with oversized heads to emphasize theatrical expression. The murder, mayhem, and marital discord of the first panel have resulted because supper was served late in a dirty pan. In the second panel, the Monkey Brand trademark presides over the two smiling and complacent heads. "Without strife / Life's sublime; / Married bliss, / Happiness," reads the copy beneath the drawing.[15] The connection made between soap and "life" and "happiness" illustrates the collective "pleasure production" in an age of spectacle and theatrical culture, where only what can be dramatized is "real." As Rachel Bowlby puts it, "'All the world's a stage' takes its characteristic twentieth-century form in [the] novel of narcissistic consumer-actors, passively drifting up and down a line whose successive stages are marked by differences in the possession of wealth and commodities" (65).

In the production of pleasure, and in the construction of a "lifestyle," costume, scenery, expressive gesture, and dialogue are a collective illusion that structures the individual consumer's reality. When Bloom gives a melodramatic recitation of his childhood to the court in "Circe," Joyce makes explicit the connection among advertising, patterns of consumption, "happiness," and the production of a "lifestyle" staged in the home:

> *[H]e wanted . . . to lead a homely life in the evening of his days, permeated by the affectionate surroundings of the heaving bosom of the family. An acclimatised Britisher, he had seen . . . through the windows of loveful households . . . scenes truly rural of happiness of*

> *the better land with Dockrell's wallpaper at one and ninepence a dozen . . . [also] model young ladies playing on the pianoforte . . . what times the strains of the organtoned melodeon Britanniametalbound with four acting stops and twelvefold bellows, a sacrifice, greatest bargain ever.* (*U*, 377, Joyce's italics)

A piano is not only something to be played in Bloom's fantasy; it is also a prop in the presence of which we prepare to read aloud the ideal script of our lives. Bloom's idea of himself as an "acclimatised Britisher" also suggests that, at least to an extent, he has been successfully targeted by the British advertising firms who were trying to create an expanded market in Ireland for British products (converting "heritage" and "tradition" into [British] "lifestyle"). British advertising is as pervasive as the weather, thus "acclimatising" Irish consumers into "Britishers."

Bowlby claims, "Individuation, in the form of a modern self-image, is inseparable from appearance" (68). Not to be able to afford "style"—not to have the means or the ability to display one's life through consumption—is to be invisible, and Molly is considerably ahead of her time in recognizing that how one looks is slowly becoming the dominant "reality" over one's invisible "reputation": "he [Bloom] says that little man he showed me without the neck is very intelligent the coming man Griffiths is he well he doesnt look it thats all I can say" (*U*, 616). Molly's somewhat cryptic dismissal ("thats all I can say") contains an implicit warning that if the public appearance of Griffiths gives her so little to comment upon, then the idea of his approaching fame ("the coming man") seems quite doubtful.

In another example, Bloom's fanciful rise to the position of mayor in the "Circe" chapter is intensely—one might say exclusively—theatrical. Indeed, his rapid fall from power can be seen, in turn, as a failure to control the spectacle of his "greatness." Once the theatrical underpinning of his role as a "natural" leader is laid bare, his audience becomes especially vicious as a result of their "reality" having been suddenly exposed as illusion. The point of a "lifestyle," as well as a political campaign, or an advertising campaign, or a career as a celebrity, is to make the performative appear normative. As Kim Devlin has pointed out in reference to Molly's dismissal of Griffiths, Molly refuses "to be impressed by arbitrarily determined cultural differences" ("The Female Eye," 117). Molly critiques the performances of others because she is, herself, a performer bent on "self"-improvement, and so she is particularly critical of failed or shoddy performances, rather than the idea of performance itself.

But Molly's most withering remarks are not for those people who perform poorly, but for those who would like to stop the show entirely: "[Mrs. Riordan] greatest miser ever was . . . let us have a bit of fun first God help the world if all the women were her sort down on bathingsuits and lownecks of course nobody wanted her to wear them I suppose she was pious because no man would look at her twice I hope Ill never be like her a wonder she didnt want us to cover our faces" (*U*, 608). Mrs. Riordan has a private source of income, and so she is well endowed in a manner that does not require the accessories of "bathingsuits and lownecks" to attract big spenders. Her invisibility ("of course nobody wanted her to wear them") gives her a "pious" view of life that is completely antithetical to the idea of a consumer-constructed lifestyle. Although Mrs. Riordan has more than enough money for "food and rent," she saves it all to pay for masses conducted after she is dead. "[L]et us have a bit of fun first" is Molly's rejection of this "pious" attitude in favor of publicly performing in the (unacknowledged) carnival of competing and staged "lifestyles" that produces the theater without footlights experienced as the reality of the everyday.

"God knows hes a change in a way," Molly says of Blazes Boylan, "not to be always and ever wearing the same old hat" (*U*, 610). Here, quite literally, Molly's physical desire is experienced as the equivalent of moving from an "old hat" to a "new" one (the promise of eventual satisfaction stimulated by the flight from one signifier to another). In this equation, eroticism may be generated by the acquisition of a new lover or a new hat, and thus shopping becomes an intercourse with objects that is nearly as stimulating as intercourse with Boylan. Indeed, in one of Molly's later thoughts, shopping becomes a type of foreplay conducted in "new" surroundings: "[I]t would be exciting going round with him shopping buying those things in a new city" (*U*, 617). But here it is interesting to note the distinction Molly makes between what she hopes will be postcoital shopping, and the precoital shopping that earlier she declined to do: "[T]he second pair of silkette stockings is laddered after one days wear I could have brought them back to Lewers this morning and kicked up a row and made that one change them only not to upset myself and run the risk of walking into him and ruining the whole thing" (*U*, 618). The difference in these two imagined shopping expeditions is that in one—the return trip to Lewers—Molly feels very much offstage vis-à-vis her later afternoon performance with Blazes Boylan. This sort of shopping is the equivalent of the backstage production that is carefully screened from the play-going audience in order that they might view the onstage scenes as being "natural" and "realistic."

It will not help Blazes Boylan to find her hosiery erotic if he is forced to recall having seen it, just hours before, crumpled in a bunch on a department store counter. Appearance and display are crucial to the "genuine fraudulence" of a modern self-image. In the same light, Raoul would not have been as impressed by the "queenly display" of "the beautiful woman" if he had bumped into her earlier, when she was arguing over the price of her *deshabille.* Leopold Bloom also recognizes the need to keep financial and hygiene matters offstage if a woman's erotic performance is to attain the necessary suspension of disbelief: "See her as she is spoil all." For his part, Blazes Boylan is always careful to present a predictable appearance that is as unified and consistent as any trademark; in fact, like a trademark (or a packaged commodity, or a theatrical performance), he is *all* appearance while betraying no visible sign of having manufactured his image. Blazes is still characterized as a "rake" by readers, but I think his evident sensitivity to the advantages of "lifestyle" make him a new-generation dandy—one who understands, unlike Griffiths, that a rhetorical style is no longer a salable commodity on an open market, and that appearance is now more visible, and thus a "more true" mark of "the coming man."

Although Boylan is "masculine" enough in his actions with Molly, the fact that he wears the clocks by which Molly "tells the time"—a direct gender reversal of the situation in "Those Lovely Seaside Girls"—suggests that, relative to his "lifestyle," he operates within the supposedly feminine sphere of attracting the "masculine" gaze through an artfully constructed appearance. The song refers to the clocks as "the latest thing," which suggests that this item of clothing, with its deliberately rapid update of embroidery design, pioneered the sort of instant fashion obsolescence that is now common to such youthful fashion items as designer jeans or athletic shoes (where the brand names or "new" features indicate publicly to any interested viewer whether the wearer possesses "the latest thing" or something that is "old hat"). The fact that boys "tell the time" by these "clocks" (and, as Molly demonstrates, girls do, too) indicates the extent to which an object (socks) becomes a sign ("clocks") in a commodity culture. This conversion exponentially increases the need to consume since the use value of a sock (something to keep one's feet warm) is replaced by the need the consumer feels to buy a new pair that features the latest clock, well before the old sock has worn out. The conversion of objects into signs is what permits the construction of a "lifestyle," where the juxtaposition of objects designates a language through which desire speaks. The need to consume "the latest thing," a need Molly frequently expresses, is based on the hope of presenting to others a carefully staged image that operates as a visual correspondent to the individual myth of the self.

Blazes is the opposite of Griffiths—the *real* "coming man"—in that he makes a strong visual impression by displaying the flamboyant lifestyle that his salary permits ("lovely stuff . . . he's certainly well off"). But, as Molly can't help noting, his verbal skills consist of a dozen or so clichés that he fits to any occasion: "Hes right enough in his way to pass the time as a joke sure you might as well be in bed with what with a lion God Im sure hed have something better to say for himself an old Lion would" (*U*, 638). Blazes is not a "joke" in terms of the current connotations of this word—as someone pathetic and hopeless—but more in the sense of the "bit of fun" that she feels the ascetic Mrs. Riordan would have outlawed if she could.[16]

The idea of "fun," in the sense of something that provides enjoyment or sensation, is basic to the philosophy of a commodity culture, where the pursuit of happiness has been refashioned not as a right, but as a duty: "Modern man *spends less and less* of life in production, and *more and more* in the continuous production and creation of personal needs and of personal well-being. He must constantly be ready to actualize all of his potential, all of his capacity for consumption. If he forgets, he will be gently and instantly reminded that he has no right not to be happy" (Baudrillard, *Selected Writings,* 48, emphasis added). "Double your pleasure, double your fun," begins a contemporary ad for chewing gum. What appears to be an invitation to increase our enjoyment of life, is in fact a rather coercive reminder that we are required to have fun and that "having fun" involves the constant trying of new experiences and sensations that double our pleasure; trying the new, of course, is the essence of a commodity culture, where the consumer must be persuaded that "life" requires a "style" of "lashing around" all the products beyond "food and rent" that fulfill his or her duty to have fun.

When Molly says of Blazes "hes a change in a way not to be always and ever wearing the same old hat," we can see that "trying" Blazes is an act of consumption before it is an act of adultery. Indeed, Baudrillard discusses a "*fun morality* whose imperative is enjoyment and the complete exploitation of all the possibilities of being thrilled, experiencing pleasure, and being gratified" (*Selected Writings,* 49). In this paradigm, Molly has a moral imperative to "try" Blazes if she is to obey the modern commandment: "Double Your Pleasure!" (Ten commandments are too confusing to market effectively, so we're down to one). Likewise, Molly is not overly excited by the idea of having the Prince of Wales as a lover because he is "old hat"; there is nothing new about him: "[H]es like the first man going the roads only for the name of a king." But a black man has enough of the requisite novelty for her to want to give it a try: "[T]hey're all made the one way only a black mans *Id like to try*" (*U*, 618, emphasis added). This is the worship of novelty, and not simply phallus worship. Any product that is "made the one way" for too long will stop selling, which is why, for example, automobiles are made a different way every year.

This operative word *try* is also what prompts Bloom's selection of *Sweets of Sin:* "Yes. This. Here. *Try*" (*U,* 194, emphasis added). One effect of commodity culture and "fun morality" is that "[a] *universal curiosity* has . . . been reawakened in the areas of cuisine, culture, science, religion, sexuality, etc. 'Try Jesus!' says an American slogan. *Everything* must be tried" (Baudrillard, *Selected Writings,* 48). In the contemporary definition of the word *try* as "experiencing something for the first time," one can only try something once; the citizen-consumer's duty to experience pleasure and try things requires the constant reconfiguration of the everyday into the new: "I wished I was one [a man] myself," Molly thinks, "for a change *just to try* with that thing they have swelling up on you so hard" (*U,* 638). It is not penis envy that prompts Molly's fantasy about being a man. She does not wish to *have* a penis, she wishes to *try* one; in fact, as far as any presumed worship of the phallus is concerned, it's rather deflating to think that Molly's impulse to have a penis—to try something new—is identical to the impulse that might also prompt her to change her brand of shampoo in order to try a new one in a differently shaped bottle.

IV. This time, you be the imperialist and I'll be the colonial subject: The politics of pleasure

The advent of a modern "lifestyle," with its paradoxical and insatiable requirement for the sensation of novelty as an everyday experience, also requires the increasingly detailed delineation and amplification of "pleasure." As Foucault has stated in a different context, the purpose of various "polymorphous techniques of power" is "to reach the most tenuous and individual modes of behavior, the paths that give it access to the rare or scarcely perceivable forms of desire, how it penetrates and controls everyday pleasure."[17] Another reason Molly would like to try being a man is that she is aware the female body has been thoroughly commodified as a source of pleasure; if she were to become a man, however, she could enjoy this commodification directly (rather than vicariously experiencing pleasure by watching the expression of a man who is looking at her): "I suppose its because they were so plump and tempting in my short petticoat he couldnt resist they excite myself sometimes its well for men all the amount of pleasure they get off a womans body" (*U,* 638). The rise of sexology at the turn of the century, and its creation of such categories as "homosexual," "pervert," and "degenerate," as well as the corresponding insistence on "heterosexuality" as normative, helped to make sexual preference part of a "lifestyle"; indeed, one way to euphemistically express disapproval of someone else's sexual practices is to say, "I don't approve of that lifestyle." Increasingly in a commodity culture, consumers visibly express how they consume products in order to make equally clear how they hope to consume others and how they hope to be consumed by them in turn.[18]

The production of everyday pleasure requires the consumption of novelty, and the degree of fun we are able to reach through this "work of consumption" (to use Wicke's phrase) is mapped out—as all current advertisers are aware—by our sexual preference, or "what turns us on" (which can also be understood as the "path" we most frequently choose to travel to reach our own "scarcely perceivable forms of desire"). Even within the "normative" practice of heterosexual intercourse, there is still a nearly endless variety of paths (a variety that *Ulysses* maps, though not comprehensively). The scientific definition of *adolescence*, for example, suggested an endless variety of products that are marketed as the appropriate fetish for all the permutations of "normal" and "perverse" sexuality (as Gerty is exquisitely aware). Lawrence Birken argues, "Sexology expressed the same conviction about the domain of the consumer, starting with the assumption of the polymorphous desiring individual who eventually specializes in particular tastes. Through specialization, individuals starting out the same fulfill their individuality."[19]

For the child growing to sexual maturity, or for the child developing his or her "own" lifestyle, the "healthy" goal in both cases is for the performative to be presented and perceived as the normative. Of course, "specialization," under the general rubric of "heterosexuality," is still "individually" expressed through strategic acts of consumption: "[T]hat black closed breeches he made me buy takes you half an hour to let them down wetting all myself always with some brandnew fad every other week" (*U*, 613). The use value and design of the black closed breeches is dubious at best ("wetting all myself always"), but Molly agrees to purchase breeches, and, despite the practical inconvenience, to wear them because she understands—albeit reluctantly—Bloom's modern duty in a commodity culture (experienced by the consumer as "need") to produce pleasure through the consumption of novelty.

But we need to notice that what is at issue for Molly is not Bloom's urge to try something new (an urge she shares), but the frequency with which he wishes to do so. All of which suggests that a power struggle over pleasure production often occurs between conflicting "lifestyles." Because the production of "personal" pleasure requires other people's labor, issues of capitalization and exploitation arise. Interestingly, it is Wanda, the dominatrix in *Venus in Furs,* who delivers a manifesto of consumerism that reinterprets Hegel's "master/slave" paradigm in terms of who consumes pleasure, and whose labor makes this consumption possible. As with economic capitalism, the goal is to produce as much profit/pleasure as possible—to spend as long as possible—at someone else's expense:

> Pleasure alone lends value to existence. . . . whoever wants to enjoy must take life gaily. . . . he dare not hesitate *to enjoy at the expense of others.* . . . He must know how to make slaves of men who feel and would enjoy as he does, and use them for his service and pleasure without remorse. . . . He must always remember this, that if they had him in their power, as he has them they would act in exactly the same way, and he would have *to pay for their pleasure* with his sweat and blood and soul.[20]

The central dynamic of Wanda and Severin's relationship in *Venus in Furs* revolves around the complex playacting of a man and a woman who blur the line between who is laboring and who is "spending." First, Severin actively persuades Wanda to dominate him; but when she grows to enjoy the role, the scenario reverses itself and soon he finds himself laboring for her pleasure. "I can't stop at make-believe, when once I begin," she tells him. "You know I hate all play-acting and comedy. You have wished it. Was it my idea or yours?" (70–71).

In still another reversal, Wanda abruptly forsakes her role as "Venus in Furs" and informs Severin about her "real" self: "[D]idn't you know that everything was only make-believe and play-acting. . . . I have played my cruel role better than you expected, and now you will be satisfied with my being a good, little wife. . . . We will live like rational people—" (131). But "being a good, little wife" turns out to be the real performance, and what she disavowed as a *performative* mode ("my cruel role") emerges as her *normative* state of being. Under the guise of being a devoted "little wife," she persuades him to be tied up one more time ("I wonder if I can still do it"); she then calls her new lover out from behind "the curtains of her four-poster bed" to administer Severin's most humiliating whipping yet. "You are indeed cruel," this lover says to Wanda. "Only inordinately fond of pleasure," she answers, a reply that supports my contention that the normative mode is any performative mode that allows for a maximization of pleasure production in any given scenario of reality. And yet, in the final reversal, it is Severin whose level of enjoyment deepens as a result of Wanda's playacting: "The sensation of being whipped by a successful rival before the eyes of an adored woman cannot be described" (137). He then proceeds to recite everyone's role and position on stage to the accompaniment of his own mounting excitement, and finishes as the star at the center of his own ultimate (pleasure) tableau.

The theatrical production of pleasure in *Venus in Furs* suggests to me that, in the midst of feeling sorry for the cuckolded Bloom, we need to entertain the idea that Molly and Blazes's afternoon performance may be, in part, a matinee staged for Bloom's pleasure. Molly suspects, while directing her own satisfactory duet with Blazes, that she may be inadvertently performing for Bloom: "[H]e has an idea about him and me hes not such a fool he said Im dining out and going to the Gaiety though Im not going to give him the satisfaction" (*U*, 610). Later, when remembering it had been Bloom who insisted on sending Milly away to be a "photo girl," her suspicions the affair with Blazes is a play directed by Leopold Bloom become even more explicit: "[O]n account of me and Boylan that's why he did it Im certain the way he plots and plans everything out" (*U*, 630). In "Circe," it is Molly who becomes a "photo girl" when Bloom asks permission from Blazes (who has invited him to "apply your eye to the keyhole . . . while I just go through her a few times") to "take a snapshot" (*U*, 462). Presumably, such a snapshot would find its way into his secret drawer along with the other staged photographs that he finds exciting.

The earliest readings of *Ulysses*—which saw Molly as immoral and Bloom as a pathetically noble man who "bears up" under the strain of being made a cuckold—may still be obscuring the possibility that Bloom, relative to the affair of Molly and Blazes, is a man more sinning than sinned against. Just as we saw with Severin, production of a painful tableau may afford a "private" pleasure for the person who appears wronged according to "normative" standards. Pleasure production for a "masculine" colonial subject is not as straightforward as it is for Raoul and the German Emperor. Bloom, as the colonial subject, cannot hope to challenge power directly, but he may design instead a scenario in which an apparently abject posture conceals the pleasure of watching others unwittingly perform under his secret direction.

Certainly in Bloom's encounter with a prostitute that I discussed earlier, he casts himself in the role of a director who hires an "actress" to recite a script he has prepared for her. Paradoxically, the business dimension of hiring a prostitute is also what makes it (potentially) erotic because the performance is paid for in advance, the actor or actress has been hired, and the question of who is to labor for whose pleasure is eliminated as a hindrance to the enjoyment of the one who is "spending." Bloom's "rehearsal" of the girl on Meath Street (who proves not ready yet for Bloom's prime time) is a precursor to the contemporary phenomenon of phone sex, in which men and women offer to recite any script the client presents—but only after obtaining the client's credit card number.[21] Still, the exchange with the girl on Meath Street is unsatisfactory for Bloom because the woman is such an unconvincing performer: "All wrong of course. My arks she called it" (*U*, 303).

In contrast, when Bloom presents a script to Molly, and in the process gets a free performance from her, he reaches a climax, but she is resentful because this particular type of playacting leaves her unsatisfied and thus feeling like an unpaid prostitute: "tell me who are you thinking of who is it tell me his name who tell me who the german Emperor is it yes imagine Im him think of him can you feel him *trying to make a whore out of me* what he never will he ought to give it up now at this age of his life simply ruination for any woman and *no satisfaction in it pretending to like it* till he comes and finish it off myself anyway" (*U*, 610, emphasis added). As Gifford and Seidman point out, the German Emperor was William I, who died in 1888—the year of Molly and Leopold's courtship—and his image dominated the newspapers at this time. Under his leadership, the new German Empire rapidly became the chief economic and military power on the continent, rivaling England's Empire.

Small wonder, then, that even sixteen years later Bloom is still excited by the erotic tableau of Raoul grabbing the beautiful woman's "opulent" curves. In calling Molly a "flower of the mountain," Bloom may have been thinking of her as unplowed countryside. In asking Molly to imagine it is the imperialistic German Emperor who is exploring and appropriating her assets ("can you feel him"), Bloom is a sheep in wolf's clothing. Accordingly, Molly calls Blazes "Raoul" in the "Circe" chapter when she invites him to come see her step out of the bathtub: "Raoul darling, come and dry me. I'm in my pelt. Only my new hat and a carriage sponge" (*U*, 461). Molly's announcement "I'm in my pelt" informs Blazes that she is naked. But it is also, as Gifford notes, an allusion to *Venus Im Pelz*. In a further echo of this novel, to "pelt" someone is to beat them unrelentingly. This refers us once more, of course, to Severin's final tableau, where his apparent complete humiliation is in fact his ultimate directorial triumph.

In contrast to all this, Molly gets no satisfaction from her performance as a woman ravaged by a German emperor. She imagines instead that she needs to hire someone herself—spend in order to "spend"—if she expects someone to perform in a prearranged manner for her enjoyment: "[U]nless I paid some nicelooking boy. . . . I'd confuse him a little . . . let him see *my garters the new ones* and *make him turn red* looking at him seduce him" (*U*, 610, emphasis added). Once again, just like "the beautiful woman," Molly links her ability to be a seductive display with her recollection of the purchase of a new pair of garters. Even when calling for Raoul/Blazes to see her in her "pelt," she announces at the same time that she is wearing a new hat.

Unlike Bloom and the girl on Meath Street, however, Molly does not enact her scenario. But if she were to do so, she would run into a contradiction identical to Bloom's problem—how can someone who has already agreed to have sex in exchange for money still convince her that he is being seduced by the irresistible display of her body packaged in a new pair of garters? Even if the boy she hires is a good actor, it is unlikely he will be able to blush on command—and yet Molly has included this as a specific stage direction! To use Devlin's term, what Molly wants from the boy is genuine fraudulence. She hopes to witness an apparently unrehearsed, involuntary, and physical expression of desire (confusion, blushing) from someone she has hired as a performer; he must convincingly present the performative as something that is normative. Buying a fantasy (performative), and then seeking to ignore the relationship of the fiscal to the physical (misrecognizing it as normative), is also basic to the experience of shopping in a modern department store; the prices are fixed to eliminate bartering, and customers are not asked to pay at the point of purchase, but only as they leave the store (with contemporary credit cards, of course, one does not pay in the store at all). This is another reason that Molly considers the act of returning her "laddered" hosiery for money as potentially fatal to an erotic mood ("run the risk of walking into him and ruining the whole thing"), and yet also imagines it would be "exciting" to go shopping with Boylan in a "new city" where she could spend at his expense.

In the same way that a manufacturer who designs a product has a particular market or audience in mind, Molly Bloom, in designing her "lifestyle" (and in her desire to improve it), also has a particular market in mind; one might even go so far as to say that Blazes Boylan receives a free sample in return for his agreement to participate in a survey of her charms. In expressing rivalry with other women, Molly thinks of Boylan this way: "[S]ee if they [other women] can excite a swell with money that can pick and choose whoever he wants like Boylan to do it 4 or 5 times locked in each others arms" (*U*, 628). With all due respect to Boylan, I think it is as unlikely that he "did it" five times as it is that Molly has—as was once believed—twenty or more lovers. What is more notable, then, is that Molly keeps increasing the number of times Boylan has reached orgasm even as she recalls, with increasing alarm, that she is getting older and stouter.

Different lifestyles require the credible presentation of different ages, and Molly feels that her increasing age is forcing her out of the lifestyle she wishes to maintain. She understands, for example, that Mrs. Riordan's age is a factor in her ascetic world view: "I hope Ill never be like her" (*U*, 608). Not surprisingly, then, each recollection of Boylan's increasingly numerous climaxes (her final reference to it is "5 or 6 times") is accompanied by a mental note of what pose she struck to bring him to it: "I gave my eyes that look with my hair a bit loose from the tumbling and my tongue between my lips up to him the savage brute" (*U*, 621). In terms of "spending" as Victorian slang for a sexual climax, we can see that Molly might also interpret Boylan's multiple orgasms as a sort of "shopping binge" that her display of herself has stimulated.

Indeed, Molly often catalogues and evaluates various features of her body—her hands, her feet, her breasts—in accordance with how capable they are of making men "spend," in the double sense of climaxing and buying her presents: "I saw his eyes on my feet going out through the turning door now how did that excite him because I was crossing them when we were in the other room. . . . my hand is nice like that if I only had a ring with the stone for my month a nice aquamarine Ill stick him for one and a gold bracelet I dont like my foot so much still I made him spend once with my foot" (*U*, 613–14). By looking back, Molly has caught the gaze of an excited consumer, and, like any good manufacturer, she is eager to know what it was about her foot (which doesn't seem like much to her) that he found so exciting. Similarly, while she is thinking about getting a man to spend money for items that might dress up her hand, Molly's thoughts return once more to her apparently undervalued foot, which, despite its unmarketable appearance to her, "made him spend once." If she could isolate what it is about her foot that is marketable, she could file this information away, or further refine it, just as she has evidently perfected "that look" which she "gives to her eyes" to make Boylan "spend." Significantly, the complaint about men that Molly voices most consistently is that there is no telling what will persuade men to spend ("they're all so different"). This, of course, is the perennial dilemma that the advertiser faces vis-à-vis the consumer.

Molly's contentment at having persuaded Boylan, as a wealthy consumer, to "spend" on her when he is free to "pick and choose" where he spends, is borne out by her silent refutation of what she takes to be Bloom's current perception of her as an unsalable commodity: "I suppose he thinks Im finished out *and laid on the shelf* well Im not nor anything like it" (*U*, 631, emphasis added). By understanding the implicit metaphor of marketing behind Molly's various strategies for getting men to spend, we can see, I think, that claiming she has the instincts of a whore misses the point. If she is a whore, then so is Blazes Boylan in his "skyblue" suit and "clocks." Indeed, so are all of us in the modern age who vie for attention through the spectacular language of lifestyle.

To have a "lifestyle" at all is to try to determine, for the sake of advancement and profit, what is currently selling and what has been remaindered to "the shelf." "What's hot and what's not" is a staple article of contemporary magazines—whether it's *Vogue* for women or *GQ* for men. In the modern world of commodity culture, where all that is visible is for sale, and where everything has an exchange value relative to the visibility of something else, the person the public labels a "whore" is really no more than what Stephen calls a "bad merchant"—someone who "buys dear and sells cheap." It is these people who draw forth all the opprobrium that our culture can muster—not because they have "sold themselves"—but because they have failed to do so for profit. When selling leads to profit, as Molly seems well aware, it covers up a multitude of sins; "prostitution" becomes "business savvy."

But if Molly has been unfairly dismissed by some readers of *Ulysses* as a prostitute at heart rather than being seen as a merchant who, like everyone else, buys cheap and sells dear, she makes a similar mistake when dismissing her famous namesake Moll Flanders: "I dont like books with a Molly in them like that one he brought me about the one from Flanders a whore always shoplifting anything she could cloth and stuff and yards of it" (*U*, 622). And yet it is only after several marriages and a great deal of bad luck, more than two hundred pages into Defoe's novel, that Moll Flanders begins to shoplift. When Molly reflects that she could "do the indifferent" to reawaken Bloom's interest in her, she is echoing the same sort of "shop talk" that Moll Flanders consistently employs: "He pursued me close after this, and as I saw there was no need to fear losing him *I played the indifferent* part with him longer than prudence might otherwise have dictated to me."[22] In looking back on her first sexual encounter with a man, Moll Flanders's primary regret is that she did not understand at that time that physical passion is just another occasion for commercial negotiation: "[I]f he had known me and how easy the trifle he aimed at was to be had [her virginity], he would have troubled his head no farther, but have given me four or five guineas and have lain with me the next time he had come at me. On the other hand, if I had known his thoughts and how hard he supposed I would be to be gained, I might have made my own terms" (27). Moll's ruminations on her "seduction" is not so much an admission of prostitution as a review of "Marketing 101": The exchange value of any "trifle," apart from its use value, will be rendered cheaper or more expensive depending on supply and demand.

Quite a bit later in the book, Moll has become a skilled negotiator and is able to "make her own terms": "I played with this lover as an angler does with a trout: I found I had him fast on the hook, so I jested with his new proposal and put him off" (125). So why does Moll end up shoplifting? For one thing, Defoe had to show her coming to no good because his reading public was not about to see her merely as a skillful negotiator. Of course, Defoe introduces so many absurdly coincidental hardships before he is able to reduce her to penury that her final downfall seems far from credible. Indeed, *Moll Flanders* can be read as Defoe's explicit inducement to women to learn to negotiate and barter if they expect to influence their destiny: "When a woman is . . . left desolate and void of counsel, she is just like a bag of money or a jewel dropped on the highway, which is a prey to the next comer" (114). Moll's problem is one that Molly shares: "I had sufficient to live on, yet had no way of increasing it" (*Moll Flanders,* 115). Both Molly and Moll are fairly adept negotiators, but both have only their physical looks and acting abilities with which to barter.

Molly is especially sensitive to the depreciation of her only capital—her body—because puberty is transforming Milly's body into the public attraction she once was: "[T]hey all look at her like me when I was her age of course any old rag looks well on you then. . . . shes always making love to my things too the few old rags I have wanting to put her hair up at 15 my powder too only ruin her skin on her shes time enough for that all her life after of course shes restless knowing shes pretty with her lips so red a pity they wont stay that way" (*U,* 631). The "capital" of a woman's appearance within a patriarchal economy, in contrast to actual money, represents capital that inevitably depreciates over the course of time, no matter how wisely it is invested ("shes pretty with her lips so red a pity they wont stay that way"). Significantly, the reason that Molly's and Milly's use of cosmetics intersect is that Milly wishes to look older and Molly to look younger. From their two ages—fifteen to thirty-three—we can see the outer limits of what we now call the "youth culture" (though one can see the nascent form of this youth culture in a popular advertising trope such as the "seaside girl").[23] The increasing mother-daughter tension between Molly and Milly needs to be understood in the context of a commodity culture where the "language of money and commodities has become an all-encompassing system—the very texture of everyday forms of ideology" (Bowlby, 25). Milly's increasing marketability amplifies Molly's sense of her own devaluation.

In the *Sunday New York Times* one section is titled "Lifestyle." In a recent edition, there was an article titled "Cards to help the tongue-tied." The reporter writes of a stationery store in the financial district of Manhattan with a special alcove called the Thoughtfulness Gallery. In this alcove is the newest generation of Hallmark cards, published under the rubrics of "Just How I Feel" and "Between You and Me." The editorial manager of Hallmark explains that "[a] lot of today's consumers are feeling a need to share their thoughts but don't find the words." The new lines of cards, she continues, "*express the stuff* we *all* want to say" (emphasis added). What does it mean when a rhetorical message titled "Just How I Feel" or "Between You and Me" is marketed for mass consumption and thus is understood to be "the stuff" we all wish to express (recall the headings of the turn-of-the-century ads: "The First Quarrel" and "Happy Reunion")? "It is what we call *universally specific,*" continues the Hallmark editor. "It's where *everyone* thinks, 'This card was really written *for me*'" (emphasis added). The final frontier of commodity culture is consciousness, where the mind, like one's living room, "talks stuff" and specific feelings are universal ("universal" within the simulacrum of a given commodity culture).

A Hallmark competitor, Carlton Cards, has introduced a "complete" modern romance line called "Couples," which is divided into four subcategories: "Falling in Love," "In Love," "Intimacies," and "Still in Love." Like Lacan's idea of the Real, the unrepresented fifth category—"Get Lost"—hovers beyond these "universally specific" expressions, and yet also serves as the prior origin of desire and anxiety that makes us misrecognize these four categories as complete. Baudrillard claims, "Consumption [is] not a function of 'harmonious' individual satisfaction . . . but rather an infinite social activity. . . . Needs are strictly specified in advance in relation to finite objects" (*Selected Writings,* 41). A customer with several cards in her hand told the *New York Times* reporter, "They capture what I feel and they save me time."

Molly, too, were she to find herself "just looking" in the Thoughtfulness Gallery, might also discover that her thoughts had been "captured." She might send Bloom the one that begins, "I Need to Feel Appreciated," and he could respond with the one titled "Please Give Me Another Chance"; like a silent movie, the scenario of "true" love rolls noiselessly forward, occasionally interrupted with titles that "capture" what the performers are thinking. In contemporary commodity culture, we are what we buy, and the more we shop, the more we are, and so we move from thing to thing—signifier to signifier—to "express the stuff we all want to say"—even though it is "the stuff" that is expressing us. Commodified desire is the consumer phenomenon known as "lifestyle," where we think we don't want what we have because we don't have what we think we want. Not surprisingly, then, in the Thoughtfulness Gallery, the card titled "I Need a Commitment" (the latest universal specific?) is sold out. But I'll conclude this chapter by citing my favorite title (as well this one as another): "This is the Real World." Yes.

6

When a Fly Gets in Your I

The City, Modernism, and Aesthetic Theory in *A Portrait of the Artist as a Young Man*

> —But we are just now in a mental world, Stephen continued. The desire and loathing excited by improper esthetic means are really unesthetic emotions. . . . Our eyelid closes before we are aware that the fly is about to enter our eye.
>
> —Not always, said Lynch critically.
>
> (*P*, 206)

> Abolish the sacred frontier which makes legitimate culture a separate universe, in order to discover the intelligible relations which unite apparently incommensurable "choices," such as preferences in music and food, painting and sport, literature and hairstyle.[1]

I. Urban-menschens: Dedalus, the Count of Monte Cristo, Superman, and Batman

Stated boldly, my project in this chapter is to reframe modernism and view it, not as a representation of modernity, but as a symptom of it. The experience of modernity is fostered by the rise of the modern city, and works of modernism do not so much convey this experience as they betray the strain of surviving it, and detail their various strategies for doing so. "What are the dangers of the forest and the prairie compared with the daily shocks and conflicts of civilization?" Baudelaire asks.[2] Indeed, the city is a forest, one rendered all the more dangerous because it appears to be the final triumph over nature. The flaneur, as Benjamin describes him, is a latter-day Natty Bumppo, wending his way over highways and through byways, his eye always alert for the easily overlooked detail that, in one instance, might warn him to take cover, or, in another instance, invite him to take charge.[3] His ability to be unerring in his distinction between these two instances will be the measure of his status as a hero to those who grow to depend upon him.

But unlike the forests in the novels of James Fenimore Cooper, where women are important only in as much as their helplessness underwrites the heroics of the male characters, women move thorough the modern forest of the city, and they do so unescorted and with their own agenda. Far from providing occasions for male heroism, they now appear as a threat to it, most obviously in the peculiarly modern incarnation of the woman as a femme fatale.[4] The certainly dangerous, yet reassuringly masculine world of the "untamed" forest becomes sexualized in a way that is both alluring and threatening to the would-be urban hero. If Natty Bumppo could take for granted the truly helpless status of the woman clinging to him, and thereupon devote all his attention to whatever was posing a threat to her, modern detectives such as Sherlock Holmes, Philip Marlowe, and Sam Spade—the urban equivalents of the pioneer—find they must investigate the damsel at the same time they try to alleviate her distress. As I discuss in more detail later, this enigmatic woman comes to stand in as a figure for the modern metropolis—alluring, yet treacherous. What I will suggest here at the outset of my discussion is that Stephen's relentless attempt to outlaw arousal as a legitimate component of aesthetic contemplation must be placed within the psychological, historical, and sociological context of modernity and the modern metropolis.

The young Stephen Dedalus—initially conceived of by Joyce as Stephen Hero—takes as his first model of ideal masculinity Dumas's Edmund Dantes, particularly in his later incarnation as the Count of Monte Cristo. Even more specifically, he fantasizes again and again that he *is* Dantes, resolutely expressing a world-weary refusal of what the formerly irresistible Mercedes never tires of offering him:

> And in his imagination he lived through an ongoing train of adventures . . . towards the close of which there appeared an image of himself, grown older and sadder, standing in a moonlit garden with Mercedes who had so many years before slighted his love, and with a sadly proud gesture of refusal, saying:
>
> —Madam, I never eat muscatel grapes. (63)

This "sadly proud gesture of refusal" is a much prized, and often reprised, strategy for Stephen; or, rather, it is a favorite fantasy, both for Stephen in particular, and male modernists more generally, of a much wished for position of calm indifference in the midst of all the conflict and temptation configured in the modern city.[5] Indeed, I read Stephen's later aesthetic theory, with its elaborate championing of a self-induced "esthetic stasis," as a more intellectualized version of Mercedes's muscatel grapes, this time configured much more generally as the "kinetic" and the "pornographic." The amount of stimulus in the modern city (pleasant or unpleasant), which is not only readily available, but in fact unavoidable, makes the posture of indifference and refusal attractive. Ideally, as in the case of Dantes, the pleasure of temptation remains ever present (Mercedes repeatedly offers the sure-to-be-refused grapes), and thus the hero is able to indulge the pleasure entailed in the temptation, not by being seduced by it, but precisely by refusing it.

Stephen's characterization of Dantes as "that dark avenger" makes more obvious my next suggestion that Dumas's Dantes, as reconceived and retrofitted by Stephen, becomes a prototype of later urban male fantasy figures such as Superman (1933) and Batman (1939).[6] Both these superheroes are known as much by the city that benefits from their presence, and over which they wield extraordinary control (Metropolis and Gotham City, respectively), as they are by their specific exploits. Another parallel with Dantes is that these urban superheroes have extraordinary resources—unlimited wealth in the case of Dantes and Batman, and nearly unlimited strength in the case of Superman—and yet they have alter egos who must try to live and love without benefit of these superpowers. An interesting difference between Dantes and Batman/Superman is that Dantes's alter ego is his former timid self (that is, not a simultaneous existence he must return to in between heroic exploits), whereas Clark Kent and Bruce Wayne are alternative realities lived within the same time frame by Superman and Batman. In a departure from Dumas's heroic paradigm, and in a foreshadowing of the Superman/Batman split, we watch Stephen, throughout *Portrait,* go from a state of timidity and bafflement to one of indomitable insouciance, and back again. One state is not prior to the other; they oscillate and coexist.

Stephen's calm refusal of Mercedes in his Superman mode is one thing, but it must be read against the counter experience of Clark Kent vulnerability when he experiences the apparent dissolution of his own identity the first time he is kissed by the ultimate distraction for a young male in the city—the prostitute: "He closed his eyes, surrendering himself to her, body and mind" (101). As I will argue, Stephen's aesthetic theory can also be read as the posture of an urban superhero, calmly rising above "kinetic" emotion in favor of "esthetic stasis." This is a particularly urban, and a particularly modern, fantasy because, as with the urban fantasies embodied in metropolitan superiors like Batman and Superman, one is able to rise above the relentless stimulation and confusion of the city and impose law and order upon its apparently unmanageable dimensions. Of course, Batman and Superman do this literally; an expected component of almost all contemporary superheroes is that they must have some capacity to fly.

In yet another curious foreshadowing of these urban superheroes, Stephen modernizes Ovid's story of Dedalus by reconfiguring flying as a way both to navigate and to put in perspective the terrifying and exhilarating experience of living in the labyrinth of a modern metropolis: "And the air is thick with their company as they call to me, their kinsman, making ready to go, shaking the wings of their exultant and terrible youth" (252). For Stephen, the labyrinth is what he designs by charting his course through it, but, because the urban environment also baffles and confuses him, it is also what designs him. Stephen, in other words, is not only the engineer who constructs the city, but also the Minotaur who is trapped within it.

Superman and Batman are called by baffled law enforcement officials when the great city, so carefully planned and constructed, appears to spawn cunning criminals who threaten to take it over completely. The villains Batman and Superman are called on to pursue are urban nightmares, figures distorted, disfigured, and maddened by the experience of living in the city. Figures like the Joker, or the Riddler, or Two-Face, are, in a sense, the unconscious of the city, particularly in the way their presence is symptomatic of something that always escapes the careful and utopian planning of architects and city planners. James Donald notes, in the context of discussing Freud's specifically urban phenomenon of the uncanny, "the modern uncanny, imagined as the labyrinth, always returns to haunt the city of light."[7]

As we will see, what haunts Stephen's aesthetic theory, composed as a well-lit City of Light with no stray alleyways of fear or desire left unilluminated, is his friend Lynch, an early graffiti artist (albeit a primitive one), who reminds Stephen, "you say that art must not excite desire. . . . I told you that one day I wrote my name in pencil on the backside of the Venus of Praxiteles in the Museum. Was that not desire?" (205). Stephen's response—"I speak of normal natures"—also highlights his impulse to construct an aesthetic theory that operates as a self-surveillance system within which individuals, by examining how they respond to art, can determine to what extent they are "normal" law-abiding citizens. "Normality" is a seductive category in its own right in Stephen's theory because it appears to map a route through the labyrinth of the modern experience, by which one is guaranteed to get neither lost nor waylaid.

The other significant metamorphosis undergone by Stephen's "dark avenger" as this male fantasy of urban omniscience makes its way into popular culture is that while Dantes uses his power to punish in a manner he alone decides upon, Superman and Batman, while possessing superpowers that would more than permit them to do the same, nonetheless pledge, repeatedly and unequivocally, to uphold law and order. The more nascent fantasy, in other words, is one of personal vengeance, whereas the later, popular, explicitly urbanized incarnation of a similar fantasy has already been recuperated into the hegemonic discourse of later capitalism. As I will discuss later, the shift can be seen as similar to the one Foucault notes, in which one moves away from a system of physically punishing the criminal in a manner related to the perceived nature of the crime and toward disciplining as a form of rehabilitation that establishes and centers upon the need for all citizens to exercise self-surveillance (thus, for later superheroes, Dantes's single-minded pursuit of personal vengeance transforms into a mandate to avenge others). This epistemic shift is embodied in the urban superhero myth in yet another way: the extraordinary power and strength of these figures are always tempered by their equally astonishing self-discipline. Whereas Dantes's extraordinary feats are made necessary by a legal system that has been corrupted and manipulated, later superheroes avenge the wrongs done to "normal" citizens, but then forgo the administration of punishment in order to promote the law as the only legitimate form of discipline because it offers the possibility of rehabilitation.

I cannot expand this line of investigation further in the confines of this book, but I have sketched it out in some detail here in order to place Stephen's aesthetic theory within the context of what I am characterizing as the male urban fantasy of physical and emotional omniscience.[8] This fantasy derives explicitly from the experience of the modern city as one that stimulates within the male subject an exhausting process of promise, anticipation, disappointment, renewed anticipation, and so on. In trying to shore up the aesthetic position as one in which, as if by magic, the observer is freed from desire and loathing, Stephen is not that different from a would-be Clark Kent explaining earnestly to his best friend how it is that he has developed X-ray vision and now knows how to fly.

II. Hurting your feelings: Aesthetic theory and self-surveillance

Because feelings are constructed as bestial, chaotic, and damnable, repressing them feels good. If affect is historically constructed, as Cvetkovitch has argued, that is, if ideological meanings are attached to physical processes, as they certainly are in Father Arnall's hell sermon, then aesthetic theory—the construction of taste, the division of high culture from low—becomes the secular equivalent of the hell sermon, in which we are asked to survey our own feelings and sensations, vis-à-vis a cultural artifact, and know whether we are in a state of grace or in danger of being cast out into the utter darkness beyond the normative (Cvetkovitch, 27). As Bourdieu states in his treatise on the history of taste, "what is at value in aesthetic discourse . . . is nothing less than the monopoly of Humanity" (491). John Fiske is even more denunciatory: "Aesthetic judgments are antipopular—they deny the multiplicity of readings and the multiplicity of functions that the same text can perform as it is moved through different allegiances within the social order."[9] I can think of no more precise an example of this than the one I have already cited, when Lynch describes his response to a statue of Venus—writing his name in pencil on her buttocks—and Stephen dismisses it with the remark "I speak of normal natures." Fiske goes on to say, "aesthetics is naked cultural hegemony, and popular discrimination properly rejects it"; this is precisely what Lynch does when he responds to Stephen's attempt to conflate feelings with instinct. Stephen claims, "Our eyelid closes before we are aware that the fly is about to enter our eye." "Not always," Lynch insists.

With the rise of mass media and the advent of commodity culture, modernist aesthetics is under a particular historical and cultural pressure because commodities insist on being enjoyed. The "aesthetics of attraction" this generates alters the concept of the subject who perceives, from someone with inviolable interiority, to someone alarmingly permeable to signs and symbols from the environment: "capitalism and the body are connected in so far as stimulating the nerves is a way of stimulating exchange. . . . The reader's [or observer's] body becomes a machine hooked into the circuit of production and consumption, rather than a disinterested entity floating above economic exigencies in search of aesthetic or moral truth."[10] Desire (divided into "perverse" and "normal") and representation (divided into the aesthetic and the pornographic) and culture (divided into high and low) are entry points for social policy and the constitution of various configurations of privilege and power. Perhaps this is a partial explanation for the current (academic) interest in pornography. As Jennifer Wicke notes, "behind the complexities of the arguments about pornography often lies a philosophical discourse about representation and education, seeing and knowing."[11]

As Foucault has argued, when overt punishment, in an epistemic shift, turns into an apparently benign discipline, the coercive power of a military or police state shifts to the need for self-surveillance: "Disciplinary power is different from punishment because its effectiveness depends on its ability to mask itself and to appear in the guise of love or self-expression."[12] D. A.

Miller notes, "[The] machinery of surveillance is set up to monitor . . . the elaborate regulation (timetables, exercises, and so on) that discipline simultaneously deploys to occupy its subjects. The aim of such regulation is to enforce not so much a norm as the normality of normativeness itself. Rather than in rendering all its subjects uniformly 'normal,' discipline is interested in putting in place a perceptual grid in which a division between the normal and the deviant inherently imposes itself."[13] Stephen's aesthetic theory, set in deliberate opposition to the pornographic or kinetic, also creates a category of normativeness, not by declaring what is normal, but by categorizing and regulating effect in a manner that gives the subject a perceptual grid by which, according to his or her own feelings, experienced as "natural," the subject watches him- or herself watching, and stands ready to condemn or discipline, with increasing severity, whatever self-surveillance experiences as an "abnormal" response. Even though Stephen is helping to set up such a system, he also seeks relief from it by declaring all response as illegitimate, except for an emotional fugue state he labels "esthetic stasis."

In the opening of book IV in *Portrait,* Stephen uses the readily available taxonomic system of the Catholic Church to carry this state over into the everyday: "Sunday was dedicated to the mystery of the Holy Trinity, Monday to the Holy Ghost, Tuesday to the Guardian Angels," and so on through the rest of the week (147). But this system is still too general to provide minute-by-minute protection, and so he surveys himself even more closely: "His day began with an heroic offering of its every moment of thought or action" (147). Here Stephen generates pleasure through intense self-surveillance, just as, in book II, he generates pleasure for himself, in a completely opposite manner, by refusing to see himself as anything but a sensual animal randomly wandering the city in a search for sensation: "It would be a gloomy secret night. . . . He would follow a devious course up and down the streets. . . . waiting for a sudden movement of his own will or a sudden call to his sinloving soul" (102). He sees himself as completely open to the wild call of the city, with no more thought to control or contour his feelings than an animal in the forest. But we should not forget that Stephen will be required to pay for his pleasure. Indeed, if we tone down the Catholic reveling in self-loathing, this passage is also a reasonable description of going to the mall just to browse around, just to immerse ourselves in a sort of interpellative orgy of appeals and promises.

Refusing self-surveillance in search of sensation is figured by Stephen as a sort of profligate and obscene spending, and the opposite pleasure of reveling in self-surveillance is likewise configured by Stephen as a sort of purchase, but this time it is grace being bought as a result of monitoring feelings, as opposed to sin being purchased as a result of letting them run riot. Appropriately, the nexus of the monetary exchange is not a prostitute in nighttown but a cash register in heaven: "Every part of his day, divided by what he regarded now as the duties of his station in life, circled about its own centre of spiritual energy. . . . every thought, word and deed, every instant of consciousness could be made to revibrate radiantly in heaven: and at times his sense of such immediate repercussion was so lively that he seemed to feel his soul in devotion pressing like fingers the keyboard of a great cash register and to see the amount of his purchase start forth immediately in heaven" (148). Finally, a store in Ireland that stays open twenty-four hours a day.

If aesthetic theory was once envisioned as a system of thought explaining the "natural" category of "beauty," I am deconstructing it in order to analyze the infrastructure of the social construction of beauty. Only then may modernist aesthetic theory be understood as the cornerstone of bourgeois hegemonic discourses that make the fictional category of the "artistic" an excuse to organize and make accessible to discipline all the chaotic responses of which the body is capable. This represents a shift from thinking about aesthetic theory as a philosophical end point to exposing it as a dynamic of self-discipline, one that resolves sexual ambivalence into an agreed-upon theory about what constitutes "beauty." What aesthetic theory elides, however, is that both logical reflection *and* physical arousal, both objective harmony *and* disconcerting fantasy, are necessary components—indeed, insatiable "drives" in Freud's and Lacan's sense of the term—in the apprehension of what is beautiful. Put more succinctly, creativity, like interpretation, *is* desire, and, not coincidentally, any theory of aesthetics interrogates desire.

Thus, we can denaturalize the theorization of what is "beautiful," regarding it not as an obvious, self-evident undertaking, but reconfiguring it as more of a process that views the body as a contested site of meaning and attempts to control it by colonizing its sensory apparatus in the service of a historically, culturally, and economically specific subjectivity, which is then reified and universalized as "human nature." Father Arnall's hell sermon sets up within Stephen an orgy of punitive self-surveillance, one in which he systematically tries to destroy his senses as pleasure receptors by overloading them with unpleasant stimuli: "Each of his senses," we are told, "was brought under a rigorous discipline" (150). But in a commodity culture, becoming a pleasure anorexic, starving oneself of images, can feel good—especially, I would like to suggest, at the turn of the century, when the modern city is virtually uncatalogued and even a tawdry bazaar in Dublin with the "magical" name of Araby brings on disorienting euphoria and nearly unbearable depression during a span of only a few days.

Joyce denaturalizes the "foundational" artistic category of aesthetic theory to reveal the way it helps to construct presumably natural entities—such as the body, sex, sexuality, gender, and identity—and appears to produce for them a myth of origin, which can then be cited as the prehistorical, precultural source of a legitimacy presented as organic and inevitable, and therefore beyond the challenge of debate. Once the relative legitimacy of feelings is beyond debate, the subject becomes, through the contested site of the body, open to the "rigours of discipline," disguised as benevolent guidance and education, within individual systems of self-surveillance. The system of self-surveillance not only becomes as "personal" as one's "feelings," it is indistinguishable from one's feelings to the point of being experienced as "just how we feel." But the manner in which meanings are assigned to feelings is what Cvetkovitch has termed a "politics of affect" (27).

In this way, feelings that are experienced as germinating from within the dominant ideology become privileged as evidence of a core self, and this, in turn, leads to their further reification into normative ideals (where, typically, they become characterized as "the way anybody would feel"). Thus, something as presumably private and unavailable to mediation as feelings help map out "within" the subject a disciplinary grid in reference to which self-surveillance can operate. It is similar to Freud's concept of the super ego, except that its dictates become cloaked as "common sense" rather than authoritative pronouncements. Of course, the same body that is mapped out by the aesthetic threatens to rescramble itself with the pornographic. Using the anthropological work of Mary Douglas, Fiske identifies aesthetic theory as performing a purification ritual: "dirt is matter out of place, and the terror it invokes in the respectable bourgeoisie derives from its power to demonstrate the fragility of the conceptual categories by which semiotic and social are exercised over unruliness and the forces of deception" (*Understanding*, 98). Commodity culture, and the city in which it operates and diffuses itself, is pornographic in the sense that it is anti-aesthetic; it generates sensation indifferent to, or deliberately transgressive of, the politics of affect that is the basis of self-surveillance. For Stephen, the aesthetic is a relief from the pornographic, but, equally, the pornographic is a relief from the aesthetic.

The pornographic generates pleasure by transgressing; the aesthetic does so by conforming. Pornography is truly "obscene" in the sense that it takes you behind the scenes of your own sensuality, shocking you with an aesthetics of attraction that is unsanctioned by the dominant hegemonic discourse of pleasure production. We censor pornography because it censors us, disturbing a system of self-surveillance we have come to rely upon as an organizing principle; feelings that are left uncategorized appear to be impulsive, reflexive, and dangerous, perhaps not even inside us at all, but something seeking to invade us from without (which is Father Arnall's basic description of Satan's goal). Indeed, Stephen experiences physical arousal as the invasion of a foreign body snaking its way into his actual body. Banished from aesthetic theory as a legitimate response, arousal returns to call into question Western culture's basic assumption of a substantive being who is presumed to be the origin and sovereign ruler of thought, feeling, and desire.

III. Sleepless in Dublin: Modernity and the ideology of the encounter

As I have already suggested, and as Jean Gagnon argues in more detail in his book *Pornography in the Urban World,* it is the city itself that is pornographic in the nonpejorative sense that the city exists in order to organize space in a manner that permits it to be eroticized for the purposes of commerce: "The city draws the look of residents and visitors alike, offering itself to be deciphered and read. It is an urban landscape which, unlike the countryside, becomes a cultural reservoir where individuals draw the representations that they more or less consciously incorporate into their lives and value-systems."[14] Oscar Wilde, in his essay "The Decay of Lying," also implies that the city alters the "nature" of subjectivity by replacing this supposedly innate nature with something like what Gagnon calls a cultural reservoir: "Nature has good intentions, of course, but, as Aristotle once said, she cannot carry them out. . . . If Nature had been comfortable, mankind would never have invented architecture. . . . Egotism itself, which is so necessary to a proper sense of human dignity, is entirely the result of indoor life."[15] The system of fictional imagery in the urban landscape, according to Gagnon, generates a particularly urban fantasy he, too, from yet another perspective, designates as an ideology of the encounter: "Whether individuals attempt to escape or embrace solitude, the city envelops us in a web of expectation of possible encounters.

In addition to the obvious case of the narrator in Joyce's story entitled "An Encounter," Stephen's constant fantasy while wandering around the city is that he will somehow meet somebody. Sometimes his fantasy is that he will sin with this person in a manner he imagines—predictably—as debasing and bestial. Wild-haired and lecherous-eyed women, of the sort the narrator of "An Encounter" remembers from the covers of pulp detective magazines, also appear to haunt the edges of Stephen's urban fantasy. At other times, he imagines encountering what amounts to the antidote of this image—a girl innocent and demure whom the Virgin Mary herself joins with him in a sinless apotheosis of satisfaction: "—Take hands, Stephen and

Emma. It is a beautiful evening now in heaven. You have erred but you are always my children" (*P,* 116).

Stephen's particular ideology of the encounter is neatly split between the kinetics of the pornographic city and the stasis of aesthetic distance from it. On the one hand, the wanton woman is the femme fatale of commodity culture, never weary of her ardent ways (as Stephen's villanelle laments), merciless, vampirish, sucking his blood, forcing him to spend again and again (and here we should recall that *spend,* in Victorian pornography, is a favorite slang term for sexual climax). The other girl, the flip side of his projection of Emma, is partially contained in the figure of Mercedes, before whom Stephen becomes a pleasure anorexic ("Madam, I never eat muscatel grapes"), immune in a priest-like manner, with both his flesh and his appetites beyond the call of all entreaties. Indeed, Stephen's habit of coupling his visits to nighttown with visits to a church might be read as a journey from the enigmatic figuration of the city as opaque and dangerous over to the Virgin Mary's reassuring refiguration of it as "a wide land under a tender lucid evening sky, a cloud drifting westward amid a pale green sea of heaven, they stood together [Stephen and Emma], children that had erred" (116).

But the importance of the urban encounter, whether it be fantasized as innocent and therefore rehabilitating, or depraved and therefore both exciting and treacherous, or something in between, is not just a topic of recent discussion. For such early students of modernity as the poet Baudelaire and the sociologist Georg Simmel, the defining experience of modernism was that of living in a modern metropolis, and the most remarked upon feature of this life was the nearly unmanageable assault of noise, illogical juxtaposition, relentless unpredictability, and enigmatic epiphanies, all made publicly available, to anyone of all classes, in a manner that was as undeniably fascinating as it was inevitably frustrating. What is so different about this experience—what makes it give rise to the symptom of modernism—is that it demands a strategy of delimitation. In the case of Stephen, one such strategy is the (imaginary) protected space of aesthetic contemplation, a space which he then is free to misrecognize as the inevitable and logical outcome of "normal nature." Alternatives to this process, which threaten to reveal it as a fantasy and a strategy, are dismissed as perverse.

As another example of a strategy of delimitation constituted by the metropolitan experience, Joyce's theory of the epiphany also might be seen as a product of, and a reaction to, the kaleidoscopic urban environment. As such, it is both derived from the experience of the city and, in as much as it influences the representation of it in art, constitutive of this same experience. If it is true, as Oscar Wilde claims, that there was no fog in London until poets and painters aestheticized it ("people see fogs, not because there are fogs, but because poets and painters have taught them"), it is equally the case that there was no one experiencing modernity as intense moments of miraculous yet bewildering clarity until Joyce's idea of the epiphany became commonplace (Wilde, 986). Another way to introduce the idea of periodization into theoretical constructs is to note that Joyce's concept of the epiphany appears to be the urbanization of Wordsworth's earlier concept of the "spot of time." Indeed, the Wordsworthian "moment" of feeling an oceanic connection to "something evermore about to be," is altered by Joyce into much more fleeting moments in which a snapshot of the permanent flux unexpectedly offers itself as a part of the whole, but only long enough to be sensed, and not nearly long enough to be contemplated or analyzed.

The individual's experience of the modern metropolis as an overwhelming assault on both sense and logic is a feature of modernity foregrounded by Baudelaire, more formally discussed at the turn of the century by the sociologist Georg Simmel, and picked up again by Benjamin at the close of the great era of modernist production. It is significant that Benjamin, not in the habit of quoting sociologists, nonetheless quotes Simmel, precisely to underline the unprecedented problem presented by the modern city to its inhabitants—how to be in a crowd of strangers, for extended periods of time, without acknowledging any of them, and without their acknowledging either you or each other: "Interpersonal relationships in big cities are distinguished by a marked preponderance of the activity of the eye over the activity of the ear. The main reason for this is the public means of transportation. Before the development of buses, railroads, and trams in the nineteenth century, people had never been in a position of having to look at one another for long minutes or even hours without speaking to one another" (qtd. in Benjamin, 35). Benjamin then draws out a point that is already implicit in Simmel's observation: The experience of modernity calls for a strategic desensitization that, in turn, fosters a unique feeling of loneliness, a type of loneliness one can feel only in a crowd.

For Baudelaire, the experience of loneliness in a crowd is unique in the history of subjectivity because the very experience that engenders the lonely feeling—observing and being jostled by a dozen or more people apparently indifferent to your existence—is also the occasion that seems capable of alleviating it by supplying, perhaps, one knowing glance from among the many oblivious ones. Benjamin compares the phenomenon of wandering through crowds, hoping for an ideal encounter, to drug addiction, particularly as regards the cycle in drug addiction of exhilaration, followed by dejection, followed by a more desperate return to the need for exhilaration. Similarly, the individual plunges himself into the crowd, frantically scanning the faces completely accessible to his gaze and yet seemingly unaware of him; his failure to make a connection drives him to experience ever more deeply the corrosive loneliness this very exercise is striving to alleviate. As Benjamin remarks, "The crowd is . . . the latest narcotic for those abandoned" (53).

As I have already implied by citing Simmel, there is nothing revisionist about characterizing the experience of moving through the crowded metropolis as an intoxicating one that promises to relieve loneliness in a manner that succeeds only in deepening it, thus initiating a cycle that immerses one further into a perpetual state of hopeless hopefulness. (As I will discuss later, in more detail, this is also the attitude of the modern consumer.) Indeed, apart from his considerable acumen as a sociologist, Simmel is also important to an appreciation of the early experience of modernity because of his status as an eyewitness, one reporting back to us from "point zero" on the unprecedented experience of the metropolis, an experience unmediated, as yet, by the useful yet distortional delimiting strategies of modernist representation.

As David Frisby notes, a primary focus of Simmel's work is "the subjective consequences of metropolitan existence."[16] Even apart from his theorizing about the experience of modernity, Simmel's description of the urban experience as "the rapid crowding of changing images, the sharp discontinuity in the grasp of a single glance, and the unexpectedness of onrushing impression" makes it clear to us, all these years later, why the most urgent requirement for the individual in the big city—very nearly a prerequisite to sanity—was "to preserve subjective life against the overwhelming power of metropolitan life" (Frisby, 115). I am trying to periodize this moment as one when the modern city was presenting an unprecedented challenge to subjectivity, and yet the effective delimiting strategies of modernist representation, which we sometimes naturalize as merely a "response" to modernity, were not yet available. As a result, the city could be a much more excruciating and exhilarating experience than it is today. Part of Joyce's ironic distance from Stephen is made possible by the fact that Joyce has begun to process the experience of modernity by setting himself the task of representing a city in literature (an underestimated organizing force behind his multiplicitous presentation of the city in *Dubliners*), whereas Stephen is still merely living in it, threatened by its institutionalized anonymity and therefore dependent upon its (apparently) boundless potential for self-affirmation.

For Simmel (and, I would argue, Stephen Dedalus), *dissociation,* paradoxically, becomes a prerequisite to *association* for individuals lonely and lost in the metropolitan crowd. The primary compensatory strategy for loneliness in the midst of a crowd is the fantasy of the chance encounter, beginning with a glance, leading from there to casual conversation, before escalating into an inarticulate but passionate union. Such an encounter takes many forms; it may be found embedded in Leopold Bloom's attempt to glimpse the white stocking of a woman about to raise her skirt in order to board a tram, an unexpected encounter which is then unexpectedly denied to him when another tram blocks his view at the precise moment he would have seen her raise her skirt. Significantly, the experience generates within him an ache of disappointment that persists throughout the day, and for which he consciously seeks compensation at later points, most notably when Gerty MacDowell arranges her skirts in such a way as to show him considerably more than her ankle. Or it might be a more or less permanent state of mind; for example, the ever-present fantasy of the young Stephen Dedalus, who walks about the city never ceasing to hope for a "holy encounter he had then imagined at which weakness and timidity and inexperience were to fall from him" (*P,* 99). Once again, an early expression of this peculiarly metropolitan fantasy is found in Baudelaire, whose sonnet "To a Passerby" claims to have discovered a rehabilitating glance of recognition—only to have it continue past: "A flash . . . then night!—O lovely fugitive, / I am suddenly reborn from your swift glance; / Shall I never see you till eternity?" (qtd. in Benjamin, 43).

Despite the lofty tone here, the reason for the failure to build a relationship from this one glance is both practical and eminently metropolitan: "Neither knows where the other goes or lives; / We might have loved, and you knew this might be!"[17] Of course, there is no independent verification of the amount of ardor in this woman's glance, but as Benjamin rather brilliantly points out, this lack of clarification is what permits the intensity of the moment: "Far from eluding the erotic in the crowd, the apparition which fascinates him is brought to him by this very crowd" (43). Once again, the experience is self-perpetuating in a peculiar way because the form of the experience renews the desire for the chance encounter even as, and precisely because, it so rapidly extinguishes all hope this *particular* encounter will prove to be the sacred event. If the experience of moving through a crowd can be self-alienating and humiliating, the fantasy of the perfect encounter occurring within the province of that same crowd "permeates [the flaneur] blissfully like a narcotic that can compensate him for many humiliations" (Benjamin, 55).

In the twentieth century, it would seem, the tantalizingly indifferent mistress of the courtly love tradition metamorphoses into the "lovely fugitive" featured in Baudelaire's chance encounter. In a sense, the perpetual nonrelationship between Clark Kent and Lois Lane freezes this moment of compensatory anticipation. Will her gaze ever meet his in recognition that he is the same man about whom she fantasizes? Her indifference to him as anything but a colleague—and not an overly bright one at that—highlights the experience of being lost and lonely in the crowded city, yet, in a manner endlessly exciting and frustrating, right next to the person who might erase the feeling by glancing his way with a slow look of dawning recognition.[18]

Although Benjamin does not develop the idea, he makes a crucial connection between, on the one hand, the fantasy of the chance encounter in the otherwise anonymous socialized space of the big city and, on the other, the experience of shopping, an experience in which goods "call out" to the passerby, in a language made more acute and seductive both by the state of mind of the individual in the city and by their attendant advertising. Thus, within the ideology of the chance encounter, we can see also a prototype for Althusser's concept of "interpellation," a theoretical concept that, like Joyce's idea of the epiphany, is exceedingly urban and should be read as a theorized reaction to the experience of modernity, and not as a universal principle of identity formation. Indeed, Althusser's example of an interpellative moment—a policeman calling out "hey, you"—is quintessentially metropolitan, especially in the unquestioned assumption that the policeman and the person he is hailing must be strangers; Althusser's policeman is not the local constable of a small village. What we need to notice is that it is the anonymity bestowed upon subjects by urban experience that leaves them predisposed to be "called" by their surroundings; their willingness to be "named" springs forth from a socially and historically specific sense that they are nameless. Their sense of being lost and lonely in the crowd predisposes them to misrecognize any form of "hailing" as equivalent to being "found."[19]

Nor is Joyce's use of the religious term *epiphany* to describe a secular, urban experience arbitrary; what makes sacred the chance encounter in the city ("Amid the deafening traffic of the town") is that while the glimpse of the divine is brief enough to torment ("A flash . . . then night!"), the certainty that it can be neither reproduced nor capitalized upon makes it eternally precious ("I am suddenly reborn from your swift glance"). If Wordsworth's spot of time seemed to promise "something evermore about to be," the urban encounter guarantees "something *nevermore* about to be"; the encounter will never be forgotten in direct proportion to the extent to which it failed to take place. "The delight of the city-dweller is not so much love at first sight as love at last sight," Benjamin remarks (43), and it is important to note how vital a role disappointment plays in the flaneur's construction of pleasure: "What makes his body twitch spasmodically is not the excitement of a man in whom an image has taken possession of every fibre of his being; it partakes more of the shock with which an imperious desire suddenly overcomes a lonely man" (46). In this sense, the activity of shopping benefits from the compensatory fantasy of the chance encounter and, indeed, caters to it, by constructing a controlled urban environment where "chance encounters" are offered in a carefully organized manner (clearly marked departments, with goods on shelves, in display cases, hanging from the ceiling, fixed to the wall).

To those who can afford to purchase things, the indulgence of an "imperious desire" which "suddenly overcomes a lonely man" can be displaced onto the modern form of shopping we now call "impulse buying." When the going gets tough—that is to say, when the delirious frustration of missed encounters and crowd-induced loneliness becomes unbearable—the tough go shopping—that is to say, they engage in preordained, easily consummated chance encounters (if you have money), as compensation. Baudelaire writes: "Like a roving soul in search of a body, [the poet] enters another person whenever he wishes. For him alone, all is open; if certain places seem closed to him, it is because in his view they are not worth inspecting" (qtd. in Benjamin, 55). Benjamin, in a startling translation, declares, "the commodity itself is the speaker here." Following upon this, he offers a reason why the urban experience of anonymity weighs particularly heavy on the impoverished shopper when he notes: "yes, the last words give a rather accurate idea of what the commodity whispers to a poor wretch who passes a shop-window containing beautiful and expensive things. These objects are not interested in this person; they do not empathize with him" (55). Walking past commodities is akin to Stephen walking past the prostitutes of nighttown; they will respond with encouragement or contempt depending on his capacity to purchase them.

For an even more accurate idea of how commodities humiliate the impoverished, we can turn, one more time, to the famous closing epiphany of Joyce's short story "Araby" and find a powerful evocation of this same moment, a moment when a young boy in love with a girl he has only spoken to once finds himself too poor to buy her anything at the bazaar. He feels, most particularly, a shame induced in him by *the object's* indomitable disinterest:

> Observing me the young lady came over and asked me did I wish to buy anything. . . . *I looked humbly at the great jars* that stood like eastern guards at either side of the dark entrance to the stall and murmured:
>
> —No, thank you.
>
> *The young lady changed the position of one of the vases*. . . . I lingered before her stall, though I knew my stay was useless. . . . I allowed the two pennies to fall against the sixpence in my pocket. . . . Gazing up into the darkness *I saw myself as a creature* driven and derided by vanity; and my eyes burned with anguish and anger. (35, my emphasis)

It is the vase itself, and its humiliating indifference to his existence, that causes him to stand before it in futile homage, only to turn away at last, feeling despised, anonymous, and insignificant—no more than a "creature." Here is a city dweller in desperate need of the interpellative experience outlined by Althusser. But in the holy church of the department store (of which the Araby bazaar is a prototype), the impoverished narrator finds that many are called, but few are chosen.

If we look back to the beginning of the story, to see what spawned this overwhelming desire to go shopping, we see that the frustration of missed "chance encounters" lies at the root of it: "Every morning I lay on the floor in the front parlour watching her door. . . . When she came out on the doorstep my heart leaped. . . . when we came near the point at which our ways diverged, I quickened my pace and passed her. This happened morning after morning. I had never spoken to her" (30). When she does speak to him finally, we see an apt example of Benjamin's point that the ideology of the magically compensatory urban encounter is easily transformed into the experience of shopping for that one thing that promises to complete us. The urban experience is nothing if not exhausting, moving from despair to exhilaration and back to despair as swiftly as a glance cast unexpectedly in one's direction.

And yet the experience is addictive, perhaps because of the extreme highs and subsequent lows brought about in a short space of time. The addictive quality is best illustrated by Baudelaire, not in one of his many descriptions of bewildering vacillations between hope and despair, but in his offhanded disgust at being in a town too rural to permit his experience of himself as a flaneur: "No shopwindows. Strolling, something that nations with imagination love, is not possible in Brussels. There is nothing to see and the streets are unusable" (qtd. in Benjamin, 50). Caught in an environment insufficiently metropolitan to intoxicate himself, he is like a man suffering from withdrawal. It is Simmel, again, at the turn of the century, and more lately Bourdieu, who argue that the aesthetic point of view in the modernist period, with its emphasis on controlling and evaluating the object from a safe (that is, "pure") perspective, bears some resemblance to the distancing strategy employed by the consumer with money to spend. For Simmel, Frisby tells us "money transactions appear to create that distance which is a necessary prerequisite for aesthetic judgement. . . . Does not 'the beautiful illusion' that is art and the aesthetic realm have its counterpart in the seemingly autonomous realm of the circulation and exchange of commodities? . . . [there is] an 'elective affinity' between the aesthetic domain and the domain of the circulation and exchange of commodities" (140). It is precisely this sociological underpinning to the supposedly "pure" gaze of aesthetic contemplation that Stephen's theory seeks to repress.

In discussing what he characterizes as the "disquiet provoked by urban space" in the experience of modernity, James Donald makes the point that against the "enlightenment aspiration to render the city transparent" and the many attempts to organize and survey it, there was "the city that people experience, a labyrinthine reality. . . . In the recesses and margins of urban space people invest places with meaning, memory and desire" (77). Whereas I have already suggested that Althusser's theory of interpellation, Joyce's concept of the epiphany, and Stephen's modernist aesthetics must be viewed within the urban context that gave rise to them, Donald makes a similar case for Freud's idea of the uncanny: "The disquieting slippage between a place where we should feel at home and the sense that it is, at some level, definitively unhomely provided the starting point for Freud's idea that the uncanny . . . is rooted in the familiar. . . . That suggests why it is necessary to make sense of the individual in the metropolis not only in terms of identity, community and civic association, but also in terms of a dramaturgy of desire, fascination and terror. This uncanny city is not out there in the streets. It defines the architecture of our apparently most secret selves" (80). In changing his character's name from "Stephen Hero" to "Stephen Dedalus," Joyce moves from a fantasy of omniscient power and complete distantiation over the city to a much more uncanny strategic engagement with the city's many winding roads and unexpected sites.

The problem with using the Count of Monte Cristo as a paradigm for moving around the city with impunity is that the experience is so insulated there can be no question of exploring, or of experiencing, the city in such a way as to have its many unexpected realities strike a chord within one's own subjectivity. This may be why latter-day urban superheroes such as Superman and Batman have their vulnerable alter egos in Bruce Wayne and Clark Kent. One gets the feeling that Stephen might have benefited from these more modernized—and urbanized—superheroes. An urban superhero who has no way of experiencing the city from our point of view has less attraction as a fantasy figure. But in addition to Dantes, Stephen designs the more vulnerable Dedalus, exploring the city as a labyrinth he has built out of his own mind, but that nonetheless retains the ability to bewilder him, to bring him face to face with a Minotaur. The world-weary Edmund Dantes is immune to the uncanny, but Stephen Dedalus is not: "He had wandered into a maze of narrow and dirty streets. . . . A trembling seized him and his eyes grew dim. . . . He was in another world: he had awakened from a slumber of centuries" (100). Recall that Freud developed his idea of the uncanny out of his experience of getting lost in the city, but getting lost in such a way that the experience of the unfamiliar was, at the same time, rooted in, and constituted by, a sense of the familiar; the uncanny takes place in a liminal space between the organized, concrete city and the chaotic, phantasmagoric interior world of the subject.

"Uncanniness" is, viewed within the urban context that spawned the concept, the experience of getting so lost as to stumble upon something hitherto unthought of, yet nonetheless utterly familiar. To have this most private feeling elicited by, and enacted within, a public space, shatters the individual's strategies of distantiation and leaves one open and vulnerable to the unmanageable onslaught of relentless stimuli always present in urban space, but most often kept at bay. This is certainly the experience of Stephen Dedalus when he comes upon the word *foetus* carved on a desk: "It shocked him *to find in the outer world* a trace of what he had deemed till then a brutish *and individual malady of his own mind*" (90, my emphasis). Following closely upon this uncanny coupling of an experience of unexpected invasion from without, with the discovery of a hitherto unimagined connection to it from within, Stephen feels the line between his presumably autonomous interior world and presumably indifferent, objective exterior world collapse: "His very brain was sick and powerless. He could scarcely interpret the letters of the signboards of the shops. . . . He could scarcely recognise as his his own thoughts . . ." (92). Here is the sudden reversal described as a component of the uncanny; what should be most familiar—his own thoughts—suddenly seem unrecognizable, and the anonymous scrawl of graffiti on a desk becomes terrifyingly familiar.

Working with the ideas of de Certeau, Donald posits what he calls a "pragmatic aesthetic through which we experience the city not only as visual culture, but above all as psychic space" (84). But it is precisely this "pragmatic aesthetic" that Stephen seeks to eliminate when he banishes the "kinetic" and the "pornographic" to the realm of what he calls, without further explanation, "improper art." Having created this category to house one sort of feeling, he then privileges, in aesthetic terms, the urban equivalent of a well-lit, frequently patrolled square. Stephen's excluded "pornographic" and "kinetic" emotion is a poorly understood uncanny feeling, such as that brought on by the word *foetus*. In his aesthetic theory he legitimates its opposite, a very canny feeling that he designates "the esthetic emotion." This feeling is "static," and, being so, thereby inaugurates an entire state of being—"esthetic stasis"—in which "the mind is arrested and raised above desire and loathing" (179). As Jake Barnes says in *The Sun Also Rises,* "isn't it pretty to think so?"[20] Stephen wants the modernist aesthetic moment to be transparent and carefully mapped out precisely as a response to the opaque, uncanny experience that characterized modernity for the citizen of a modern metropolis. "The modern uncanny," Donald writes, "imagined as the labyrinth, always returns to haunt the city of light" (83).

Equally, the modern experience haunts the edges of Stephen's aesthetic theory, and even smuggles itself into the heart of it in the figure of the irrepressible Lynch: "If I am to listen to your esthetic philosophy give me at least another cigarette. I don't care about it. . . . Damn you and damn everything. I want a job of five hundred a year. You can't get me one" (207). Lynch might be willing to visit Stephen's rarefied aesthetic perch, but, as he never fails to remind himself and Stephen, you can't live there any more than you can live in a perpetual state of grace (something Stephen has already tried and failed to do). If it is a commercial-free zone that serves as a refuge from the city, it is equally a place where you can neither earn money nor spend it, neither desire nor express this desire. Lynch may admire the engineering that has gone into the construction of Stephen's "esthetic stasis," but clearly he feels bound to point out dwelling within it is neither fun nor profitable.

In discussing Simmel's essay "The Metropolis and Mental Life," Donald identifies Simmel's "modern metropolitan man" as having "two main aspects to his personality. One is defensive: the blase intellectualising self that provides some protection against the shock of exorbitant stimuli. The other aspect is more expressive, but again in a specifically modern way: it identifies a form of conduct, or an exercise of liberty, that manifests itself in an aesthetics of self-creation" (80). What is fascinating to me about the walk Stephen and Lynch take together is that they each correspond to these two aspects. Stephen, of course, is the distant intellectualizing self, and we can easily imagine how experiences, such as the one in which he encountered the word *foetus,* serve to underwrite his strategy of intellectualizing. Lynch, on the other hand, is the interactive one: eating dung, writing his name on the buttocks of statues, demanding cigarettes, and yearning for a well-paying job, the better to secure his fantasy to be a man about town with the ways and means to enjoy what it has to offer.

It is not only in their mannerisms that Stephen and Lynch appear to be the two aspects of Simmel's metropolitan personality, but also in the marked counterpoint embodied in their dialogue:

> —But what is beauty? asked Lynch impatiently. Out with another definition. Something we see and like! Is that the best you and Aquinas can do?
>
> —Let us take woman, said Stephen.
>
> —Let us take her! said Lynch fervently. (208)

The blase intellectual flaneur, indifferently strolling past the idea of "woman," walks beside the girl watcher, alert for someone to see and like; the deliberately canny side by side with the irrepressibly uncanny; Jekyll conversing with Hyde; the two aspects of the personality of metropolitan man debating each other.

IV. Forgive me, Mastercard, for I have gone shopping: A Catholic in the modern city

The final social reality to be factored into my cultural reading of Stephen's aesthetic theory is the urban experience most particular to him: that of being raised an Irish Catholic in the rapidly modernizing city of Dublin. Another reason Stephen fears the physical, kinetic world is that he is trying to save himself from Father Arnall's hell, a place where the flesh is at risk of being systematically and exhaustively tortured if the sinner's fleshly cravings are inflamed by some image that flies in at the eyes before his soul can blink. "He was in mortal sin," he reflects, and adds, significantly to my reading, "it could happen *in an instant.* But how so quickly?" (139, my emphasis). Notice he appears to be in agreement with Lynch. The fly enters the eye—desire enters the I—before one blinks; or, rather, the desire to sin is stimulated by something seen, before one can even think or decide either to keep looking or to look away.

The Catholic concept of mortal sin, in which one is held guilty for thinking sinful thoughts, is badly out of synch with the reality of the visual landscape of the modern city, with its commercialized and eroticized space, all devoted to entering the eye in such a way as to reconfigure the I (again, one can see here a basis for interpellation, Althusser's urbanized concept of the relationship between subjectivity and ideology). For a modern Catholic boy accountable to his stern God for sinning in thought as well as in deed, modernity in general, and the urban landscape in particular, is a hellhole of stimulation the founding fathers of the Catholic Church never could have imagined or predicted.

Stephen's answer to how it happens "in an instant" and "so quickly" is explicitly rendered as something entering his eye before he blinks: "But how so quickly? By seeing or by thinking of seeing. The eyes see the thing, without having wished first to see. Then in an instant it happens. But does that part of the body understand or what?" (139). The sudden entering of stimulation from the object of desire—Baudelaire's imperious desire—convulses the "I" much as a fly would the eye. Stephen, in his penitent moments, experiences it as the unexpected and unwelcome invasion of a foreign body. He therefore views that part of himself that responds to this sensual ambush as a foreign, snaky thing—living in his body, feeding off it like a parasite, but somehow distinct: "Was that then he or an inhuman thing moved by a lower soul than his soul? His soul sickened at the thought of a torpid snaky life feeding itself out of the tender marrow of his life and fattening upon the slime of lust" (140). Desire is seen as an internal vampire sucking away at his life's blood, fattening itself with the slimy by-product of his lustful thoughts.

Vampire imagery is a central trope of the experience of commodity culture and of modernity because the modern city, like the vampire, seduces the subject into opening up his wallet or her purse and, while exciting a disorienting mixture of pleasure and terror in the half-willing victim, feeds on the life force embodied there, either in the form of blood or money. Nowadays, we call it going shopping, and we have a lot of humorous ways of depicting the experience of being hypnotized into spending more than we earn; but we must not imagine the subject of early modernism had any such collectively endorsed way to articulate the experience of modernity as anything but the sort of bewildering yet mesmerizing process we see taking over the narrator of "Araby": a frightened boy who shows up at the bazaar, in a semi-trance, staring at the tawdry entrance with awe because it "displayed the magical name [Araby]" (*D*, 34).

And yet, despite the evident amount of pleasure, the underside of guilt, shame, and punishment that follows hard upon this experience is succinctly summed up by Father Arnall: "How [the damned] will rage and fume, to think that they have lost the bliss of heaven for the dross of earth . . . *for a tingling of the nerves*" (129, emphasis mine). The urban landscape is pornographic to the wandering, hopeless Stephen, helplessly experiencing the way it contours his affective responses as the kinetic reflexive action of an inutterably bestial dimension of his subjectivity; Dublin itself becomes the antithesis of what Araby represented: "The letters of the name of Dublin lay heavily upon his mind, pushing one another surlily hither and thither with slow boorish insistence. . . . The body that was his stood, listless and dishonoured, gazing out of darkened eyes, helpless" (111). Both the narrator of "Araby" and Stephen Dedalus thrill to the many siren calls of the city, but, for both, their object of desire inflames them only because it is a *missed* encounter, love at *last* glance. What seemed at last to represent freedom from loneliness turns into a despised signifier of exhausted hopes and futile enthusiasms.

But let us try to put the early experience of the city and commodity culture yet further into a Catholic context. Mortal sin, if we were to translate it into what Stephen might call the language of the marketplace, is wanting something without being able to afford to buy; sinning in thought, though not yet in deed, is the essence of commodity culture. The state of unrest Stephen alternately laments and wallows in is the experience of a turn-of-the-century adolescent wandering through an urban center of signs designed to eroticize space and formulate an atmosphere conducive to the consumption of goods, which appear to embody what is lacking in one's social relations—what Marx calls the commodity. An important organizing principle in *Portrait* is that Stephen's experience of the city is intensified by the fact that he began his life outside of Dublin, in an environment so rural that the story wherein he imagines himself as Baby Tuckoo features as its dominant image, not a tram rattling past on a city street, but a moocow coming along the road. Stephen's development is figured in quite a few ways in *Portrait,* but one of the major engines of change is his combination of shock, consternation, and delight upon encountering the modern city.

Indeed, the city is described not in geographical terms at all, but only in relation to how it felt to him to be in it: "Dublin was a new and complex sensation" (66). This sensation, represented by the city, yet embodied within himself, is so new and complex that he treats it like the labyrinth designed by his namesake, Dedalus: "In the beginning he contented himself with circling timidly round the neighbouring square" (66). The biblical echo, "in the beginning," alerts us to the fact that the urban world is all before Stephen. Only at this point does he begin to show signs of the modern consumer, an urban wanderer lost yet mesmerized in a constellation of signs, signs alerting him to inarticulate feelings of discontentment and yet, at the same time, and in a manner indistinguishable from this discontentment, inaugurating the hopeful fantasy of the chance encounter: "A vague dissatisfaction grew up within him as he looked on the quays and on the river and on the lowering skies and yet he continued to wander up and down day after day as if he really sought someone that eluded him" (66).

What we have here is a portrait of Baudelaire's flaneur as a young boy. But as a young man, and as a young man recently brought to the city, his sense of some ultimate encounter, evermore about to be, just around the corner, maybe in the next shop window, eventually tips over into an exhausted state of sullen disappointment: "though they passed a jovial array of shops lit up and adorned for Christmas, his mood of embittered silence did not leave him. . . . The causes of his embitterment were many, remote and near. He was angry with himself for being young and prey of restless foolish impulses" (67). Whereas earlier he made a pretend cave of Monte Cristo on his kitchen table and imagined himself as the calm, methodical avenger, Edmund Dantes, now he is inundated with the eroticized atmosphere of the urban landscape, his desires so numerous, so diffuse, and so intangible that "inarticulate cries and the unspoken brutal words rushed forth from his brain to force a passage. His blood was in revolt. He wandered up and down [the city streets]. . . . He moaned to himself like some baffled prowling beast. He wanted to sin with another of his kind. . . . He felt some dark presence moving irresistibly upon him from the darkness. . . . He stretched out his arms in the street to hold fast the frail swooning form that eluded him and incited him" (99–100). Never has a character in literature so badly needed to go shopping. But Stephen knows nothing of this, any more than his religious instructors do. Their insistence that desiring things in thought is a mortal sin, a disgusting tingling of the nerves, in punishment for which each of his five sense will be ingeniously tortured forever, has caused this poor young Irish flaneur to experience the dawning of the commodity age as an apparently self-induced psychosis of squalid madness and unregenerate sinning.

Indeed, Father Arnall's description of hell has a curious theme running though its numerous scenarios of pain: Devils will torment sinners with repetitious recitals of all their inadequacies, detail all their failures, chronicle missed opportunities, amplify self-doubt, magnify imperfections. But what is this really? This is your average Head and Shoulders dandruff shampoo commercial, whose slogan, worthy of the demonic taunting of a particularly loathsome devil, is: "You never get a second chance to make a first impression." Absolution is offered in the form of a product, after you have done penance, or paid for it. You've seen this commercial: The woman looks up on the bus. The chance encounter she's dreamed of—that Stephen dreams of, Mercedes, muscatel grapes, and all the rest—is about to ensue, but the man who was to initiate the moment looks away; he sees dandruff on her shoulders, and we know, from the fiendishly tight close-up of her face presented by the camera, we know from her death-like expression of regret and remorse, that all her ambition and hopes will henceforth unceasingly mock her as she begins her pathetic crawl toward the welcome death and annihilation she will gratefully embrace. Or, she can buy the shampoo, and, in the process, buy peace of mind that when the chance encounter occurs, she will be perfectly poised to meet it. This is only one example among many; the possibility of having the longed-for chance encounter occur, only to find you have missed it, is a central nightmare in modern advertising, indicating, by its regular presentation, the importance of keeping alive the fantasy of the ideal encounter as a way to cope with the crowd-induced loneliness of the metropolitan experience.

In the cruel democracy of commodity culture, poverty does not disqualify you from seeing all that is unavailable to you. Accordingly, the only times Stephen is at peace in *Portrait,* the only times he is free from the inarticulate longing that changes him into a baffled prowling beast, are those times immediately after confession, when he has purged himself—at least until he leaves the confessional—of all the sinful urges promoted by the city ("How simple and beautiful was life after all!"); those times immediately after visiting a prostitute and wallowing in the fantasy of the chance encounter ("In her arms he felt that he had suddenly become strong and fearless and sure of himself"); or those infrequent times—only once in the novel, actually—when he finds himself flush with his essay prize money, amounting to thirty-three pounds ("For a swift season of merrymaking the money of his prizes ran through Stephen's fingers"). Immediately upon receiving his prize money, his ability to pay both eclipses his sense he should pray and grants him pardon from the ever-restless fantasy of the chance encounter: "Great parcels of groceries and delicacies and dried fruits arrived from the city. . . . his trousers' pockets bulged with masses of silver and copper coins. . . . He . . . wrote out resolutions . . . pored upon all kinds of price lists. When he could do no more he drove up and down the city in trams" (97–98). Riding the trams, I would suggest, is the best and swiftest way to visit and revisit every point of commercial interest in the city.

Significantly, this activity replaces his previous use of idle time: wandering the streets as a baffled prowling beast. Instead of first sinning, then praying, he is buying, then paying. But, when the money runs out, we learn "the season of pleasure came to an end" (98). Joyce summarizes Stephen's spending spree with the fascinating notion of modern consuming as a way to generate pleasure *as climate,* to dwell within an exhilarating storm of sanctioned sensation. He is so involved in the process of satisfying himself—however spuriously—that he is insulated, for "a season," from the other dimension of the city: the systematic promotion of dissatisfaction coupled with products that offer salvation. Advertising, like religion, depends upon the truism "man does not live by bread/goods alone"; he needs scripture/advertising as well. As soon as Stephen's money dwindles, however, the "wasting fires" spring up again: "He burned to appease the fierce longings of his heart before which everything else was idle and alien" (98). As in "Araby," the desire to consume consumes the everyday, in favor of a longed-for apotheosis of complete satisfaction.

But also, once again, Stephen fails to make any connection between the "pornographic," or the "kinetic," landscape of the modern city and what he misunderstands as the appalling relentlessness of his own body's mindless and inexplicable cravings: "Beside the savage desire within him to realise the enormities which he brooded on nothing was sacred" (98–99). At the same time, Stephen continues to fantasize fondly about an innocent encounter, one which he deliberately opposes to this urge: "Only at times, in the pauses of his desire, when the luxury that was wasting him gave room to a softer languor, the image of Mercedes traversed the background of his memory. . . . A tender premonition touched him of the tryst he had then looked forward to and in spite of the horrible reality which lay between his hope of then and now, of the holy encounter he had then imagined at which weakness and timidity and inexperience were to fall from him. Such moments passed" (99).

The image of Mercedes always accompanies a fantasy of control, of taking no more than he needs, of being self-sufficient, neither sinful nor in debt, neither guilty nor full of longing. In economic terms, this seems a fantasy based on use value, a system in which everything costs what it appears to be worth. It is a fantasy of indomitable wholeness based upon, and signified by, calm and resolute refusal in the face of the desirable: "Madam, I never eat muscatel grapes." It is worth noting, too, that when this fantasy is ascendant, Dublin becomes "sunny Marseilles," and its reality as a "new and complex sensation" is transformed into a simple village path running past Mercedes's idyllic rural abode: "a small whitewashed house in the garden of which grew many rosebushes" (63).

In dramatizing Stephen's presentation of his aesthetic theory, Joyce deconstructs aesthetic theory in order to expose it as a regulatory regime that monitors subjectivity, criminalizes "perversion" (after first constructing it), and, through the guise of a supposedly neutral exploration of "the beautiful," provides the entry point for the policing of desire. Joyce shows aesthetic theory must be designated as asexual in order that it might also pose as ahistorical. By showing Stephen Dedalus in the throes of inventing a modernist aesthetics, Joyce shows him systematically vacuuming out dirt—the erotic—from such a theory, in order to create a sanctioned space, one that is free from the relentless seductions and importunities of the modern urban landscape. It is a sanctioned space similar to what the Catholic Church promises to a priest; the artist, like the priest, will be able to listen to the confessions of sin, be immersed in vertiginous scenarios of fantasy and desire, and yet remain coolly indifferent within what Stephen calls, when he contemplates what it would be like to become a priest, a "magical immunity." If being a priest means enjoying the confessions of girls and women while remaining immune from sin and desire—the sacred incarnation of an urban Superman—then Stephen feels he may have a vocation. Stephen's figuring of the artist as "a priest of the eternal imagination," in other words, is not just a clever metaphor; the recitation of his aesthetic theory to Lynch is less an attempt to understand the artist than it is to be ordained in the sense of being immunized from the constant interpellations made by the kinetically charged cityscape to what he misperceives as his sin-loving flesh.

Indeed, Stephen's studied indifference when recounting his aesthetic theory is routed in an instant, not by the clamoring city, which it is designed to keep at bay, but by Lynch's remark: "Your beloved is here" (215). Instantly he is flooded with bitterness brought on by having seen her flirt with a real priest instead of confiding her sinful thoughts to him, a self-ordained priest of the eternal imagination made mysteriously immune from the pornographic and the kinetic by the holy word of his own aesthetic theory: "She had no priest to flirt with, . . . remembering how he had seen her last. Lynch was right. His mind, emptied of theory and courage, lapsed back into a listless peace" (216).

The collapse that has taken place between the world of art and the marketplace might also be characterized with reference to what Haug calls "commodity aesthetics."[21] On the one hand, "beauty" is still understood as an appearance that appeals to the senses, but, on the other, commodity aesthetics denotes "a beauty developed in the service of the realization of exchange-value, whereby commodities are designed to stimulate in the onlooker the desire to possess and the impulse to buy. . . . The transformation of the world of useful objects into commodities triggers instinctual responses, and is the functional means by which not only the world of sensual objects but also human sensuality itself is remoulded again and again" (Haug, 8). Use value in capitalism, according to Baudrillard, is nowhere in existence except as nostalgia, and as an alibi for exchange value; Mercedes and the Virgin Mary, and the effect of confession itself, are the aesthetic equivalents of use value: innocent, capable of holy encounters, a commercial-free zone where everything becomes exactly what it appears to be.[22]

In contrast, the commodity aesthetics generated by exchange value turn this same "tender tryst" into an encounter with the femme fatale, who seems to become a figure for both the city itself and commodity culture in general: "A figure that seemed to him by day demure and innocent came towards him by night through the winding darkness of sleep, her face transfigured by a lecherous cunning, her eyes bright with brutish joy" (99). This movement from innocence to depravity is reminiscent of the vampirish transformation Bram Stoker chronicled in *Dracula.* Indeed, the vampire myth is a central trope of the experience of modernity and the commodity aesthetics of the city, particularly with its ideology of the tantalizing yet addictive and, eventually, destructive urban encounter; Dracula, after all, is determined to move from rural Transylvania to the big city of London.

Vampirism is also the trope to which Marx turns when searching for a way to describe how capital, the undead, mesmerizes its victims by transforming innocent use value—if there ever was such a thing—into the alternately heavenly and hellish world of disorienting pleasure production and fatal attractions spawned by exchange value: "Capital is dead labour, which, vampire-like, lives only by sucking living labour, and lives the more, the more labour it sucks."[23] When Stephen finds himself in nighttown in *Portrait,* he is not in search of the innocent use value he fantasizes as Mercedes waiting for him in her little house; instead, he is immersing himself in the much more delirious sensation of exchange value: "He would pass by them [the prostitutes] calmly waiting for a sudden movement of his own will or a sudden call to his sinloving soul from their soft perfumed flesh. . . . he prowled in quest of that call" (102). This is not universal sexuality, but a historically specific technocracy of sensuality. What we are invited to witness is the way human sensuality has been molded by commodity aesthetics, and how human need and instinct structures are altered under the impact of a continuously changing prospect of satisfaction offered by commodities. With the rise of commodity culture and the subordination of use value to exchange value, and the attendant fetishization of the object it brought about, having a "normal nature" becomes a difficult pose.

What Stephen describes as "prowling in quest of that call" is his attempt to design a sexual encounter that approximates the ideology of the transforming encounter promised by the fantasy of exchange value. Earlier, he had envisioned his encounter with Mercedes as one in which "he would fade into something impalpable under her eyes and then, in a moment, he would be transfigured. Weakness and timidity and inexperience would fall from him in that magic moment" (65). Significantly, this encounter appears to happen, finally, but only when his "sinloving flesh" has been "called" by a prostitute's soft perfumed flesh: "In her arms he felt that he had suddenly become strong and fearless and sure of himself" (96). Later, he will achieve a similar moment, after his confession, when the pressure of the communion wafer on his tongue generates a state of well-being identical to that of the pressure of the prostitute's tongue in his mouth. Stephen in sin or Stephen in a state of grace craves the same thing: an ideal encounter with the commodified product—prostitute or communion wafer. In this regard, the only difference between going shopping or "buying" a prostitute and going to confession is that, on the one hand, shopping and sex are guilt free as long as you have money, and, on the other, confession is free, but you have to feel guilty to indulge in its forgiveness. The communion wafer is indeed, as Bloom is the first to notice, the longest selling and most successful product in the world. What is Coca Cola against its two-thousand-year ad campaign, with testimonials from Matthew, Mark, Luke, and John?

V. Beauty *is* the I of the beholder: Aesthetic theory and marketing strategies

Stephen delivers his theory while walking through the noisy streets of Dublin, apparently indifferent to the almost constant interruptions pressing in on him on all sides: "A long dray laden with old iron came round the corner . . . covering the end of Stephen's speech with the harsh roar of jangled and rattling metal. Lynch closed his ears and gave out oath after oath till the dray had passed" (209). Stephen, however, waits patiently for the noise to subside, and continues without a break in his line of reasoning. In this scene alone—Stephen waiting imperturbably, Lynch with both hands over his ears, cursing in a frenzy—we have an example of someone dissociating from the city and someone right next to him painfully registering every nuance of its jangling reality. The city intrudes on Stephen's aesthetic discourse metaphorically as well, as when he overhears wealthier classmates discussing their future earning potential as doctors:

> There's plenty of money to be made in a big commercial city.
> —Depends on the practice. (216)

The aesthetic point of view is a refuge from modernity from an economic standpoint as well.

Stephen's ability to resume his thought, as though no tram had intervened, further reveals his aesthetic posture as a strategy of distantiation couched within a philosophical point of view. As Pierre Bourdieu argues, "this pure aesthetic is indeed the rationalization of an ethos: pure pleasure, pleasure totally purified of all sensuous or sensible interest, perfectly free of all social or fashionable interest, as remote from concupiscence as it is from conspicuous consumption" (493). If, as Simmel's work also claims, "the particular form of intellectuality appropriate to metropolitan existence is one which reacts with indifference to external shocks and a whole field of possible interactions," then the privileged position of the "pure" gaze of aesthetic contemplation is also the fantasy of complete protection from the addictive rhythm of the assaulting and seductive effects of the big city on the individual (qtd. in Frisby, 115).

In Bourdieu's sociological reading of a modernist aesthetic point of view, he finds the construction of what we might term a "commercial-free zone," within which the observer can view with impunity the permanent flux of stimuli in the big city landscape, and do so without succumbing to what Baudelaire and Benjamin describe as "shocks," or what Baudelaire calls "imperious desires" (the sort Stephen tries to denigrate and dismiss as "kinetic emotions"). This gets us closer to the implicit question embedded within the question of "what is Stephen's aesthetic theory," and that is the more sociologically, historically, and economically based question of "why such an emphasis on aesthetic theory in the modernist period?"

Or, put more bluntly, and with a direct emphasis on *Portrait* as an example of this general phenomenon, if Stephen fancies himself an artist, why not create instead of pontificate? The contouring influences on his aesthetic theory cannot be appreciated without first asking why the necessity for it, and why the urgency to express it in the city streets to a bemused and inattentive friend? Everyone seems to know, from teachers to stray students passed on the street, that Stephen is "planning" a work on aesthetic theory.

Equally, Lynch makes it clear that the oration Stephen delivers to him is only the latest one of a series. For Stephen, theorizing about aesthetics is not so much a work of scholarship in progress as it is a way of life, a means of coping, and a fantasy of immunity from the experience of modernity. And, of course, once approached this way, the "nature" of the theory will not appear as "natural," but as constructed. As Gane argues in discussing Bourdieu's sociological reading of aesthetic theory, "the aesthetic point of view defines a social superiority which is misrecognised as being in the nature of the art work itself. It is the aesthetic point of view . . . that creates the aesthetic object while simultaneously proclaiming the social position of the beholder" (qtd. in Bourdieu, 148). Of course, Stephen's social standing has been steadily slipping since the opening of the novel, and one of my answers to the question of why Stephen disseminates an aesthetic theory with such personal urgency, and why he insists, like some sort of philosophical Ancient Mariner, on stopping people passing by to tell it, is that he is, as he admits in his less self-confident moments, feeling increasingly destabilized by his declining social and economic status—literally from first son of a Cork landowner to very nearly homeless—and one way to deny that is to assume the aesthetic point of view as the only remaining posture of social superiority he can afford.

In order to adopt this posture at the outset, Stephen performs a bit of noblesse oblige that is bizarre, considering his own increasingly desperate circumstances:

> At the foot of the steps they halted and Stephen took a packet of cigarettes from his pocket and offered it to his companion.
>
> —I know you are poor, he said.
>
> —Damn your yellow insolence, answered Lynch. (204)

Far from being as flush as this regal gesture implies, Stephen wanders through the noisy streets of Dublin expounding his theory because he cannot afford to go shopping. The interpellative call of every shopwindow he passes must be refuted by a valorization of the (imagined) pure gaze of the aesthetic point of view. Thus modernist aesthetics in general, and Stephen's in particular, evidence an urban strategy of distantiation. The presumably "pure" aesthetic gaze (what Stephen calls "static" emotion) is the corollary of the presumably "impure" gaze (what Stephen calls "kinetic" or "pornographic") of the consumer.

Safely ensconced within the perspective of the aesthetic gaze, one is able to experience, to use Bourdieu's terms, a "pure pleasure" that is, at the same time, "a pleasure totally purified of all sensuous or sensible interest." The fantasy, for the subject of commodity culture, seems to be one where the shopper can enjoy the pleasure of advertisements urging consumption, while at the same time remaining immune to the sense of lack and longing simultaneously produced alongside this pleasure. This is *necessarily* a fantasy because, as Benjamin makes clear when discussing Baudelaire's "To a Passerby," the sense of loss and consequent longing, far from undermining the pleasure, actually constitutes it. In "the high point of the encounter . . . the poet's passion seems to be frustrated but in reality bursts out of him like a flame" (43).

In offering his response to the question of why the mediatory category of the aesthetic was so intricately constructed and elaborated in modernism, Terry Eagleton describes it as "an isolated enclave within which the dominant social order can find an idealized refuge from its own actual values of competitiveness, exploitation and material possessiveness."[24] This is accurate as far as it goes, but I am suggesting this is a two-way street, and those who have been dispossessed of the material means necessary to dwell within "the dominant social order" still may at least *appear* to be qualified to do so if they philosophize and attempt to naturalize this "idealized refuge," as though they still required its ideological blandishments. Being "natural" is a pose, and Stephen must naturalize the privileged category of aesthetic contemplation not, as Eagleton might suggest, because he is a member of the dominant class, but because he no longer is.

In a way, Stephen is continuing a class strategy his father, Simon, began when he first found himself drifting toward bankruptcy: send his boy to Clongowes, where other children have fathers who are magistrates, and give his son the educational wherewithal to participate in the dominant class's investment in a "pure" aesthetic gaze, even as one's ability to invest financially in anything continues to dwindle. Certainly by the time of the trip to Cork with his father, it is dawning on Stephen that this is the only legacy he can expect. Indeed, the genesis of Stephen's aesthetic distinctions is less Aristotle or Aquinas, as he would have Lynch and others think, and more the intensely humiliating trip he took with his father to Cork. Ostensibly, this was a homecoming trip on which Simon brings along his eldest son as proof to his old schoolmates that he has continued to prosper in Dublin. The real purpose of the visit, however, is that Simon's rapidly increasing insolvency continues to force him to sell off the land that once underwrote his family's claim to a secure position within the dominant culture of the Irish Catholic middle class. Furthermore, no one in Cork, however much they humor Simon, appears to be in any doubt about this. Stephen is in the thankless position of being brought along as proof of his father's prosperity, even when the result of the trip will be to make his own financial future, and thus his eventual social status, even more bleak.

Even as Stephen Dedalus strives to shore up the line between "high" and "low" culture, his description of the "pure" aesthetic gaze actually describes one of the central problems of modernity that modernism attempts to engage: the conflation of the presumably universal observer, contemplating the aesthetic object, and the consumer in the modern metropolis, powerfully attracted to the aura of advertised products in the modern marketplace. The requirements Stephen insists must be met before an object might be regarded as "artistic" are the same requirements a commodity must meet before it can be considered marketable to the consumer. For example, Stephen's hypothetical aesthetic observer must first achieve emotional stasis in order to witness "the soul of the commonest object" as it "leaps out" and becomes "radiant."

In *Stephen Hero,* Stephen discusses arbitrary "found" objects one might encounter in a walk through the city, such as a basket, which is certainly not an advertised commodity, and yet, within the context of modern consumerism, Stephen's theory about such an object is similar to what Haug has termed "commodity aesthetics," and the concept of the moment when the object achieves its epiphany is comparable to Benjamin's description of objects achieving an "aura." Stephen's moment of aesthetic stasis is analogous to the moment when the consumer is prompted to buy; the moment when the subject feels interpellated; the moment when modern man in the metropolis experiences the uncanny sense that the never before seen corresponds to what he has not yet thought, but nonetheless knows. The desire and loathing Stephen is sure he has eliminated in the moment of "aesthetic stasis" are sublimated before the aura of the contemplated object causes it to take on the dimensions of something we can imagine as what we need to eliminate anxiety, incertitude, and timidity. The effect on Stephen of a prostitute's kiss, which made him feel "strong and fearless and sure of himself," is analogous to Bloom's imagined moment when an advertisement perfectly designed "to cause passers to stop in wonder" also achieves its radiance: "They [the prostitute's lips, but, also, in my reading, Bloom's "sole unique advertisement"] pressed upon his brain as upon his lips as though they were the vehicle of a vague speech" (96). If Stephen's perfect work of art resembles not only a perfect kiss, or a perfect confession, but also Bloom's perfect advertisement, then the impulse to pay or pray, consume or worship, to lust after or to long for, all have much in common.

Notes

Introduction

1. Karl Marx, *Capital* (New York: International, 1967).

2. James Joyce, *Dubliners,* ed. R. Scholes and A. Walton Litz (New York: Viking Press, 1969), 32. All other quotes from *Dubliners* will be cited in the text.

3. Stanislaus Joyce, *My Brother's Keeper* (New York: Viking Press, 1958), 23.

4. Thomas Richards, Jennifer Wicke, Cheryl Herr, and Franco Moretti are among the first to discuss systematically the discourse of advertising and commodity culture in Joyce. Thomas Richards, *The Commodity Culture of Victorian England: Advertising and Spectacle, 1851–1914* (Stanford: Stanford University Press, 1990). Jennifer Wicke, *Advertising Fictions: Literature, Advertisement, and Social Reading* (New York: Columbia University Press, 1988). Cheryl Herr, *Joyce's Anatomy of Culture* (Chicago: University of Illinois Press, 1986). Franco Moretti, *Signs Taken for Wonders: Essays in the Sociology of Literary Forms* (London: Verso, 1983). Recent essays on the topic of Joyce and advertising or commodity culture are included in a special double issue of the *James Joyce Quarterly* 30.4/31.1 (1993), devoted to Joyce and advertising, edited by Garry Leonard and Jennifer Wicke. Other important essays include: Jennifer Wicke, "'Who's She When She's At Home?': Molly Bloom and the Work of Consumption," *James Joyce Quarterly* 28.4 (1991): 749–64. Joseph Heininger, "Molly Bloom's Ad Language and Goods Behavior: Advertising as Social Communication in *Ulysses,*" in *Molly Blooms,* ed. Richard Pearce (Madison: University of Wisconsin Press, 1994). For a discussion of the relationship among economics, gender, and the social construction of reality, see Mark Osteen, *Making Both Ends Meet: Economics in Ulysses* (Syracuse: Syracuse University Press, 1995). For a thorough discussion of popular literature in *Dubliners, Exiles,* and *Portrait,* see R. B. Kershner, *Joyce, Bakhtin, and Popular Literature: Chronicles of Disorder* (Chapel Hill: University of North Carolina Press, 1989).

5. James Joyce, *Stephen Hero,* ed. John J. Slocum and Herbert Cahoon (New York: New Directions, 1963), 213.

6. James Joyce, *A Portrait of the Artist as a Young Man,* ed. Chester G. Anderson (New York: Viking, 1968).

7. James Joyce, *Ulysses,* ed. Hans Walter Gabler et al. (New York and London: Garland Publishing, 1984, 1986), 592. In paperback by Garland, Random House, Bodley Head, and Penguin.

8. Edward Mott Wooley, *The Art of Selling Goods* (Chicago: American Business Man, 1907). All other references to this work will be cited in the text.

9. Louis Althusser, "Ideology and Ideological State Apparatuses," in *Lenin and Philosophy and Other Essays* (New York: Monthly Review, 1971). For a recent and useful overview of the current status of theories of ideology, see Mike Cormack, *Ideology* (Ann Arbor: University of Michigan Press, 1992). For examples of how theories allowing for the negotiating with a dominant ideology might be applied, see John Fiske, *Reading the Popular* (Boston: Unwin Hyman, 1989). Fiske is specifically interested, as I am, in how ideology is evaded, undermined, and subsumed by the subject.

10. Michel de Certeau, *The Practice of Everyday Life,* trans. Steven Rendall (Berkeley: University of California Press, 1984), xix. It is here that de Certeau makes his distinction between "tactics" and "strategies," an idea that has become central to any theory seeing the subject as negotiating with dominant ideology: "I call a 'strategy' the calculus of force-relationships which becomes possible when a subject of will and power (a proprietor, an enterprise, a city, a scientific institution) can be isolated from an 'environment'. . . . I call a 'tactic,' on the other hand, a calculus which cannot count on a 'proper' (a spatial or institutional localization), nor thus on a borderline distinguishing the other as a visible totality" (xx). For example, the dominant ideology represented by a department store employs "strategies" to attract and direct subjects (customers), while these customers respond with "tactics." Strategies tend to develop and exploit space, while a tactic "depends on time—it is always on the watch for opportunities that must be seized 'on the wing'. . . . It must constantly manipulate events in order to turn them into 'opportunities'."

11. See Jean Baudrillard, *Selected Writings,* ed. Mark Poster (Stanford: Stanford University Press, 1988). What I am describing here is similar to Baudrillard's important idea of advertising as the "simulacrum" of reality included by advertising discourse. Baudrillard's concept of the hyperreal is important to my argument as well, and the following passage may serve as an introduction: "The era of simulation is . . . everywhere initiated by the interchangeability of previously contradictory or dialectically opposed terms. . . . All the great humanist criteria of value, all the values of a civilization of moral, aesthetic, and practical judgement, vanish in our system of images and signs. Everything becomes undecideable" ("Symbolic Exchange and Death," 128). Although I find Baudrillard's idea of the hyperreal fascinating and useful, I also find that he idealizes what he calls "the great humanist criteria of value"; he presents it as something that somehow existed "pure" and "intact" before modern advertising obscured it. But, just as advertising rearranged—rather than "destroyed"—what masquerades as "essential womanhood," advertising offered a new way to fictionalize the "truth." My approach to advertising grants the Lacanian premise that subjectivity itself is a fantasy, and, as such, any intervention with this fantasy might sustain something like "false consciousness," but might equally interact with the fantasy of subjectivity in a way that is powerfully transformative.

12. All these theorists, in different ways, concern themselves with the moment of

decoding as it takes place for each subject confronted with an ideological "call" or interpellation. Their interactive models for subject/object relations serve as the theoretical infrastructure of my discussion. The following selections give some idea of the relevance of each theorist to my explication of commodity culture as it relates to Joyce's fiction: "The Presence and circulation of a representation . . . tells us nothing about what it is for its users. We must first analyze its manipulation by users who are not its makers" (de Certeau, *The Practice of Everyday Life,* xiii). "The truth about consumption is that it is a function of production and not a function of pleasure, totally collective" (Baudrillard, *Selected Writings,* 46). Of course, my improvement upon Baudrillard is to argue pleasure *is* a production. "For the patriarchal order is indeed the one that functions as the organization and monopolization of private property to the benefit of the head of the family. . . . How, then, can the analysis of women's exploitation be dissociated from the analysis of modes of appropriation?" (Luce Irigaray, *This Sex Which Is Not One,* trans. Catherine Porter [Ithaca: Cornell University Press, 1985], 83). "[H]istory is not a text . . . our approach to it and to the Real itself necessarily passes through its prior textualization, its narrativization in the political unconscious" (Fredric Jameson, *The Political Unconscious: Narrative as a Socially Symbolic Act* [Ithaca: Cornell University Press, 1981], 35). "For the real truth of the matter . . . is that there is no such thing as relatively independent spheres of circuits: production is immediately consumption and a recording process . . . , without any sort of mediation, and the recording process and consumption directly determine production" (Gilles Deleuze and Felix Guattari, *Anti-Oedipus: Capitalism and Schizophrenia,* trans. Robert Hurley, Mark Seem, and Helen R. Lane [Minneapolis: University of Minnesota Press, 1989], 4). "[Commodity fetishism consists in] the relation between a structured network and one of its elements: what is really a structural effect, an effect of the network of relations between elements, appears as an immediate property of one of the elements, as if this property also belongs to it outside its relation with other elements" (Slavoj Zizek, *The Sublime Object of Ideology* [London: Verso, 1989], 24). "With respect to the object *a,* at once image and pathos, the subject feels himself to be in an imaginary situation of otherness . . . the object is the object of desire only by virtue of being the end-term of the fantasy" (Jacques Lacan, "Desire and the Interpretation of Desire in Hamlet," in *Literature and Psychoanalysis: The Question of Reading, Otherwise,* ed. Shoshana Felman [Baltimore: Johns Hopkins University Press, 1982], 73).

13. Discussions of Lacan's concept of "lack" are far too numerous to mention, but the following description by Kaja Silverman begins to make the connection between this insatiable lack and a commodity culture anxious to suggest possible ways to close it: "Not only does language provide the agency of self-loss, but cultural representations supply the standard by which that loss is perceived. We look within the mirror of those representations—representations which structure every moment of our existence—not only to discover what we are, but what we can never hope to be and (as a consequence) hopelessly desire. . . . The subject not only learns to desire within the symbolic order; it learns what to desire. It is there taught to value only those objects which are culturally designated as full and complete. . . . Lacan

indicates that the subject's desires are manufactured for it" (*The Subject of Semiotics* [New York: Oxford University Press, 1983], 177). The discourse that "teaches" is advertising, and, as such, it is a religious discourse because it offers a version of "wholeness" that must be supported both by an act of faith and by a constantly maintained relationship with the "religion" of consumption.

14. Michel Foucault, *The History of Sexuality: Volume I, An Introduction* (New York: Random House, 1986), 45. Throughout this volume, Foucault argues that "pleasure" has a history, and that it is a construction that seeks to elide the very power configuration that creates the sensation of pleasure: "Power operated as a mechanism of attraction; it drew out those peculiarities over which it kept watch. Pleasure spread to the power that harried it; power anchored the pleasure it uncovered."

15. Joe Voelker and Thomas Arner, "Bloomian Pantomime: A. J. Dowie and the 'Messianic Scene'," *James Joyce Quarterly* 27.2 (1990): 283–91. See Voelker and Arner's fascinating article about the historical American evangelist Alexander J. Dowie. Voelker and Arner review contemporary newspaper accounts concerning the "ministry" of the actual Dowie in order to demonstrate Joyce's use of the devices and tropes of pantomime in his depiction of Bloom's rise to fame in the "Circe" episode. In the course of their essay, Voelker and Arner quote the actual Dowie's insistence that he was the new Elijah (reported in the *New York Times* on June 3, 1901): "'I am Elijah the prophet, who appeared first as Elijah himself, second as John the Baptist, and who comes in me, the restorer of all things'. . . . After this pronouncement, the Irish papers followed the American in paying ironic tribute to Dowie's business abilities by dubbing him 'Profit' Elijah . . . and Bloom's first thought when he is handed the Elijah throwaway in 'Lestrygonians' is 'Paying game'" (288). Of course the presence of the throwaway in *Ulysses,* and its intricate relationship to the racehorse "Throwaway," as well as "the dark horse" Bloom, all suggest that advertising is the new (improved!) testament, and Bloom the adman is its true prophet (in direct contrast to the false "Profit," Alexander J. Dowie).

16. Bonnie Kime Scott, ed., *The Gender of Modernism: A Critical Anthology* (Bloomington: Indiana University Press, 1990), 2. Scott's fascinating anthology makes clear that anxiety about gender roles is an issue specifically repressed in what came to be understood as "modernism." What I have noticed, in my own reading through the anthology, is that many of these unacknowledged architects of modernism (most of them women) seem more comfortable than men when it comes to nominating the astonishing energy of popular culture and commodity culture as a valid topic for supposedly "high art." Indeed, were they to listen in on the lopsided aesthetic debates of Stephen Dedalus and Lynch, their sympathies might well lie (as I believe Joyce's do) with the fig-eating, groin-rubbing Lynch. H.D. notes, for example, in a clear tone of invitation to the would-be artist, "there is plenty of pornographic literature that is interesting and amusing" (99). Of course, Ezra Pound's credo "make it new" is absolutely central to the goal of advertising. The "language of the marketplace" was forever generating novelty ("making it new") in order to establish a "language" of goods by which the consumer might express him- or

herself. Indeed, McCracken's description of the eighteenth century seems to have more than a passing resemblance to the aesthetics of modernism: "With the growth of fashion grew an entirely new habit of mind and pattern of behavior. Increasingly, aesthetic and stylistic considerations took precedence over utilitarian ones. That an object had not exhausted its usefulness was no longer sufficient grounds for its preservation. . . . This development represents a triumph of style over utility, of aesthetics over function" (19). The deprivileging of "utility and function" may correspond to the deprivileging of "plot" and "characterization" in modernist texts.

17. Recent books devoted to the generally neglected history of commodity culture in modern times include: Neil McKendrick, John Brewer, and J. H. Plumb, *The Birth of a Consumer Society: The Commercialization of Eighteenth-Century England* (Bloomington: Indiana University Press, 1982); Chandra Mukerji, *From Graven Images: Patterns of Modern Materialism* (New York: Columbia University Press, 1983); Rosalind H. Williams, *Dream Worlds: Mass Consumption in Late Nineteenth Century France* (Berkeley: University of California Press, 1982); Grant McCracken, *Culture and Consumption* (Bloomington: Indiana University Press, 1988). In the conclusion of his chapter "The Making of Modern Consumption," McCracken states: "It is a curiosity for the sociology of knowledge that the role of the consumer revolution in the 'great transformation' was so long and systematically ignored. . . . The history of consumption has no history, no community of scholars, no tradition of scholarship. . . . it is 'neonatal'" (28). Such a description seems applicable to the related topic of Joyce, advertising, and commodity culture. Rob Shields, ed., *Lifestyle Shopping: The Subject of Consumption* (New York: Routledge, 1992). Shields describes (citing de Certeau as his authority) the sort of approach that is needed in the study of consumption; it is an approach featured at several points in my book: "There is a need . . . to treat consumption as an active, committed production of self and of society which rather than assimilating individuals to styles, appropriates codes and fashions, which are made into one's own" (2).

In addition, there are numerous unscholarly histories, which are fascinating and valuable, both for their reproduction of advertisements now lost and for their forthright assertions about what advertising was understood to be. These include: Frank Presbrey, *The History and Development of Advertising* (New York: Doubleday, Doran, and Co., 1929); E. S. Turner, *The Shocking History of Advertising!* (London: Michael Joseph, 1952). I use several turn-of-the-century ad manuals (including *The Art of Selling Goods,* a copy of which was a part of Joyce's Trieste library), as well as various "histories" to reveal how the development of ideas relevant to advertising rarely improve upon what Leopold Bloom was espousing in 1904.

18. R. B. Kershner, *Joyce and Popular Culture* (Gainesville: University Press of Florida, 1996). See Kershner's excellent and detailed introduction, which discusses the history of critical interest in the phenomenon of "popular culture" in Joyce scholarship.

19. Thomas Richards, *Commodity Culture,* 7. All other references to this work will be cited in the text.

20. Qtd. in Rosalind Williams, *Dream Worlds,* 72.

21. Very recently, there has been quite a bit of work on commodity culture and Joyce from the postcolonial point of view. See the special issue "Joyce and the Police," *Novel* 29.1 (1995). See also the special issue "Joyce and Advertising," *James Joyce Quarterly* 30.4/31.1 (1993), eds. Jennifer Wicke and Garry Leonard.

22. Rob Shields, ed., *Lifestyle Shopping,* 2. All other references to this work will be cited in the text.

23. Margorie Perloff, "Modernist Studies," in *Redrawing the Boundaries: The Transformation of English and American Literary Studies,* ed. Stephen Greenblatt and Giles Gunn (New York: Modern Language Association, 1992), 156.

24. In her book *Idylls of the Marketplace: Oscar Wilde and the Victorian Public* (Stanford: Stanford University Press, 1986), Regina Gagnier makes the point that men who shared homosexual desire referred to themselves not as "gay" or "homosexual" but as "modern" (51). The desire of men for men was publicly communicated through fashion and patterns of an understood blend of "sexual preference" and "customer selection." The famous example of this is the wearing of a green carnation. As Joseph Valente has pointed out, Stephen's musing, "'But you could not have a green rose. But perhaps somewhere in the world you could' (P12)—unmistakably recalls Wilde's famous 'green carnation,' which was the symbol . . . of the artifice of the imagination . . ." ("Thrilled by His Touch: Homosexual Panic and the Will to Artistry in *A Portrait of the Artist as a Young Man,*" *James Joyce Quarterly* 31.3 (1994): 171). As I argue in my book, this is also a gesture toward the artifice of constructing oneself as a "man," and the necessity of the advertising/consumer dynamic ("lifestyle") to do so. Kershner was one of the first Joyce scholars to offer a detailed look at both writers; see "Wilde and Joyce on Shakespeare," *Texas Studies in Language and Literature* 20 (1978). More recently, the connection between Joyce and Wilde has been explored by Zack Bowen with a specific emphasis on popular culture, "Wilde about Joyce," in Kershner, ed., *Joyce and Popular Culture,* 105–15.

25. Oscar Wilde, *The Importance of Being Earnest, The Complete Works of Oscar Wilde* (Bristol, England: Parragon Books, 1995), act 3. All other references to this work will be cited in the text.

26. Oscar Wilde, *The Picture of Dorian Gray, The Complete Works of Oscar Wilde* (Bristol, England: Parragon Books, 1995), 101. All other references to this work will be cited in the text.

27. David Pierce, *James Joyce's Ireland* (New Haven: Yale University Press, 1992), 27. Pierce reprints this page of the *Irish Homestead,* surrounded by these ads.

28. In Lacanian theory, the subject is dependent on a Symbolic Order that must neither shift, nor reveal itself to be what, in fact, it is: a representation of reality, and not the whole of what is real. Lacan insists the process of understanding the world, and our experience of it, through symbols, always leaves something out because it never perfectly embodies what it is understood to signify. The individual tries to act like a signified—something coherent and whole prior to language—but he or she is, in fact, a floating signifier forever masquerading as a signified. This something that

is left out is what Lacan calls "the Real"—some rem(a)inder of the Imaginary Order that escapes representation within the Symbolic Order, and so remains a threat to the fictional unity of identity. The construction of a "lifestyle" is a way to manage this threat, but, at the same time, it is a way also to playfully subvert "naturalized" identity constructions.

Chapter 1

1. *International Standard Bible Encyclopedia* (Grand Rapids, Mich.: William B. Erdman's, 1988).

2. *Encyclopedia Judaica* (Jerusalem: Keter Publishing House, 1971), 452.

3. Jennifer Wicke makes a similar point in her book *Advertising Fictions,* 13. "Single ads are evanescent, ephemeral structures; of more moment to my argument is the reshaping of cultural discourse as a whole by the massive presence of a huge archive of advertisement."

4. Fredric Jameson, *The Political Unconscious,* 35.

5. Other popular expressions (in America, at least) include "Born to Shop"; "Shop till you drop"; and "When the going gets tough, the tough go shopping."

6. Jean Baudrillard, *Selected Writings,* 13. "'Free to be oneself' in fact means: free to project one's desires onto produced goods. 'Free to enjoy life' means: free to regress and be irrational, and thus adapt to a certain social organization of production."

7. Wicke also states that Bloom thinks of "Sandow's ads as if they were a potential cure for the abuses of history. . . . Moments of historical clarity are slippages in Bloom's internal text—advertising rushes into the breach to reclaim him as subject" (*Advertising Fictions,* 126). My emphasis here is somewhat different since I am pointing out that advertising supports the illusion of individual autonomy by presenting the consumer's individual experience as something outside of, and superior to, the currently accepted narratives of "History." For a thorough look at Sandow as a historical entity and mass-media phenomenon, see Kershner, "The World's Strongest Man: Joyce or Sandow?" *James Joyce Quarterly* 30.4/31.1 (1993–94): 667–96.

8. Lacan's concept of the "Real" as that which continues to exist beyond representation is a central subtext of my discussion of the "simulated universe" of advertising and the consumer's "myth of the self": "what the unconscious does is to show us the gap through which neurosis recreates a harmony with a real—a real that may well not be determined" (Jacques Lacan, *The Four Fundamental Concepts of Psychoanalysis* [New York: W. W. Norton, 1981], 22). The "Real," like all of Lacan's theoretical concepts, is complex and dependent on other terms for its full significance. Ragland-Sullivan's description of the Real in reference to Lacan's seminars on Joyce emphasizes that the Real is beyond representation, even though representation constantly tries to symbolize it: "language produces a Real which does not have any corresponding reality. . . . Lacan emphasized that without an internalized representation of a border or an identity limit, a subject is open to the chaos of the Real which wreaks havoc on subjects who have little or no sense of a self that has a name

and some characteristic properties" (Ellie Ragland-Sullivan, "Lacan's Seminars on James Joyce: Writing as Symptom and 'Singular Solution'," in *Psychoanalysis and . . .*, ed. Richard Feldstein [New York: Routledge, 1982], 79.

9. Jules David Law argues: "An unspecifiable movement of self-objectification and self-alienation characterizes Gerty's experience of erotic arousal and, implicitly, Bloom's as well. Yet because of the patriarchal context in which Gerty's erotic discourse emerges, her sexuality apparently must be domesticated or contained before the narrative can be returned to Bloom's perspective. . . . Bloom conceives of his self-objectification as an experiment or as a type of experience, while Gerty conceives of self-objectification as a goal" ("'Pity They Can't See Themselves': Assessing the 'Subject' of Pornography in 'Nausicaa'," *James Joyce Quarterly* 27.2 [1990]: 226). Law's analysis here is insightful and accurate. I would only point out that "the patriarchal context" that dominates Gerty's point of view has its source in the pastiche of advertising lingo that permits Gerty to "make sense" of her past. Bloom is able to "conceive of his self-objectification as an experiment" because he has not been instructed by ads on how to view him"self" solely in terms of how he imagines the opposite sex sees him; nor does his financial future depend upon his learning to do so. One gender distinction that advertisements promote is that women must buy designated products in order to make themselves more "feminine." Men, on the other hand, are able to regard the degree of their ability to purchase whatever they want as sufficient proof of their degree of "masculinity."

Luce Irigaray puts this gender distinction in the marketplace in provocatively stark terms, and locates it as the central feature of both economic exchange and gender: "The exchanges upon which patriarchal societies are based take place exclusively among men. Women, signs, commodities, and currency always pass from one man to another; if it were otherwise, we are told, the social order would fall back upon incestuous and exclusively endogamous ties that would paralyze all commerce. . . . Heterosexuality is nothing but the assignment of economic roles: there are producer subjects and agents of exchange (male) on the one hand, productive earth and commodities (female) on the other" (*This Sex Which Is Not One*, 192).

Trevor Williams also makes several cogent observations about the "commodification" of relationships in *Dubliners:* "Mrs. Mooney regards marriage as 'reparation' or payment for Bob Doran's 'consumption' of her daughter; and Mrs. Kearney's obsession with the contract to pay her daughter converts Kathleen into a 'service' (and thus a form of commodity)" ("Resistance to Paralysis in *Dubliners*," *Modern Fiction Studies* 35.3 [1989]: 444).

10. Qtd. in Frank Presbrey, *The History and Development of Advertising*, 317.

11. This point was made by Kimberly Devlin on a panel I chaired on Joyce and advertising at the International James Joyce Symposium in Monte Carlo, in 1990.

12. Qtd. in E. S. Turner, *The Shocking History of Advertising!*, 63. All other references to this work will be cited in the text.

13. Qtd. in Diana Hindley and Geoffrey Hindley, *Advertising in Victorian En-*

gland, 1837–1901 (London: Wayland, 1972), 28. All other references to this work will be cited in the text.

Chapter 2

1. Michel de Certeau, *The Practice of Everyday Life,* xix. All other references will be cited in the text.

2. Don Gifford, *Joyce Annotated: Notes for Dubliners and A Portrait of the Artist as a Young Man* (Berkeley: University of California Press, 1982), 66.

3. Diana Hindley and Geoffrey Hindley, *Advertising in Victorian England,* 108.

4. Barbara Kruger, "I shop, therefore I am," *Love for Sale: The Words and Pictures of Barbara Kruger* (New York: H. N. Abrams, 1990), 36.

5. Cited as one of the examples in the definition of *ephemeral* in the *OED.*

6. Fritz Senn, "History as Text in Reverse," in *Joyce and the Subject of History,* ed. Marc A. Wollaeger, Victor Luftig, and Robert Spoo (Ann Arbor: University of Michigan Press, 1996), 53.

7. Marc A. Wollaeger, "Reading *Ulysses:* Agency, Ideology, and the Novel," 101.

8. Fredric Jameson, "Postmodernism and Consumer Society," in *The Anti-Aesthetic: Essays on Postmodern Culture,* ed. Hal Foster (Seattle: Bay Press, 1983), 120.

9. E. Ann Kaplan, *Rocking around the Clock: Music Television, Postmodernism, and Consumer Culture* (New York: Methuen, 1987), 47.

10. Michel de Certeau, *Heterologies: Discourse on the Other,* trans. Brian Massumi (Minneapolis: University of Minnesota Press, 1986), 216.

11. Jacques Lacan, *Speech and Language in Psychoanalysis,* trans. Anthony Wilder (Baltimore: Johns Hopkins University Press, 1968), 23.

12. Cheryl Herr, "Ireland from the Outside," in *Joyce and the Subject of History,* 210.

13. For a thorough analysis of "personal" and "historical" narrative in the "Nestor" chapter, see my essay "Joyce and Lacan: The Twin Narratives of History and His[S]tory in the 'Nestor' Chapter of *Ulysses,*" in *Joyce and Contexts,* ed. Vincent Cheng and Timothy Martin (Cambridge: Cambridge University Press, 1992).

14. Jean Baudrillard, "The Ecstasy of Communication," in *The Anti-Aesthetic: Essays on Postmodern Culture,* ed. Hal Foster (Washington: Bay Press, 1983), 133.

Chapter 3

1. Ferruccio Farina, *Venus Unveiled* (Leicester, England: Magna Books, 1989), 11.

2. Linda Williams, *Hard Core: Power, Pleasure, and the "Frenzy of the Visible"* (Los Angeles: University of California Press, 1989), 30. All other quotations from this work will be cited in the text.

3. Paul Hammond, *French Undressing: Naughty Postcards from 1900 to 1920* (London: Bloomsbury Books, 1976), 8. All other quotations from this work will be cited in the text.

4. Robert J. Stoller, *Observing the Erotic Imagination* (New Haven: Yale University Press, 1985), 67. All other quotations from this work will be cited in the text.

5. See, for example, Anonymous, *A Man and a Maid* (New York: Grove Press, 1968). This is perhaps one of the best known examples of what amounts to a genre of pornography. Scenarios of female resistance, followed precipitously by impassioned acquiescence, form the basic pleasure construct of this turn-of-the-century pornographic classic. In the novel, a man lures various women (first and foremost the fiancée who jilted him) to a specially equipped sound-proof room (a confessional?) and then causes them to "confess" their "secret" sexual desires. Their confession is involuntary in that it is conveyed through a bodily manifestation of physical excitement, which the women verbally deny, at first, and then heartily acknowledge. What amounts to kidnapping and rape on the part of the man is rationalized and excused as merely an activity that provides the women with what they "really" want. The postcoital attitude of the women is uniformly one of gratitude.

6. Michel Foucault, *History of Sexuality: Volume I, An Introduction,* 45.

7. "Leda and the Swan," *The Poems of W. B. Yeats,* ed. Richard Finneran (New York: Macmillan, 1983), 214–15.

8. In another startling intersection of the sacred and profane, or of "pornography" and commodity culture, a woman compliantly agreeing to act out the narrative of a man is the essence of the extremely lucrative business of "phone sex." One can, for instance, call in to hear a variety of tapes, all advertising a complex and bewildering array of pleasure constructions. Typically, in the advertisement inviting the consumer to call, a model is shown holding the telephone with a declaration of her particular state of desire printed above. "I'm young . . . I'm lonely . . . I'm innocent." Others feature moods rather than circumstances: "I'm angry with you." Others announce a strategically enticing cry for help: "I can't get my boots off . . . will you help me?" Such constructions, were they to be collected, catalogued, and categorized, would offer a compendium of "perversions" every bit as comprehensive as all the "perversions" described by such sexologists as Krafft-Ebing and Ellis. The technology of the telephone has been grafted onto that of photography to produce the "talking" erotic postcard.

9. Margot Norris cites the assertion, first made by Freud and seconded by Lacan, that there is, as Norris paraphrases it, "an inherent pathology in human sexuality." Her description of the difficulty of mutual desire is relevant to what I am calling in this chapter the problem of pleasure: "[E]ven in adult love relations, men and women find the pursuit of desire . . . elusive except by a series of complex symbolic maneuvers" (Norris, 489). My further contention is that commodity culture, in an infinite variety of ways, offers any given product as the centering symbol of a pleasurable configuration of desire, and thus becomes a historically specific manufacturing device we might dub the semerotic pleasure machine. What is home without (fill in the blank)? Incomplete. With it, an abode of bliss. Were human sexuality not inherently pathological, if pleasure did not have a constantly shifting history and

constitution, commodity culture, as we know it, would be impossible even to imagine.

10. There is a subtle implication here that what Gabriel confidently recognizes as a "mood" may be the first gesture of what Gretta might normally present as a performance for his benefit. Likewise, his question "I think I know what's wrong" appears to be a verbal cue for an erotic game that Gretta knows well. But she cannot enter into the familiar dialogue on this night; hence her sudden and (to Gabriel) astonishing departure from a well-rehearsed script.

11. Bram Dijkstra, *Idols of Perversity: Fantasies of Feminine Evil in Fin-de-Siecle Culture* (New York: Oxford University Press, 1986), x.

12. Stephen's temptress, as characterized in his villanelle—"are you not weary of ardent ways"—is a type of excessive female desire leading to the exhaustion of the male. Such a figure, also seen as the femme fatale in salon paintings at the turn of the century, causes the man to "spend" until he is utterly depleted. Through this typology, insatiable and excessive female desire becomes associated with the potentially destructive allure of commodity culture; both forces—female sexuality and advertising—threaten to stimulate the man interminably, thus causing him to "spend" until he is dead. This connection is made, indirectly, in "Araby," when the narrator travels to the bazaar, under a powerful yet inexplicable compulsion to buy he knows not what for the young woman who has physically aroused him.

Chapter 4

1. Mark Schechner, *Joyce in Nighttown: A Psychoanalytic Inquiry into Ulysses* (Berkeley: University of California Press, 1974), 161–62; Fritz Senn, "Nausicaa," in *James Joyce's Ulysses,* ed. Clive Hart and David Hayman (Berkeley: University of California Press, 1974), 277–311. Fritz Senn, for example, says "Gerty MacDowell is the latest avatar of the temptress in Joyce's fiction. . . . *A Portrait* presents its own gallery of temptresses, leading up to the vision in Chapter 4 and the villanelle of Chapter 5" (284).

2. Hugh Kenner, *Ulysses* (Baltimore: Johns Hopkins University Press, 1980), 106. "Withdrawing all human jostle like the tide, it shows Bloom utterly alone, in a rest between two crowded episodes, 'Cyclops' where drinkers throng, 'Oxen of the Sun' where noisy students drink."

3. Suzette Henke, "Gerty MacDowell: Joyce's Sentimental Heroine," in *Women in Joyce,* ed. Suzette Henke and Elaine Unkeless (Chicago: University of Illinois Press, 1983), 132.

4. Maria Susanna Cummins, *The Lamplighter,* ed. Nina Baym (New Brunswick: Rutgers University Press, 1988). *The Lamplighter* had been published in 1854, and though it was reprinted for years, it finally went out of print—and out of favor—in the 1920s. Joyce, who was a reluctant student of the vagaries of publishing, must have been intrigued by this novel, which is one of the earliest examples of what we now routinely call "a runaway bestseller." "What is the mystery of these innumerable editions of the *Lamplighter*?" Hawthorne grumbles in a letter to his publisher.

Nina Baym tells us: "While *The Scarlet Letter* sold under 10,000 copies in Hawthorne's lifetime, *The Lamplighter* sold 40,000 copies in its first month alone and 60,000 more before it had been out for a year" (ix). The fact that women might not take as their role model a character who is systematically humiliated her entire adult life for a single sexual experience seems to have puzzled Hawthorne.

5. Kimberly Devlin, "The Romance Heroine Exposed: 'Nausicaa' and *The Lamplighter,*" *James Joyce Quarterly* 22.4 (1985): 383. Other references to this essay will be cited in the text.

6. Thomas K. Richards, "Gerty MacDowell and the Irish Common Reader," *ELH* 52.3 (1985): 761.

7. Devlin notes this distinction between the two Gertrudes, although she does not explore the discourse of advertising in this chapter as a possible reason for this difference: "Gerty reads the fashion magazines and beauty columns that inevitably promote the artful attention to personal appearance condemned by Maria Cummins" ("Romance Heroine," 389).

8. Jacques Lacan, "Seminar of 21 January 1975," in *Feminine Sexuality, Jacques Lacan and the Ecole Freudienne,* ed. Juliet Mitchell and Jacqueline Rose (New York: W. W. Norton, 1985), 164. All other references to this work will be quoted in the text.

9. Judith Williamson, *Decoding Advertisements,* 63–65. See Williamson for a more detailed discussion of the way in which advertisements can be seen as illustrating the Imaginary and Symbolic Order of Jacques Lacan: "Once the boundary between the Imaginary and the Symbolic has been crossed, it is impossible to return. . . . Ads set up, in your active relationship towards them, the fictional creation of an impossibly unified self. . . . In offering us symbols as the objects of unity they ensnare us in a quest for the impossible." All other references will be quoted in the text.

10. Kimberly Devlin argues: "Gerty conceives of herself as object, fashioning herself as an attractive sight through her elaborate apparel and carefully contrived poses" ("The Female Eye: Joyce's Voyeuristic Narcissists," in *New Alliances in Joyce Studies,* ed. Bonnie Kime Scott [Newark: University of Delaware Press, 1988], 135). My reading endorses Devlin's insight, but seeks to add to it by showing how advertisements have taught Gerty to present her sexuality as a "package."

11. In *Commodity Culture,* Thomas Richards makes a very good case that Gerty is posing as a "seaside girl." In my reading, a "seaside girl" is merely the most current incarnation of what Lacan calls "The Woman." I do not refute Richards's point, which I think is accurate and fascinating from a historical point of view, but I wish to demonstrate Gerty's psychological complicity in the process of her own commodification.

12. Teresa de Lauretis, *Alice Doesn't: Feminism, Semiotics, Cinema* (Bloomington: Indiana University Press, 1984), 10.

13. See Richards, "Gerty MacDowell," 762. Here is where I differ from Richards, who says, "Gerty fails to see that she is dealing with a social relation between human beings and supposes instead that she is dealing with a relation between things." Lacan's point is that the sexual relation, in the speaking being, does not take place

in the biological register, but in the cultural one. When we approach a partner, we imagine the other as corresponding to the Other, which constitutes our fictional unity. At least to this extent, there is no such thing as a straightforward "social relation between human beings."

14. Qtd. in Stephen Heath, "Joan Riviere and the Masquerade," in *Formations of Fantasy,* ed. Victor Burgin, James Donald, and Cora Kaplan (New York: Methuen, 1986), 52. Also, the reader interested in antecedent theories to Lacan's theory of "The Woman" should read Joan Riviere's 1929 essay "Womanliness as a Masquerade" in this same collection, pp. 35–45.

15. Fritz Senn, "Nausicaa," 218.

16. Even at modern-day beach resorts such as Fort Lauderdale, men and women surround themselves with a constellation of heavily advertised products (towels, sunglasses, beer, sun-tan lotion, hair products, T-shirts, beach bags), which serve to announce their proximity to a media-endorsed standard of "femininity" or "masculinity." As Margate and Brighton became popular, much concern was expressed in the popular press, particularly along the lines of courtship. Because the beach was relatively "classless" compared to the city, working girls were teased by stories in such magazines as *Forget Me Not* (which had a special "Seaside" issue every August), where wealthy young men fell in love with them beyond the watchful eye of a mother, and the engagement was secure before the return to town. A story entitled "How I Got My Sisters Married," which ran as a serial throughout the summer of 1904, is subtitled "The Love Affairs of the Misses Frobisher at the Seaside." In it, an enterprising younger brother spots a "Harrow man" and conspires to put him in the way of his sister at every opportunity.

17. As one travel book about England puts it: "And so to Margate, seaside metropolis of Kent. . . . It boasts what the advertisements call 9G miles of 'glorious sands,' but, even more important and sensible, a whole district called 'Dreamland,' where 20 hitherto useless acres were eventually covered with facilities for holiday fun and games. . . . It is a pastiche of Brighton, imitation seaside Palladian of the most revolting type, but executed on such a grand scale that, like the baroque when coated on really thick, it succeeds by its very excess of enormity" (Donald Cowie, *England: The Land and the People* [South Brunswick, England: A. S. Barnes, 1972], 51).

The seaside resort itself is an advertised commodity where "[t]he space of leisure had been sexualized. . . . seaside resorts successfully integrated sexual practice into the practice of consumption. . . . At some resorts, such as Brighton and Bournemouth, the advertisers virtually outnumbered the bathers" (Richards, *Commodity Culture,* 228). In such a place, Richards maintains, "the stress falls on leisure time, impulse buying, non-partisan quiescence, and a therapeutic ethos of individual fulfillment through a manufactured utopia of commodities" (235). As an advertising man, Bloom recognizes the potential of featuring (that is to say, packaging) Molly's voice and figure in such an atmosphere: "Tour the south then. What about English wateringplaces? Brighton, Margate. Piers by moonlight. Her voice floating out. Those lovely seaside girls" (*U,* 148).

18. In her book *Loving with a Vengeance* Tania Modleski makes the point that popular culture written for women often instructs women on how to attract the male gaze without having her actions appear intentional: "A heroine must not even understand sexual desire, for knowledge entails guilt. . . . the novels often place her in circumstances where she can work on the male's sexual desires and yet not be held responsible for 'the consequences'. One of the authors' favorite devices is to make the heroine sick, or even unconscious. That way, she can parade around in pajamas or even be stripped and changed by the hero. . . . what Harlequins are read for is the way they deal with the contradiction between the ideal situation and real life. . . . This is even less tolerable than it might at first seem, for once women are aware of being suspected, they must try to make themselves look innocent, and, of course, in manipulating appearances, they forfeit the very possibility of innocence" (*Loving with a Vengeance: Mass-Produced Fantasies for Women* [New York: Methuen, 1984], 51–52). As I try to show, Joyce may have been particularly fascinated with the song "Those Lovely Seaside Girls" because the women are first shown as "ideal" types of "femininity," and then their seasickness in the final verse of the song "strips" them of all the devices they used to "manipulate" this "ideal" appearance.

19. Florence Walzl, "Dubliner: Women in Irish Society," in *Women in Joyce,* 34.

20. In a letter to Stanislaus, Joyce satirizes the "kindly committee" that has set up a laundry in order to employ former prostitutes: "The phrase Dublin by Lamplight means that Dublin by lamplight is a wicked place full of wicked and lost women whom a kindly committee gathers together for the good work of washing my dirty shirts" (*Selected Letters of James Joyce,* ed. Richard Ellmann [New York: Viking Press, 1975], 130).

21. Gifford glosses *mots* as prostitutes, while Wall, in his *Anglo-Irish Glossary,* corrects this and refers to them more as attractive women or actresses. But it still seems fair to say Paddy Dignam, Jr., regards them as sexually available, while a woman such as Miss Dunne seems more inclined to view similar images with an eye toward how the women manage to make themselves attractive to men, and available for courtship and marriage, without crossing the line and appearing "loose" or "cheap."

22. As Richards points out, "the narrative uses terms of manufacture as attributes rather than as extrinsic qualities. . . . one of the few punctuated appositives in the chapter names Gerty by an extrinsic quality, her shoe size: 'but she never had a foot like Gerty MacDowell, a five, and never would'" (*Commodity Culture,* 228). I would like to emphasize that these standard measurements not only buoy up Gerty's sense of well-being, they do so by allowing her to insist the very shape of her foot is "superior" to that of other women's.

23. Catch phrases from late-twentieth-century hit songs frequently feature a refrain that expresses the frustration of being in a marketplace where there is constant looking with no touching: "You can't touch this" (M. C. Hammer); "You want it all, but you can't have it" (Depeche Mode); "You can look but you'd better not touch" (Bruce Springsteen).

24. Stephen Dedalus is also highly tuned to any mention of women's clothing:

"The names of articles of dress worn by women or of certain soft and delicate stuffs used in their making brought always to his mind a delicate and sinful perfume. . . . It had shocked him too when he had felt for the first time beneath his tremulous fingers the brittle texture of a woman's stocking" (*P,* 155). In the case of both Stephen and Bloom, the implication is that items of "feminine" fashion deployed in the sexual marketplace (such as hosiery and underwear) have already been erotically encoded by advertisements. Information about "certain soft and delicate stuffs used in their making," for example, almost certainly comes from advertisements in ladies' magazines, which discussed such matters in endless detail.

25. In a contemporary "Bloomsday Souvenir" edition of the *Evening Press,* an ad for Clery's department store applauds Gerty's exhaustive shopping expedition, entirely omitting that the item she finally found was "slightly shopsoiled." Our emotional attachments to objects are so complex that "defects" in merchandise are as persistently elided as "defects" in personal appearance.

26. The unmarried Maria still seems to imagine herself as someone "out on spec"; consequently, she is puzzled when young men seem not to notice her: "She thought she would have to stand in the Drumcondra tram because none of the young men seemed to notice her" (*D,* 102).

27. I am using *tactic* here in the specialized sense of de Certeau, as discussed previously. *Tactics* and *strategies* are two terms for which de Certeau offers a detailed definition in his attempt to highlight the political dimension that is present in each "trivial" act of consumption: "A tactic insinuates itself into the other's place, fragmentarily, without taking it over in its entirety, without being able to keep it at a distance. It has at its disposal no base where it can capitalize to its advantages, prepare its expansions, and secure independence with respect to circumstances. . . . Strategies, in contrast, conceal beneath objective calculations their connection with the power that sustains them from within the stronghold of its own 'proper' place or institution" (*The Practice of Everyday Life,* xx). Clearly, Gerty practices "tactics" that give her a brief respite from her cultural and economic position—oppressed as she is by both British colonialism and the mental colonialism of British advertising.

28. See Cheryl Herr's discussion of the song "My Girl's a Yorkshire Girl," also alluded to in *Ulysses.* In line with my analysis of "Those Lovely Seaside Girls," Herr states, "there is no difference between Cissy Caffrey and Zoe, between a Dublin girl and a Yorkshire one; both English and Irish workers share the same institutional oppressions" (*Joyce's Anatomy of Culture,* 209). The "seaside girls" are not factory workers, but, as Herr goes on to suggest, women's fashion can be experienced as a form of oppression: "the fashion column lingo that Gerty MacDowell feeds from . . . suggests the connection between oppressive cultural institutions and the seemingly innocent code system of fashion" (209). I would also point out that the "Yorkshire Girl" is presented as a sort of trademark in this song, and it is this prized trademark, rather than the actual "girl," that causes three different men to vie for the privilege of "owning" such a valuable commodity.

29. Qtd. in Gavin Weightman and Steve Humphries, *The Making of Modern*

London, 1815–1914 (London: Sidgwick and Jackson, 1983), 49. Weightman emphasizes the fact that "Regent Street" was specifically designed as a sort of shopping mall of the latest fashions, hairstyles, and cosmetics: "Butchers, greengrocers and the like were not to be allowed to trade there. Regent Street was not, in the way it is now, a main road in London: rather, it was a genuine shopping centre in which the rich could park their carriages and parade up and down, the ladies popping into shops between the fashionable hours of two and four in the afternoon, while their footmen waited outside" (*The Making of Modern London,* 49).

30. Richards talks about how advertising has "changed the shape of women's anatomy by making that body normative and compulsory" (*Commodity Culture,* 241). But one needs to be very precise here. Advertising persuades women to buy products to reshape (often temporarily, as in the case of corsets) their body in accordance with a represented standard. In today's sexual market, literally changing the shape of one's face and body is possible as plastic surgery begins to advertise its services to people who want to look more "beautiful."

31. Herr doesn't specifically analyze these lyrics in her discussion, but she makes a fascinating point that the pantomimes of this time often featured tableaux that displayed a profusion of commodity goods in a style quite like that of a modern department store. In the "Dick Whittington" pantomime there is even a "Procession of Trades," and Cheryl Herr comments: "These jobs, evidently arranged in order of increasing importance and judging by the programme, supplying some highly visible advertisement for local tradespeople . . ." (128). This connects, as Herr points out, to the march of the beatitudes in "Circe," which includes "Barnum" and "Buy Bull" (commerce as the new "bible"). The denouement of the pantomime occurs when the hero acquires enough money to freely shop for himself, and triumphantly leads his new love among all the merchandise that previously had been a source of frustration (Adam and Eve sent forth into the brave new world of advertised things). In a foreshadowing of the future, the most spectacular, expensive, and eagerly awaited pantomime was always the Christmas show. Before the event, newspapers ran feature stories detailing the mounting costs of the production. Nowadays, we have the Radio City Music Hall Christmas Show as well as the (televised) Macy's Thanksgiving Day parade.

32. For an excellent assessment and critique of Irigaray's theory, see Toril Moi, *Sexual/Textual Politics* (London: Routledge, 1988): "Irigaray's failure to consider the historical and economic specificity of patriarchal power, along with its ideological and material contradictions, forces her into providing exactly the kind of metaphysical definition of woman she declaredly wants to avoid. She thus comes to analyse 'woman' in idealist categories, just like the male philosophers she is denouncing" (148). What Joyce does in "Nausicaa" is present a woman in the very style of language that popular culture uses to "essentialize" what a "woman" should be; he then shows us gaps in this discourse of supposedly "natural womanhood" through which we can glimpse a historical female subject who is struggling to survive (we might say "limping along") in a heavily mediated environment of patriarchal economic reality, where only those women who successfully masquerade as

"feminine" gain access (as married women) to any degree of financial security. To put this another way, Irigaray's tendency to "essentialize" women is not convincing, but her discussion of gender in terms of "modes of appropriation" is invaluable when analyzing a text such as *Ulysses,* which so deliberately resists idealistic and ahistorical representations of all those "big words" such as "woman," "man," "history," and, of course, "true love."

Chapter 5

1. Jean Baudrillard, *Selected Writings,* 21.

2. Rosalind H. Williams, *Dream Worlds,* 21. Williams also uses the word *lifestyle* anachronistically in order to describe the phenomenon in nineteenth-century France that was generally described—by contemporary writers—as "the democratization of luxury": "When in the late nineteenth century alternative models of consumption—alternative lifestyles, to use contemporary parlance—arose, they supplanted rather than replaced the aristocratic model" (21). Significantly, the image of Queen Victoria became a ubiquitous trademark of advertised goods.

3. Rachel Bowlby, *Just Looking: Consumer Culture in Dreiser, Gissing, and Zola* (New York: Methuen, 1985), 28. All other references will be cited in the text.

4. Jennifer Wicke, "Molly Bloom and the Work of Consumption."

5. *New York Times,* April 7, 1991.

6. Jacques Lacan, *Four Fundamentals,* 75. Lacan makes it clear that the gaze is not manifested solely by our reaction to seeing someone who sees us; we react to objects, windows, or anything that triggers the urge to comprehend who we are by imagining what we look like to the Other: "The gaze is not located just at the level of the eyes. The eyes may very well not appear, they may be masked. The gaze is not necessarily the face of our fellow being, it could just as easily be the window behind which we assume he is lying in wait for us. It is an x, the object when faced with which the subject becomes object" (*Four Fundamentals,* 220).

7. Jules David Law, "Simulation, Pluralism, and the Politics of Everyday Life," in *Coping with Joyce: Essays from the Copenhagen Symposium,* ed. Morris Beja and Shari Benstock (Columbus: Ohio State University Press, 1989), 197. All other references will be cited in the text.

8. M. R. Booth, *Victorian Spectacular Theatre, 1850–1910* (Boston: Routledge and Kegan Paul, 1981), 64. All other references will be cited in the text.

9. I am indebted to Cheryl Herr's book *Joyce's Anatomy of Culture* for much of my understanding of the relationship between Joyce's depiction of gender and the popular theater of his time.

10. Kim Devlin, "Pretending in 'Penelope': Masquerade, Mimicry, and Molly Bloom," in *Molly Blooms,* ed. Richard Pearce (Madison: University of Wisconsin Press).

11. Peter Brooks, *The Melodramatic Imagination: Balzac, Henry James, Melodrama and the Mode of Excess* (New Haven: Yale University Press, 1976), 48. All other references will be cited in the text.

12. "The beautiful woman" can also be seen as a complex example of Irigaray's theory that the woman acts as an economic conduit through which men communi-

cate to other men the "spending" of sexuality as well as the "spending" of consumerism. Linda H. Williams points out that the moment in contemporary pornographic films where the male actor climaxes is called "the money shot." At this same moment, the female actor is portrayed, illogically enough, as achieving equal orgasmic pleasure just by looking: "'The Money shot' could thus finally be viewed as that moment when the male 'homosexual' economy falters, most reverts to an absolute and unitary standard of value" (*Hard Core,* 210).

13. Another scenario he recalls as exciting is the pornographic mutoscope titled "a dream of wellfilled hose"—also a staged image where a commodity (hosiery) allows a woman to become a spectacle of abundance ("wellfilled"). This, in turn, produces erotic pleasure and results, in the "Nausicaa" chapter, in the "spending" of Bloom's "wellfilled hose."

14. The advertising strategy illustrated by the Diano ad has changed very little over the years. As I discuss elsewhere, brassiere and girdle ads in America in the 1950s made such comments as "[a] body is not a figure. A body is what you're given, a figure is what you make of it," and "make your torso more so" ("'The Woman Is Perfected': Sylvia Plath and *Mademoiselle,*" *College Literature* 19 (1992): 60–82). Just a few months ago, an ad in the *New York Times* urged women to upgrade their wardrobes with tight-fitting skirts with the statement "Improve your bottom line."

15. Looking back from the perspective of the age of television, we can see the "Monkey Brand Melodrama" as a precursor to a much more complex, but essentially similar phenomenon known as the daytime soap opera. The continual melodrama of the show is punctuated by the commercials, which, in direct contrast to the endlessly unfolding story of the soap opera, present a mini-crisis that is resolved, in thirty seconds, by the introduction of the product.

16. A recent pop-psychology term, retrospectively appropriate for Mrs. Riordan, is "pleasure anorexic"; the term was coined to describe people who reacted to the conspicuous consumption of the 1980s by cutting back their use of commodities and "luxury" items. The term further implies that the subject derives a sense of identity by denying him- or herself "popular" or "stylish" objects. Finally, the term insists that only consumption of the "new" produces enjoyment ("doubles" one's "fun"), and therefore the refusal to consume is also a willful self-denial of pleasure. But "pleasure anorexics," in their attempt to do away with "lifestyle," still must define themselves in direct relation to the phenomenon they wish to banish.

Mrs. Riordan, for example, may "perversely" enjoy restricting her degree of mass consumption, but when Parnell is denounced by the priesthood, her complex and enduring rage is acted out for Stephen's benefit in a manner he has never forgotten: "Dante had ripped the green velvet back off the brush that was for Parnell one day with her scissors and had told him that Parnell was a bad man" (*P,* 16). Indeed, if Simon Dedalus is to be credited, Mrs. Riordan's self-imposed austerity is thoroughly implicated in the wealth of imperialism and commodity culture: "But he had heard his father say that she was a spoiled nun and that she had come out of the convent in the Alleghanies when her brother had got the money from the savages for the trinkets and the chainies" (*P,* 35). Gifford reports: "According to Ellmann, Mrs.

Riordan's real-life counterpart had been on the verge of becoming a nun in America when her brother, who had made a fortune out of trading with African natives, died and left her 30,000 pounds" (145). Mrs. Riordan's very vocal refusal to "lash it around" is motivated, at least in part, because the commodity culture she disparages made her wealthy in the first place.

17. Michel Foucault, *The History of Sexuality: Volume I, An Introduction,* 11.

18. Even more to the point, a new brand of condom, just released on the marketplace, is called "Life Styles"; the use of the plural is an attempt on the part of the marketer to appeal to as wide a variety of sexual practices among potential consumers as possible.

19. Lawrence Birken, *Consuming Desire: Sexual Science and the Emergence of a Culture of Abundance, 1871–1914* (Ithaca: Cornell University Press, 1988), 50.

20. Leopold Von Sacher-Masoch, *Venus in Furs* (New York: Sylvan Press, 1947), 135–36, emphasis added. All other references will be cited in the text.

21. In a skit I saw on the television show *Saturday Night Live,* the performative dimension of phone sex was wonderfully highlighted by showing the hired woman as a housewife who "talks sexy" to a man who cannot see her, while scurrying around the kitchen getting supper ready for her family. "I'm so hot you wouldn't believe it," she tells her breathless caller while bending over to check on the meat loaf that is in the oven.

22. Daniel Defoe, *The Fortunes and Misfortunes of the Famous Moll Flanders* (New York: New American Library, 1964), 27, emphasis added. All other references will be cited in the text.

23. In his discussion of the "Nausicaa" episode of *Ulysses,* Thomas Richards discusses the relationship between the definition of "adolescence" and turn-of-the-century advertising (*Commodity Culture,* 205–48).

Chapter 6

1. Pierre Bourdieu, *Distinctions: A Social Critique of the Judgement of Taste,* trans. Richard Nice (Cambridge: Harvard University Press, 1984), 6. All other references will be cited in the text.

2. Qtd. in Walter Benjamin, *Charles Baudelaire: A Lyric Poet in the Era of High Capitalism* (London: NLB, 1973).

3. As Benjamin points out, rather startlingly, Baudelaire frequently cited Cooper's novels as an influence on his conceptualization of the man in the modern city as a similar sort of pioneer, one who is set down in the midst of apparent chaos, yet learns to discern patterns by noting the meaningful juxtaposition of seemingly insignificant details: "The poetry of terror of which the American woods with their hostile tribes on the warpath encountering each other are so full—this poetry which stood c. in such good stead attaches in the same way to the smallest details of Parisian life. The pedestrians, the shops, the hired coaches, or a man leaning against a window—all this was of the same burning interest to the members of Peyrade's bodyguard as a tree stump, a beaver's den, a rock, a buffalo skin, an immobile canoe, or a floating leaf was to the reader of a novel by Cooper" (Benjamin, 42).

4. The idea of the vamp in cinema, and the femme fatale in literature and art, is linked, I would argue, to the effect of the modern metropolis on the construction of masculine subjectivity. For an overview of the genesis of the femme fatale, see Patricia Bade. For a look at the popularity of this figure in salon paintings of the time, with dozens of reproductions, see Bram Dijkstra, *Idols of Perversity,* and Virginia Allen, *The Femme Fatale: Erotic Icon.* None of these works, however, explores what I am able to discuss only briefly in this chapter: the connection between the femme fatale as a figure of both desire and fear, and the exhilarating/frightening experience of modernity for the metropolitan man.

5. Bonnie Kime Scott has assembled a group of works by women writers that makes it clear their experience of modernity was distinct from that of their male counterparts (Bonnie Kime Scott, ed., *The Gender of Modernism*). Scott's collection does not particularly highlight the different way the city was experienced, but I would suggest the female equivalent of the flaneur moved through the city much less randomly. Mrs. Dalloway, for example, declares at the outset of Woolf's novel, "she would buy the flowers herself" (Virginia Woolf, *Mrs. Dalloway* [New York: Harcourt, 1925], 3). And this is precisely what she proceeds to do, without fuss or fanfare. Likewise, Miss Kilman enters a department store to buy petticoats and, though full of thoughts about herself and her relationship to Clarissa, arrives at the correct section (guided by Elizabeth) virtually unaware of her surroundings. In contrast to Benjamin's concept of the flaneur, there is a sense that women in public spaces see themselves as expressly on an errand; they have a place to go and a plan to get them there. Jean Rhys's characters, to offer another example, exhibit none of the wanderlust so typical of Stephen, and seem to regard the public space of the city as one that must be carefully mapped out and precisely navigated: "I have been here five days. I have decided on a place to eat in at midday, a place to eat in at night, a place to have my drink in after dinner. I have arranged my little life" (Jean Rhys, *Good Morning, Midnight, The Complete Novels* [New York: Norton, 1985], 347).

6. Alan Clark and Laurel Clark, *Comics: An Illustrated History* (London: Green Publishing Company, 1992). Although Superman did not appear as a character until 1938, he was conceived as an idea in 1933 (Clark and Clark, 11). Since Stephen refers to Edmund Dantes as "the dark avenger," it is worth noting a now-forgotten early superhero, the Crimson Avenger. He is already an example of someone devoted to the plight of others: "Friend of the needy, foe of the underworld." The "underworld" is the urban labyrinth, confusing and uncanny, that threatens to undermine the "City of Light." For a discussion of Superman and Batman as interesting reflections of the construction of masculine subjectivity in modernism, see Peter Middleton, *The Inward Gaze: Masculinity and Subjectivity in Modern Culture* (New York: Routledge, 1992).

7. James Donald, "The City, The Cinema: Modern Spaces." In Chris Jencks, *Visual Culture* (New York: Routledge, 1995), 83. All other references to this text will be cited in the text.

8. The antithesis of the urban superhero, but nonetheless a figure destined to survive the modern metropolis, is Charlie Chaplin's "tramp." It is precisely the

tramp's inability to be urbanized that affords him a sort of magical immunity from the grinding hustle and bustle of the city. It is significant, perhaps, that Stephen's fantasy of himself as an urban superhero has left him exhausted and disillusioned in *Ulysses,* while the resilience of Leopold Bloom seems much more like the enduring flexibility of Charlie Chaplin's tramp.

9. John Fiske, *Understanding Popular Culture* (New York: Routledge, 1989), 130. All other references will be cited in the text.

10. Ann Cvetkovitch, *Mixed Feelings: Feminism, Mass Culture, and Victorian Sensationalism* (New Brunswick: Rutgers University Press, 1992), 21. All other references will be cited in the text.

11. Jennifer Wicke, "Through a Gaze Darkly: Pornography's Academic Market," in *Dirty Looks: Women, Pornography, Power,* ed. Pamela Church Gibson and Roma Gibson (London: British Film Institute, 1993), 63.

12. Michel Foucault, *Discipline and Punish: The Birth of the Prison,* trans. Alan Sheridan (New York: Pantheon Books, 1977), 41.

13. D. A. Miller, *The Novel and the Police* (Berkeley and Los Angeles: University of California Press, 1988), 18.

14. Jean Gagnon, *Pornography in the Urban World,* trans. James Boake (Toronto: Art Metropole, 1986), 25. All other references will be cited in the text.

15. Oscar Wilde, *Complete Works,* 970.

16. David Frisby, *Simmel and Since: Essays on Georg Simmel's Social Theory* (New York: Routledge, 1992), 115. All other references will be cited in the text.

17. Technology has created an electronic ability to indulge the ideology of the encounter, from phone sex to e-mail romances to interactive chatlines, where disembodied voices create a new kind of "crowd," and the hope of "making contact" runs high.

18. As one of the readers of this book in manuscript pointed out, Lois and Clark Kent/Superman got married on the recent show; but shortly after that came the announcement the show had been canceled, and the quote from a nameless television executive in my local TV guide was: "We never should have let them get married. The show went downhill fast from that point on."

19. Louis Althusser, "Ideology and Ideological State Apparatuses," 1971), 127–86. Indeed, Althusser's important work on ideology might also be seen as a way to elaborate a strategy of distantiation from the confusion of modernity. His characterization of ideology as "a representation of the imaginary relationship of individuals to their real conditions of existence" might be read as the lived relation between men and their urban environment—or, to paraphrase Simmel, ideology is the institutionalized form of a dissociation that makes association possible (152–53).

20. Ernest Hemingway, *The Sun Also Rises* (New York: Charles Scriber, 1926), 241.

21. W. F. Haug, *Critique of Commodity Aesthetics: Appearance, Sexuality and Advertising in Capitalist Society* (Minneapolis: University of Minnesota Press, 1986). All other references will be cited in the text.

22. This point is made throughout Baudrillard's work, most notably in *Simula-*

tions (New York: Semiotext(e), 1983). Baudrillard is of particular importance to my attempt to "urbanize" the theories and practices of modernism because of his frank recognition—already nascent in Stephen Hero's theory of the epiphany—that it is the object that rules over the subject. He abandons a metaphysics of the subject, and argues instead for the subject as the effect of a metaphysics of the object. Baudrillard sees something sinister in this, though I prefer de Certeau's more even-handed look at how the subject, with individual "tactics," reacts to the class issues and social relations implicit, yet denied, in the ideological "strategy" represented by objects in capitalism (*The Practice of Everyday Life,* xix). In the sense that there is always something about the subject that the commodity cannot place under erasure, the subject has an existence apart from this reified object in as much as it continues to embody the social relations everywhere suppressed in the commodity.

23. Karl Marx, *Capital,* vol. 1, 342.

24. Terry Eagleton, *The Ideology of the Aesthetic* (Cambridge, Mass.: Basil Blackwell, 1990), 111.

Bibliography

Allen, V. *The Femme Fatale: Erotic Icon.* New York: Whitson, 1983.

Althusser, L. "Ideology and Ideological State Apparatuses." In *Lenin and Philosophy and Other Essays.* 127–86. New York: Monthly Review, 1971.

Anonymous. *A Man and a Maid.* New York: Grove Press, 1968.

Bade, P. *Femmes Fatales: Images of Evil and Fascinating Women.* London: Ash, 1979.

Baudrillard, J. "The Ecstasy of Communication." In Foster, *The Anti-Aesthetic.*

———. *Selected Writings.* Ed. Mark Poster. Stanford: Stanford University Press, 1988.

———. *Simulations.* New York: Semiotexte, 1983.

Benjamin, W. *Charles Baudelaire: A Lyric Poet in the Era of High Capitalism.* London: NLB, 1973.

Birken, L. *Consuming Desire: Sexual Science and the Emergence of a Culture of Abundance, 1871–1914.* Ithaca: Cornell University Press, 1988.

Booth, M. R. *Victorian Spectacular Theatre, 1850–1910.* Boston: Routledge and Kegan Paul, 1981.

Bourdieu, P. *Distinctions: A Social Critique of the Judgement of Taste.* Trans. Richard Nice. Cambridge: Harvard University Press, 1984.

Bowen, Z. "Wilde about Joyce." In Kershner, ed., *Joyce and Popular Culture.*

Bowlby, R. *Just Looking: Consumer Culture in Dreiser, Gissing, and Zola.* New York: Methuen, 1985.

Brooks, P. *The Melodramatic Imagination: Balzac, Henry James, Melodrama and the Mode of Excess.* New Haven: Yale University Press, 1976.

Burgin, V., J. Donald, and C. Kaplan, eds. *Formations of Fantasy.* New York: Methuen, 1986.

Cheng, V., and T. Martin, eds. *Joyce and Contexts.* Cambridge: Cambridge University Press, 1992.

Clark, A., and L. Clark. *Comics: An Illustrated History.* London: Green Publishing Company, 1992.

Comay, Joan, and Ronald Brownrigg. *Who's Who in the Bible.* New York: Bonanza Books, 1980.

Cormack, M. *Ideology.* Ann Arbor: University of Michigan Press, 1992.

Cowie, D. *England: The Land and the People.* South Brunswick, England: A. S. Barnes, 1972.

Cummins, M. S. *The Lamplighter.* Ed. Nina Baym. New Brunswick: Rutgers University Press, 1988.

Cvetkovitch, A. *Mixed Feelings: Feminism, Mass Culture, and Victorian Sensationalism.* New Brunswick: Rutgers University Press, 1992.

de Certeau, M. *Heterologies: Discourse on the Other.* Trans. Brian Massumi. Minneapolis: University of Minnesota Press, 1986.

———. *The Practice of Everyday Life.* Trans. Steven Rendall. Berkeley: University of California Press, 1984.

Defoe, D. *The Fortunes and Misfortunes of the Famous Moll Flanders.* New York: New American Library, 1964.

de Lauretis, T. *Alice Doesn't: Feminism, Semiotics, Cinema.* Bloomington: Indiana University Press, 1984.

Deleuze, G., and Felix Guattari. *Anti-Oedipus: Capitalism and Schizophrenia.* Trans. Robert Hurley, Mark Seem, and Helen R. Lane. Minneapolis: University of Minnesota Press, 1989.

Devlin, K. "The Female Eye: Joyce's Voyeuristic Narcissists." In Scott, ed., *New Alliances in Joyce Studies.*

———. "The Romance Heroine Exposed: 'Nausicaa' and *The Lamplighter.*" *James Joyce Quarterly* 22.4 (1985): 67–81.

Dijkstra, B. *Idols of Perversity: Fantasies of Feminine Evil in Fin-de-Siecle Culture.* New York: Oxford University Press, 1986.

Donald, J. "The City, The Cinema: Modern Spaces." In Jencks, ed., *Visual Culture.*

Eagleton, T. *The Ideology of the Aesthetic.* Cambridge, Mass.: Basil Blackwell, 1990.

Encyclopedia Judaica. Jerusalem: Keter Publishing House, 1971.

Farina, F. *Venus Unveiled.* Leicester, England: Magna Books, 1989.

Felman, S., ed. *Literature and Psychoanalysis: The Question of Reading, Otherwise.* Baltimore: Johns Hopkins University Press, 1982.

Fiske, J. *Reading the Popular.* Boston: Unwin Hyman, 1989.

———. *Understanding Popular Culture.* New York: Routledge, 1989.

Foster, H., ed. *The Anti-Aesthetic: Essays on Postmodern Culture.* Washington: Bay Press, 1983.

Foucault, M. *Discipline and Punish: The Birth of the Prison.* Trans. Alan Sheridan. New York: Pantheon Books, 1977.

———. *The History of Sexuality: Volume I, An Introduction.* New York: Random House, 1986.

Frisby, D. *Simmel and Since: Essays on Georg Simmel's Social Theory.* New York: Routledge, 1992.

Gagnier, R. *Idylls of the Marketplace: Oscar Wilde and the Victorian Public.* Stanford: Stanford University Press, 1986.

Gagnon, J. *Pornography in the Urban World.* Trans. James Boake. Toronto: Art Metropole, 1986.

Gibson, P., and R. Gibson, eds. *Dirty Looks: Women, Pornography, Power.* London: British Film Institute, 1993.

Gifford, D. *Joyce Annotated: Notes for Dubliners and A Portrait of the Artist as a Young Man.* Berkeley: University of California Press, 1982.

Gifford, D., with Robert Seidman. *Ulysses Annotated: Notes for James Joyce's Ulysses.* Berkeley: University of California Press, 1988.

Greenblatt, S., and Giles Gunn, eds. *Redrawing the Boundaries: The Transformation of English and American Literary Studies.* New York: Modern Language Association, 1992.

Hammond, P. *French Undressing: Naughty Postcards from 1900 to 1920.* London: Bloomsbury Books, 1976.

Hart, C., and D. Hayman, eds. *James Joyce's Ulysses.* Berkeley: University of California Press, 1974.

Haug, W. F. *Critique of Commodity Aesthetics: Appearance, Sexuality and Advertising in Capitalist Society.* Minneapolis: University of Minnesota Press, 1986.

Heath, S. "Joan Riviere and the Masquerade." In Burgin, Donald, and Kaplan, eds., *Formations of Fantasy.*

Heininger, J. "Molly Bloom's Ad Language and Goods Behavior: Advertising as Social Communication in *Ulysses.*" In Pearce, ed., *Molly Blooms.*

Hemingway, E. *The Sun Also Rises.* New York: Charles Scriber, 1926.

Henke, S. "Gerty MacDowell: Joyce's Sentimental Heroine." In Henke and Unkeless, eds., *Women in Joyce.*

Henke, S., and E. Unkeless, eds. *Women in Joyce.* Chicago: University of Illinois Press, 1983.

Herr, C. "Ireland from the Outside." In Wollaeger, Luftig, and Spoo, eds., *Joyce and the Subject of History.*

———. *Joyce's Anatomy of Culture.* Chicago: University of Illinois Press, 1986.

Hindley, D., and G. Hindley. *Advertising in Victorian England, 1837–1901.* London: Wayland, 1972.

International Standard Bible Encyclopedia. Grand Rapids, Mich.: William B. Erdman's, 1988.

Irigaray, L. *This Sex Which Is Not One.* Trans. Catherine Porter. Ithaca: Cornell University Press, 1985.

Jameson, F. *The Political Unconscious: Narrative as a Socially Symbolic Act.* Ithaca: Cornell University Press, 1981.

———. "Postmodernism and Consumer Society." In Foster, ed., *The Anti-Aesthetic.*

Jencks, C. *Visual Culture.* New York: Routledge, 1995.

Joyce, J. *Dubliners.* Ed. R. Scholes and A. Walton Litz. New York: Viking Press, 1969.

———. *A Portrait of the Artist as a Young Man.* Ed. Chester G. Anderson. New York: Viking Critical Library, 1968.

———. *Selected Letters of James Joyce.* Ed. Richard Ellmann. New York: Viking Press, 1975.

———. *Stephen Hero.* Ed. John J. Slocum and Herbert Cahoon. New York: New Directions, 1963.

———. *Ulysses.* Ed. Hans Walter Gabler, et al. New York and London: Garland

Publishing, 1984, 1986. In paperback by Garland, Random House, Bodley Head, and Penguin.

Joyce, S. *My Brother's Keeper.* New York: Viking Press, 1958.

Kaplan, E. A. *Rocking around the Clock: Music Television, Postmodernism, and Consumer Culture.* New York: Methuen, 1987.

Kenner, H. *Ulysses.* Baltimore: Johns Hopkins University Press, 1980.

Kershner, R. B. *Joyce, Bakhtin, and Popular Literature: Chronicles of Disorder.* Chapel Hill: University of North Carolina Press, 1989.

———. "Wilde and Joyce on Shakespeare." *Texas Studies in Language and Literature* 20 (1978), 215–25.

———. "The World's Strongest Man: Joyce or Sandow?" *James Joyce Quarterly* 30.4/31.1 (1993–94): 667–96.

———, ed. *Joyce and Popular Culture.* Gainesville: University Press of Florida, 1996.

Kruger, B. "I shop, therefore I am." *Love for Sale: The Words and Pictures of Barbara Kruger.* New York: H. N. Abrams, 1990.

Lacan, J. "Desire and the Interpretation of Desire in Hamlet." In Felman, ed., *Literature and Psychoanalysis.*

———. *The Four Fundamental Concepts of Psycho-Analysis.* New York: W. W. Norton, 1981.

———. "Seminar of 21 January 1975." In Mitchell, ed., *Feminine Sexuality.*

———. *Speech and Language in Psychoanalysis.* Trans. Anthony Wilder. Baltimore: Johns Hopkins University Press, 1968.

Law, J. D. "'Pity They Can't See Themselves': Assessing the 'Subject' of Pornography in 'Nausicaa'." *James Joyce Quarterly* 27.2 (1990): 219–39.

———. "Simulation, Pluralism, and the Politics of Everyday Life." In *Coping with Joyce: Essays from the Copenhagen Symposium,* ed. Morris Beja and Shari Benstock. Columbus: Ohio State University Press, 1989.

Leonard, G. "Joyce and Lacan: The Twin Narratives of History and His[S]tory in the 'Nestor' Chapter of *Ulysses.*" In Cheng and Martin, eds., *Joyce and Contexts.*

———. *Reading Dubliners Again: A Lacanian Perspective.* Syracuse: Syracuse University Press, 1993.

———. "'The Woman Is Perfected': Sylvia Plath and *Mademoiselle.*" *College Literature* 19.2 (1992): 60–82.

Leonard, G., and Jennifer Wicke, eds. *James Joyce Quarterly* 30.4/31.1 (1993). Special Issue: "Joyce and Advertising."

Lyotard, J. F. *Postmodern Condition.* Minneapolis: University of Minnesota Press, 1982.

Marx, K. *Capital.* Vol. 1. New York: International, 1967.

McCracken, G. *Culture and Consumption.* Bloomington: Indiana University Press, 1988.

McKendrick, N., John Brewer, and J. H. Plumb. *The Birth of a Consumer Society: The Commercialization of Eighteenth-Century England.* Bloomington: Indiana University Press, 1982.

Middleton, P. *The Inward Gaze: Masculinity and Subjectivity in Modern Culture.* New York: Routledge, 1992.

Miller, D. A. *The Novel and the Police.* Berkeley and Los Angeles: University of California Press, 1988.

Mitchell, J., and J. Rose, eds. *Feminine Sexuality, Jacques Lacan, and the Ecole Freudienne.* New York: W. W. Norton, 1985.

Modleski, T. *Loving with a Vengeance: Mass-Produced Fantasies for Women.* New York: Methuen, 1984.

Moi, T. *Sexual/Textual Politics.* London: Routledge, 1988.

Moretti, F. *Signs Taken for Wonders: Essays in the Sociology of Literary Forms.* London: Verso, 1983.

Mukerji, C. *From Graven Images: Patterns of Modern Materialism.* New York: Columbia University Press, 1983.

Norris, M. "Ibsen and 'The Dead'." *MFS* 35.3 (1989): 478–96.

Osteen, M. *Making Both Ends Meet: Economics in Ulysses.* Syracuse: Syracuse University Press, 1995.

Pearce, R. "Joyce and the Police." *Novel* 29.1 (1995): 5–137.

———, ed. *Molly Blooms.* Madison: University of Wisconsin Press, 1994.

Perloff, M. "Modernist Studies." In Greenblatt and Gunn, eds., *Redrawing the Boundaries.*

Pierce, D. *James Joyce's Ireland.* New Haven: Yale University Press, 1992.

Presbrey, F. *The History and Development of Advertising.* New York: Doubleday, Doran, and Co., 1929.

Ragland-Sullivan, Ellie. "Lacan's Seminars on James Joyce: Writing as Symptom and 'Singular Solution'." In *Psychoanalysis and . . . ,* ed. Richard Feldstein. New York: Routledge, 1982.

Rhys, J. *Good Morning, Midnight. The Complete Novels.* New York: Norton, 1985.

Richards, T. *The Commodity Culture of Victorian England: Advertising and Spectacle, 1851–1914. Stanford: Stanford University Press, 1990.*

———. "Gerty MacDowell and the Irish Common Reader." *ELH* 52.3 (1985): 41–56.

Schechner, M. *Joyce in Nighttown: A Psychoanalytic Inquiry into Ulysses.* Berkeley: University of California Press, 1974.

Scott, B. K., ed. *The Gender of Modernism: A Critical Anthology.* Bloomington: Indiana University Press, 1990.

———. *New Alliances in Joyce Studies.* Newark: University of Delaware Press, 1988.

Senn, F. "History as Text in Reverse." In Wollaeger, Luftig, and Spoo, eds., *Joyce and the Subject of History.*

———. "Nausicaa." In Hart and Hayman, eds., *James Joyce's Ulysses.*

Shields, R., ed. *Lifestyle Shopping: The Subject of Consumption. New York: Routledge, 1992.*

Silverman, K. *The Subject of Semiotics.* New York: Oxford University Press, 1983.

Stoller, R. J. *Observing the Erotic Imagination.* New Haven: Yale University Press, 1985.

Turner, E. S. *The Shocking History of Advertising!* London: Michael Joseph, 1952.

Valente, Joseph. "Thrilled by His Touch: Homosexual Panic and the Will to Artistry in *A Portrait of the Artist as a Young Man.*" *James Joyce Quarterly* 31.3 (1994): 167–88.

Voelker, Joe, and Thomas Arner. "Bloomian Pantomime: A. J. Dowie and the 'Messianic Scene'." *James Joyce Quarterly* 27.2 (1990): 283–91.

Von Sacher-Masoch, L. *Venus in Furs.* New York: Sylvan Press, 1947.

Walzl, F. "Dubliner: Women in Irish Society." In Henke and Unkeless, eds., *Women in Joyce.*

Weightman, G., and Steve Humphries. *The Making of Modern London, 1815–1914.* London: Sidgwick and Jackson, 1983.

Wicke, J. *Advertising Fictions: Literature, Advertisement, and Social Reading.* New York: Columbia University Press, 1988.

———. "Molly Bloom and the Work of Consumption." In Pearce, ed. *Molly Blooms.*

———. "Through a Gaze Darkly: Pornography's Academic Market." In Gibson and Gibson, eds., *Dirty Looks.*

———. "'Who's She When She's At Home?': Molly Bloom and the Work of Consumption." *James Joyce Quarterly* 28.4 (1991): 749–64.

Wilde, O. *The Complete Works of Oscar Wilde.* Bristol, England: Parragon Books, 1995.

Williams, L. *Hard Core: Power, Pleasure, and the "Frenzy of the Visible."* Los Angeles: University of California Press, 1989.

Williams, R. *Dream Worlds: Mass Consumption in Late Nineteenth Century France.* Berkeley: University of California Press, 1982.

Williams, T. "Resistance to Paralysis in *Dubliners.*" Modern Fiction Studies 35.3 (1989): 437–57.

Williamson, J. *Decoding Advertisements: Ideology and Meaning in Advertising.* New York: Marion Boyars, 1978.

Wollaeger, M. "Reading *Ulysses:* Agency, Ideology, and the Novel." In Wollaeger, Luftig, and Spoo, eds., *Joyce and the Subject of History.*

Wollaeger, Marc, Victor Luftig, and Robert Spoo, eds. *Joyce and the Subject of History.* Ann Arbor: University of Michigan Press, 1996.

Wooley, E. M. *The Art of Selling Goods. Chicago: American Business Man, 1907.*

Yeats, W. B. *The Poems of W. B. Yeats.* Ed. Richard Finneran. New York: Macmillan, 1983.

Zizek, S. *The Sublime Object of Ideology.* London: Verso, 1989.

Index